Fo

Berlin

M000279409

*To Cesar
from Mother
Elaine.
March 1995*

Parts of this book appear in *Fodor's Germany*

Fodor's Travel Publications, Inc.
New York • Toronto • London • Sydney • Auckland

Grateful acknowledgment is made to the following for permission to reprint previously published material: "Seeing Is Believing," by Christopher Hope. Reprinted by permission of *The New Republic* © 1989, The New Republic, Inc.

Fodor's Berlin

Editor: David Low
Contributors: Christopher Billy, Paula Consolo, George Hamilton, Michael Kallenbach, Graham Lees, Marcy Pritchard, Linda K. Schmidt, Robert Tilley
Creative Director: Fabrizio La Rocca
Cartographer: David Lindroth
Illustrator: Karl Tanner
Cover Photograph: Blaine Harrington III

Design: Vignelli Associates

Special Sales

Fodor's Travel Publications are available at special discounts for bulk purchases for sales promotions or premiums. Special editions, including personalized covers, excerpts of existing guides, and corporate imprints, can be created in large quantities for special needs. For more information, contact your local bookseller or write to Special Markets, Fodor's Travel Publications, 201 East 50th Street, New York, NY 10022. Inquiries from Canada should be directed to your local Canadian bookseller or sent to Random House of Canada, Ltd., Marketing Department, 1265 Aerowood Drive, Mississauga, Ontario L4W 1B9. Inquiries from the United Kingdom should be sent to Fodor's Travel Publications, 20 Vauxhall Bridge Road, London, England SW1V 2SA.

MANUFACTURED IN THE UNITED STATES OF AMERICA
10 9 8 7 6 5 4 3 2 1

Contents

Maps

Foreword

We would like to express our gratitude to the German National Tourist Board, German Information Center, Berlin Tourist Office, GermanRail, Inc., Lufthansa German Airlines, LTU International Airways, and KD German Rhine Line for their help and support. Special thanks go to Hedy Wuerz, Helga Brenner-Khan, Birgit Fickert, Jan Friedrich, Lucille Hoshabjian, Jan Myers, Rudolf Masata, Michael Brodersen, Gisela Höppner, and Hubert Wegmann.

While every care has been taken to assure the accuracy of the information in this guide, the passage of time will always bring change and, consequently, the publisher cannot accept responsibility for errors that may occur.

All prices and opening times quoted here are based on information supplied to us at press time. Hours and admission fees may change, however, and the prudent traveler will avoid inconvenience by calling ahead.

Fodor's wants to hear about your travel experiences, both pleasant and unpleasant. When a hotel or restaurant fails to live up to its billing, let us know and we will investigate the complaint and revise our entries where the facts warrant it.

Send your letters to the editors of Fodor's Travel Publications, 201 East 50th Street, New York, NY 10022.

Highlights and Fodor's Choice

Highlights

For visitors from abroad on their first arrival in Berlin, crossing over into the East at **Checkpoint Charlie** used to be an unnerving experience. You were not allowed to cross unless your papers were in order. The tension would quickly mount as stern-looking border guards examined documents, checked identities, then motioned visitors through a security tract with automatic doors that opened with a buzz. Now, with the Cold War divide gone and the East German flag furled, the first thing those same visitors want to do is see where all this used to happen. Vestiges of Checkpoint Charlie remain—the original signboard marking the border and some barbed wire to protect token sections of the Berlin Wall from being chipped down. Russian and Polish emigrés sell papier-maché Gorby dolls and jars of cheap dried caviar, all under cigarette billboards stating this is "now Marlboro country" and it is time to "Test the West."

The remaining pieces of the **Berlin Wall,** in central Mühlenstrasse between the Jannowitzbrücke and Oberbaumbrücke bridges, and at Bernauerstrasse in Wedding (where a "wall museum" has been proposed), have been left standing as a historic reminder of what once divided Berlin. The scar left by the Wall and the border fortifications is still visible, but for much of its length the strip of land beside it resembles a huge building site as developers set about putting it to new uses.

Changes are taking place in Berlin as quickly as reunification of the two Germanys in October 1990. Week after week and month after month, city planners, investors, and bulldozers appear anew. The pace of change is faster than even the most cynical Berliner imagined. West Berliners always boasted about their fashionable shopping street the Kurfürstendamm—the locals call it the Ku'damm—with its 2 miles of conspicuous consumption and often seedy nightlife. But now there's the **Unter den Linden** in the East, steeped in history and being restored to its former glory. The huge **Meissen** porcelain showroom is still there, as is, for the time being, the ex–Soviet embassy, fronted by a bust of Lenin.

New investment is pouring into the area all the time, and large embassies that were formerly in the western part of the city are now taking their places on Unter den Linden. Banks, showrooms for cars, travel agencies, and fashionable stores are opening their doors, as well. Next door to the Deutsche Staatsoper (State Opera House), the Opera Café has become a bustling meeting place about 8:30 to midnight. It's amusing to watch the clientele, particularly those stern German ladies in their fitted hats, filling up on fattening pastries and whipped cream.

Since the beginning of 1992 the Staatlichen Museen zu Berlin, the Prussian cultural seat, has been re-created, and now oversees museum activities all over Berlin. Much of the work has yet to be completed, including the merging of museums and collections of the formerly divided city. The plan at the moment is to move as much as possible from western Berlin to **Museum Island** in the eastern part of the city. A competition will be launched to rebuild a new museum, no later than 1994, with the specific aim of redesigning public access to Museum Island. Museum experts predict that the situation will remain in flux until at least 1995.

The hotel and restaurant scene in eastern Berlin is in upheaval as the official government trustees—the Treuhand—struggle with the enormous task of returning state-confiscated and -run properties to their former owners or selling them off to private entrepreneurs and corporate-operated chains. We've tried to keep up with the changes as much as possible, but it's always a good idea to call in advance before heading for that highly touted eastern Berlin hotel or restaurant; it may have changed ownership or name, or it may have closed down completely.

New restaurants, most with western Berlin–style management and financial backing, are springing up in eastern Berlin. Coffee shops and hotels are also opening as fast as possible, and businesses that suffered under Communist rule are learning quickly about a free market economy, good service, and what it means to get a decent tip. The **former Jewish quarter,** surrounding the Oranienburgestrasse Synogogue, is now being restored to its former self, and new restaurants, such as **Beth Café** (Tuchokslystr. 40), **Kolbo** (Augustr. 77/8), and **Café Oren** (Oranienburgestr. 28) have opened in the neighborhood; these establishments serve Middle Eastern cuisine and sometimes kosher food.

Berlin has witnessed a nightclub revival, especially in the east, with **Clarchens Ballhaus** (Auguststr. 24–5) experiencing a rebirth in popularity. The **Globus** (Leipzigerstr. at Otto Grottewohlstr.), formerly a notorious club named Tresor that was closed by the authorities, is now one of Berlin's "in" places, with hip hop, acid jazz, and ragga. The **Planet** (Kopernickerstr. 52), a mecca of the Euro techno scene, is another trendy spot for night owls.

A popular musical based on the life of Marlene Dietrich, titled *Where Have All the Flowers Gone*, opened in April 1993 at the **Theater am Kurfûrstendamm** (Kurfurstendamm 206). This show is one of the first musicals in a long time to originate in Germany. Although contemporary musicals are not usually successful in Berlin, the play appears destined to run for years, and travel agents are including the show as part of tourist packages.

Fodor's Choice

No two people will agree on what makes a perfect vacation, but it's fun and helpful to know what others think. We hope you'll have a chance to experience some of Fodor's Choices during your visit to Berlin and eastern Germany. For detailed information about each entry, refer to the appropriate chapters of the book.

Castles and Palaces

Albrechtberg, Meissen

Schloss Charlottenburg, Berlin

Schloss Sanssouci, Potsdam

Spandauer Zitadelle, Berlin

Wartburg castle, Eisenach

Zwinger Palace, Dresden

Churches

Berliner Dom, Berlin

Deutscher Dom and Französischer Dom, Berlin

Dom, Magdeburg

Marienkirche, Berlin

Nikolaikirche, Berlin

Nikolaikirche, Leipzig

Thomaskirche, Leipzig

Memorable Sights

Berlin from the top of the Funkturm, Alexanderplatz

Climbing the terraces at the base of Schloss Sanssouci, Potsdam

Facing the Schauspielhaus on Gendarmenmarkt, Berlin

The modern Kaiser Wilhelm Gedächtniskirche, Berlin, at night

Strolling down Unter den Linden, Berlin

Monuments and Memorials

Berlin Wall remains

Brandenburger Tor, Berlin

Buchenwald concentration camp, outside Weimar

Frauenkirche, Dresden

Kaiser Wilhelm Gedächtniskirche, Berlin

Neue Wache, Berlin

Pergamon Altar, Pergamonmuseum, Berlin

Museums

Ägyptisches Museum, Berlin

Gemäldegalerie, Dahlem, Berlin

Museum der Bildenden Künste, Leipzig

Grüne Gewölbe, Dresden

Neue Nationalgalerie, Berlin

Pergamonmuseum, Berlin

Sempergalerie Collection, Dresden

Restaurants

Bamberger Reiter, Berlin (*Very Expensive*)

Frühsammer's restaurant an der Rehwiese, Berlin (*Very Expensive*)

Ermeler-Haus, Berlin (*Expensive*)

Sekundogenitur, Dresden (*Moderate*)

Wirtshaus Moorlake, Berlin (*Moderate*)

Auerbachs Keller, Leipzig (*Inexpensive*)

Blockhaus Nikolskoe, Berlin (*Inexpensive*)

Zur Letzten Instanz, Berlin (*Inexpensive*)

Hotels

Bristol Hotel Kempinski, Berlin (*Very Expensive*)

Dresdner Hof, Dresden (*Very Expensive*)

Hotel Bellevue, Dresden (*Very Expensive*)

Hotel Berlin, Berlin (*Very Expensive*)

Elephant, Weimar (*Expensive*)

Schweizerhof Berlin, Berlin (*Expensive*)

Auf der Wartburg, Eisenach (*Moderate*)

Charlottenhof, Berlin (*Moderate*)

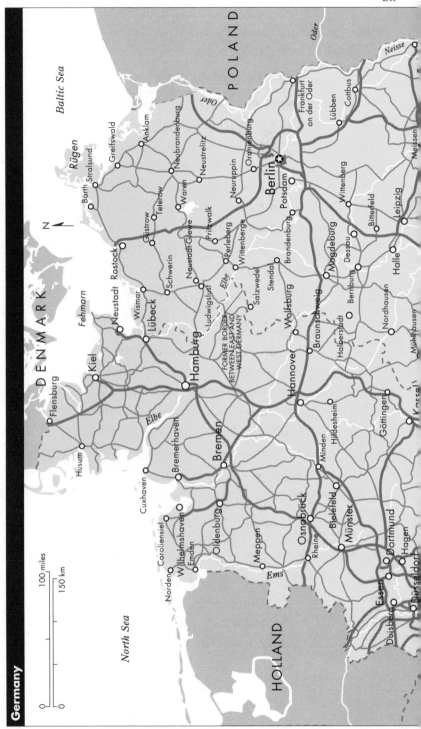

Germany

North Sea

Baltic Sea

DENMARK

HOLLAND

POLAND

Berlin

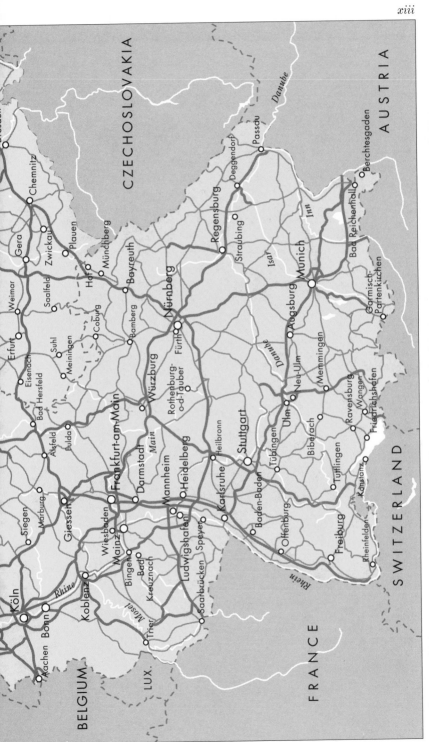

Allee

Molkestr.

Entlastungsstr.

Unter den Linden

Otto Grotewohlstr.

Friedrichstr.

Karl-Liebknecht-Str.

Rathausstr.

Marx-
Engels
Pl.

Gendarmen-
markt

Wallstr.

Leipzigerstr.

Potsdamerpl.

FORMER LOCATION OF BERLIN WALL

Oranienstr.

Wilhelmstr.

Friedrichstr.

Lindenstr.

Ritterstr.

Potsdamerstr.

Schönebergerstr.

Möckernstr.

Prinzenstr.

Gitschinerstr.

Möckernstr.

Urban - str.

Yorckstr.

Yorckstr.

Gneisenaustr.

Baerwaldstr.

Monumentenstr.

Kreuzbergstr.

Mehringdamm

Volkspark
Hasenheide

N

Victoria
Park

Kolonnenstr.

Dudenstr.

Columbiadamm

0   750 yards

0   750 meters

World Time Zones

MONDAY
SUNDAY

+12 | +13

International Date Line

-10

-11

+11

+12

-9

-7

-8

-6

-10

-11

-4

-3

-5

-4

-3:30

-4

-5

-4

-3

-3

-3

| +11 | +12 - | -11 | -10 | -9 | -8 | -7 | -6 | -5 | -4 | -3 | -2 |

Numbers below vertical bands relate each zone to Greenwich Mean Time (0 hrs.).
Local times frequently differ from these general indications,
as indicated by light-face numbers on map.

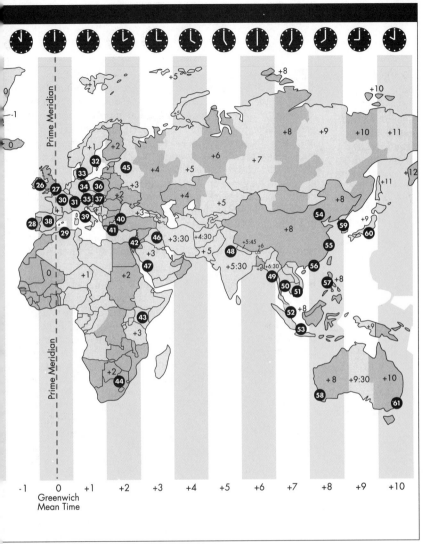

Mecca, **47**
Mexico City, **12**
Miami, **18**
Montréal, **15**
Moscow, **45**
Nairobi, **43**
New Orleans, **11**
New York City, **16**

Ottawa, **14**
Paris, **30**
Perth, **58**
Reykjavík, **25**
Rio de Janeiro, **23**
Rome, **39**
Saigon (Ho Chi Minh City), **51**

San Francisco, **5**
Santiago, **21**
Seoul, **59**
Shanghai, **55**
Singapore, **52**
Stockholm, **32**
Sydney, **61**
Tokyo, **60**

Toronto, **13**
Vancouver, **4**
Vienna, **35**
Warsaw, **36**
Washington, D.C., **17**
Yangon, **49**
Zürich, **31**

Introduction

By Robert Tilley

British-born Robert Tilley lives in Germany and is a broadcast and print journalist whose work has appeared in German and British publications.

Berlin isn't a city at all, really—it's more like a country. It's certainly a way of life, a state of mind. Take Heine's word for it. The German poet wrote: "[Berlin] . . . just provides the gathering place for a lot of people, among them many of intellect, for whom it's quite immaterial where they are." In more prosaic terms, Germany's new capital, restored to its old status, is an amorphous, sprawling conurbation. The size of a small European state (and bigger than Andorra, Liechtenstein, or San Marino), it's a patchwork quilt of eight towns, 59 villages, and 27 farms and estates, fused together in 1920 to form Greater Berlin, nearly 900 square kilometers and with a city border 234 kilometers (138 miles) in length, longer than the railway line connecting it with the nearest western German city, Hanover.

Berlin's way of life? The history of Berlin has molded its lifestyle in a way that no other European city can match: imperial capital; meeting point of European culture and all forms of artistic expression; refuge for oppressed minorities; 1920s pleasureground; home of German fascism; military citadel flattened by war, occupied by victorious armies, and then rent asunder by a 28-mile-long wall that divided it into two halves that symbolized the Cold War confrontation between Western democracy and communist totalitarianism. And in no other European city can you see historical influences so evidently at work in the way it functions. The Berliners really do live from day to day, with a phlegmatic, unconventional but at the same time practical approach to life that's the despair of other Germans. Goethe thought them to be an "audacious lot."

The Berliners are born survivors, an attribute that makes them excellent business people: sharp, quick-witted, inquisitive, outgoing, and—as you'll undoubtedly find as a visitor—warmhearted hosts. Their humor is naturally sardonic and self-deprecatory, a dry form of wit with instant appeal to Americans and British. When did you ever hear reference to German humor? Yet the Berliner *Schnauze*, or Berlin wit, is renowned beyond German borders and respected even by those who feel its sometimes cruel lash. Its acerbic tone was to be savored in the graffiti that decorated the hated Wall, and wonderfully captured by the most famous spray-painted and prophetic line: "Will the last one over please switch out the lights."

You can find examples of Berlin wit all over the city, and not all of them are contemporary. Several historical monuments are deliberately humorous in style, most notably the equestrian statue of Frederick the Great on Unter den Linden, in which the figures of his two outspoken critics Lessing and Kant are positioned under the horse's tail. Frederick was a typical Berliner, so hospitable a host that guest rooms at his Potsdam palace, Sanssouci, outnumbered his own chambers.

Berlin flourished under Frederick's enlightened rule, but the city was already a great German capital when he ascended the throne in 1740. It's a young city by European standards, beginning life in the early Middle Ages as two trading communities on and around the Spree River island where eastern Berlin's great museums now stand, the so-called Museumsinsel. The island was called Cölln and a nearby riverbank settlement, Berlin. The Margrave Heinrich the Tall combined them into one administrative town in 1307, and it is from that date that the city's history really begins. Paradoxically, several other areas of what is now Greater Berlin are older—Spandau and Köpenick, for instance. Until 1920 they nurtured their own, independent, histories, and even today they zealously guard their ancient traditions. You'll hear their denizens say that they are "off to Berlin" when talking about a shopping trip or an outing to the theater in the city center. Several Berlin parish churches are far older than the city of which they are now a part.

Berlin is a city of churches, most of them Protestant. Ironically, Berliners fiercely resisted the Reformation, and in 1524 the Prince-Elector Joachim Nestor banned Luther's New Testament. His successor, Joachim II, opened the gates of Berlin to the Reformation. A century later, the city was again caught up in religious strife, suffering heavily in the Thirty Years' War, which swept a destructive course through much of Germany. It was at the height of the war that Berlin's first great ruler, the Prince Elector Friedrich Wilhelm, took power, laying the foundation of the Prussian-Brandenburg state. It was Friedrich Wilhelm who first welcomed to Berlin the foreign refugees who were to play such a major role in creating the vibrant city we know today. He encouraged the Huguenots to settle there, and they brought badly needed skills that helped the city increase the volume of its trade sixfold within 10 years.

In those days Berlin's rulers lived in what is now the eastern part of the city, in a palace badly damaged in World War II and later blown up by East Berlin's then communist masters. An enduring, grand reminder of that chapter of Berlin history is the famous avenue, Unter den Linden, once a tree-lined riding path connecting the palace with the royal hunting grounds of the present Tiergarten park.

It was Friedrich Wilhelm's successor, the Prince Elector Friedrich III, who began the construction of Berlin's most famous palace, the Charlottenburg, intending it to serve as a summer residence in the sylvan peace of the western reaches of the expanding city. Friedrich was the first of the highly cultured rulers to whom Berlin will be ever indebted, and he is the true father of the Prussian state. Under his enlightened rule arose academies of arts and sciences, and the theater and music flourished. Small wonder that he won the favor of the German Emperor Leopold, who bestowed on him the title of King of Prussia.

Friedrich was crowned in 1701 in Königsberg, but he chose Berlin as his royal residence. He dipped deep into the city and state coffers to finance the kind of court he thought worthy of the new kingdom of Prussia—too deep for the likes of his ascetic son Friedrich Wilhelm I. When his father died, the funeral was the last display of Prussian pomp for 27 years. Friedrich Wilhelm initiated a severe austerity program, diverting money into the equivalent of a modern defense budget, which he regarded as essential for the security of the new Prussian state. The people dubbed him their "Soldier King."

Friedrich Wilhelm's death swung the pendulum back again. His son Friedrich II—Frederick the Great—possessed his grandfather's aesthetic sensibilities, and under his 46-year rule Berlin flourished as never before. The monumental grandeur of Berlin (and of nearby Potsdam) began to take shape under such architects as Georg von Knobelsdorff, and Frederick's court attracted the cream of European artistic talent; Voltaire came for a visit and stayed three years.

Frederick's successor, his nephew Friedrich Wilhelm II, continued the work of building Berlin into a leading European cultural and political capital. The architects Carl Langhans and Karl Friedrich Schinkel gave Berlin its Neoclassical stamp, with Langhans building its most famous structure, the Brandenburger Tor. But 15 years after the completion in 1791 of the massive victory arch, Napoléon and his troops marched through it, heralding two years of occupation of the city by the French. Napoléon robbed the arch of its crowning sculpture, the Quadriga, but Berlin won it back again in 1814.

The industrial age brought further problems for Berlin. A simmering cauldron of discontent, its source being workers, students, and intellectuals, boiled over in 1848 into open rebellion, pressuring the Prussian court into unparalleled concessions. There was a reactionary backlash, however, and the freedoms won by the Berlin proletariat were lost again in an undemocratic constitution that was to last until 1918. In the latter half of the 19th century, industrialization brought Berlin remarkable prosperity but also enormous poverty. By the turn of the century more than 1,000 factories had been established in Berlin and railways and canals had been built, but alongside them sprung up overcrowded tenements in which nearly two million people eked out miserable existences.

Meanwhile, Prussia's military victories over Austria and France paved the way for German unification (1871) and Prussian dominance over the new nation. Piloted by Bismark, the country was largely conservative and militaristic, but Berlin, steadily becoming a modern capital, remained resolutely liberal. Thus revolution was never far away, and in November 1918, after Germany's defeat in World War I, it broke out again, forcing the abdication of Kaiser Wilhelm II.

Berlin flourished anew during the Weimar Republic that followed. During that brief, heady burst of democracy, Berlin became a cultural and entertainment capital as well. The joyous 1920s brought to prominence the likes of Bertholt Brecht, Kurt Weill, Erich Kastner, George Grosz, Fritz Lang, Marlene Dietrich, and a thousand other names that made this period a golden age for Berlin.

But it was an ephemeral time, an incandescence that ended in dark years of recession, runaway inflation, social unrest, and the rise of fascism. We all know what followed. Berlin was destined for damnation: Hitler's militaristic capital, bombed to ruins and then occupied by the Red Army, cut in four ways like a cake by the victorious Allies, then split into two zones and finally divided for nearly three decades by a hideous wall.

The fall of the Wall in November 1989, and the demise of the communist regime that built it, opened the way for Berlin's rebirth as the premier city of Germany and the restoration of its status as capital of the nation. The debate over the merits of Bonn and Berlin was long and often passionate, but there was never really any doubt about the outcome. The selection of Berlin by the German Bundestag in June 1991, was more of an emotional vote than a political or economic one, and an impassioned speech by interior Minister Wolfgang Schäuble is given the credit by grateful Berliners for swinging the vote their way. Historic Berlin—the city of the first Prussian king and of Frederick the Great—has returned to claim its birthright.

Lawmakers have given the government 12 years to make the move from Bonn. It won't be an easy time, for even several years after the fall of the Wall Berlin is still a divided city, cleft no longer by a physical barrier but by the differences created by the parallel development of the capitalist West and the communist East. In the long run, however, the unifying forces must inevitably succeed and Berlin will emerge as an even more extraordinary metropolis, growing by the early 21st century into the largest and most powerful industrial city between the Atlantic and the Urals. The infrastructures that took shape in the two halves of Berlin give the city a sound foundation, not only economically but culturally. After inheriting three opera houses and more than a dozen world-class museums, newly united Berlin is set to become Germany's cultural capital and an important

European center of the arts. The Reichstag, historic seat of the German imperial parliament, will return to its old function, and around the century-old building, on the now-open banks of the Spree River, will arise a new suburb of administrative buildings. Part of the land that once served as the mined border between East and West Germany will be developed, with office blocks, parks, and gardens springing up where armed guards and dogs once patrolled.

As champions of Bonn have pointed out, every long-term advantage of shifting the capital to Berlin will be more than matched by immediate drawbacks. "Enormous economic and social challenges face the city as it wrestles with the problems thrown up by unification and the task of resuming its premier position within Germany," said a leading German economist. "Berlin . . . will inevitably attract great amounts of investment capital, entrepreneurship, labor, and know-how, but the attendant complications are likely to be awesome." At press time, unemployment was still high as eastern Berlin's creaking economic base was jacked up to western levels, and as western Berlin lost the special tax status it enjoyed as a divided and isolated city. However, with construction booming in eastern Berlin, many are finding work rebuilding part of the city, which is in desperate need of restoration.

Adding to the strains—but also contributing greatly to Berlin's fascination—is its great ethnic diversity, a modern manifestation of the open society that the city has always encouraged. More than a quarter of a million foreigners from 156 countries have made their home in Berlin, half of them Turks (Berlin, wags say, is Turkey's second-largest city). The Turks, who have made the district of Kreuzberg virtually their own, were lured to Berlin by the availability of relatively high-paying jobs on automobile assembly lines, in factories, and under conditions the Germans disdained. They contributed greatly to the German economic boom of the 1960s and 1970s, and it's a measure of Berlin's openness that their integration is almost complete. Less assimilated but nonetheless integral to everyday Berlin are the Third World refugees, the dropouts (West Berliners were exempted from the draft) and junkies, the punks and skinheads, the has-beens and ne'er-do-wells who find in this big-hearted metropolis a tolerance missing in most other German cities.

Yes, Berlin has its problems, and they're going to multiply. But it has the human and humane resources to solve them and make Berlin a great German—indeed, a great European—capital once again.

1 Essential Information

Before You Go

Government Tourist Offices

Contact the German National Tourist Office at 122 E. 42nd St., 52nd Floor, New York, NY 10168, tel. 212/661–7200; or 11766 Wilshire Blvd., Suite 750, Los Angeles, CA 90025, tel. 310/575–9799.

In Canada 175 Bloor Street East, North Tower, Suite 604, Toronto, Ontario M4 W3R8, tel. 416/968–1570.

In the United Kingdom Nightingale House, 65 Curzon Street, London W1Y 7PE, England, tel. 071/495–3990.

Tours and Packages

Should you buy your travel arrangements to Berlin packaged or do it yourself? There are advantages either way. Buying packaged arrangements saves you money, particularly if you can find a program that includes exactly the features you want. You also get a pretty good idea of what your trip will cost from the outset. For most destinations, you have two options: fully escorted tours and independent packages. However, independent packages are most common and few escorted tours include Berlin alone but instead combine it with other German cities and European capitals.

Escorted tours typically mean having limited free time and traveling with strangers. Escorted tours are most often via motorcoach, with a tour director in charge. Your baggage is handled, your time rigorously scheduled, and most meals planned. Escorted tours are therefore the most hassle-free way to see a destination, as well as generally the least expensive.

Independent packages allow plenty of flexibility. They generally include airline travel and hotels, with certain options available, such as sightseeing, car rental, and excursions. Independent packages are usually more expensive than escorted tours, but your time is your own.

While you can book directly through tour operators, you will pay no more to go through a travel agent, who will be able to tell you about tours and packages from a number of operators. Whatever kind of package you choose, be sure to find out exactly what is included, such as taxes, tips, transfers, meals, entertainment, and ground transportation. Ask about the level of hotel used, where it is located, the size of rooms, the kinds of beds, and the amenities available, such as pool or room service. Ask about cancellation penalties. Nearly everyone charges them, and the only way to avoid them is to buy trip-cancellation insurance. Your travel agent should sell it. Also ask about the single supplement. Some operators allow you to avoid this surcharge by agreeing to be matched up with a roommate of the same sex, even if one is not found by departure time. Remember that a program that has features you won't use, whether for rental sporting equipment or discounted museum admissions, may not be the most cost-wise choice for you. Don't buy a Rolls-Royce, even at a reduced price, if all you want is a Chevy!

Fully Escorted Tours Escorted tours are usually sold in three categories: deluxe, first-class and tourist, or budget-class. The most important differences are the price and the level of accommodations. Some operators specialize in one category, while others offer a range. Consider **Maupintour** (Box 807, Lawrence, KS 66044, tel. 913/843–1211 or 800/255–4266) in the deluxe category; **Caravan Tours** (401 N. Michigan, Suite 3325, Chicago, IL 60611, tel. 312/479–4040 or 800/CARAVAN), **Globus** (95-25 Queens Blvd. Rego Park, NY 11374, tel. 718/268–7000 or 800/221–0090), **Lufthansa,** the German airline (tel. 800/645–3880), **Olson-Travelworld** (Vox 10066, Manhattan Beach, CA 90226, tel. 310/546–8400 or 800/421–5785), and **Trafalgar Tours** (21 E. 26th St., New York, NY 10010, tel. 212/689–8977 or 800/854–0103) in the first-class category; and **Cosmos**, a corporate cousin of Globus, at the same address, in the budget class. Escorted programs that include Berlin are also available from **American Airlines Fly AAway Vacations** (tel. 800/321–2121) and **United Airlines' Vacation Planning Center** (tel. 800/328–6877).

Independent Packages Independent packages, which travel agents call FITs (for Foreign Independent Travel), are offered by airlines, tour operators, and any number of other companies, from large established ones to small, new entrepreneurs. **Lufthansa** (*see above*) also has Berlin packages as well as fly/drive and rail/drive programs. Also look into programs from **Delta Dream Vacations** (tel. 800/872–7786), **Globetrotters** (139 Main St., Cambridge, MA 02142, tel. 617/621–9911 or 800/999–9696), **SuperCities** (Box 1789, Minneapolis, MN 55440, tel. 402/498–8234 or 800/333–1234), **Travel Bound** (599 Broadway, New York, NY 10012, tel. 212/334–1350 or 800/456–8656), and **United Airlines' Vacation Planning Center** (*see above*).

Their programs come in a wide range of prices based on levels of luxury and options—in addition to hotel and airfare, sightseeing, car rental, transfers, admission to local attractions, and other extras. Note that when pricing different packages, it sometimes pays to purchase the same arrangements separately, such as when a rock-bottom promotional airfare is being offered. Again, base your choice on what's available in your budget for the destinations you want to visit.

Special-Interest Travel Special-interest tours that focus on Berlin specialize in opera, wines, and river cruises, among other topics. Special-interest programs may be fully escorted or independent. Some require a certain amount of expertise, but most are for the average traveler with a particular interest and are usually hosted by experts in the subject matter. When the program is escorted, it enjoys the advantages and disadvantages of all escorted programs; because your fellow travelers are apt to be passionate or knowledgeable about the subject, they can prove as enjoyable a part of your travel experience as the destination itself. The price range is wide, but in general they cost more—sometimes a lot more—than independent packages because of the expert guide and the special activities.

Museums **Travel Concepts** (62 Commonwealth Ave, Suite 3, Boston, MA 02115-1815, tel. 617/266–8450) will custom-design to Germany an art, history, or other type of cultural program for groups of 15 or more.

Opera **Dailey-Thorp Travel** (330 W. 58th St., New York, NY 10019, tel. 212/307–1555; book through travel agents) has opera programs that include Berlin.

River Cruises **Köln-Düsseldorfer (KD) Rivers Cruises of Europe** (Suite 317, 170 Hamilton Ave., White Plains, NY 10601, tel. 914/948–3600; in eastern U.S., 800/346–6525; in western U.S., HI, AK, 800/858–8587) has an Elbe River cruise that visits Berlin.

Wine-Tasting **DER Tours** (11933 Wilshire Blvd., Los Angeles, CA 90025, tel. 310/479–4140 or 800/782–2424; book through travel agents) has a "Rhine and Wine" program that includes Berlin.

U.K.-Based Operators **Cresta Holidays** (Cresta House, Victoria St., Altrincham, Cheshire WA14 1ET, tel. 061/927–7000) has flight/hotel packages and special offers. **DER Travel Service** (18 Conduit St., London W1R 9TD, tel. 071/408–0111) offers package holidays by air, car, or rail with 3–10 nights in Berlin, Christmas and New Year's packages, and shopping weekends to Berlin's Christmas markets. **GTF Tours** (182–186 Kensington Church St., London W8 4DP, tel. 071/229–2474) has flight/accommodation packages to Berlin for one or more nights. **Hamilton Travel Ltd** (6 Heddon St., London W1R 7LH, tel. 071/439–3199) offers economical scheduled fares to Berlin. **Scandinavian Seaways** (Scandinavia House, Parkeston Quay, Harwich, Essex CO12 4QG, tel. 0255/241234) handles a 5-day package to Berlin, with sightseeing tours and a New Year's festive holiday. **Sovereign Cities** (Groundstar House, London Rd., Crawley, West Sussex RH10 2TB, tel. 0293/547700) has flight/hotel packages to Berlin from two to seven nights, with optional excursions. Moswin Tours (21 Church St., Oadby, Leicester LE2 5DB, tel. 0533/719922) offers "Advent in Berlin" among a large selection of escorted trips and tailor-made holidays to Germany.

When to Go

It's always high season in Berlin. Even in its most dismal month—cold, wet February—the city entices thousands of visitors from all over the world to its glittering annual film festival. Nonetheless, the spring and summer months from April through September are the best times for a visit. In December and January, you might find yourself trudging around the city's sights through ankle-deep snow, while the weather in March and October is unpredictable. Since Berlin does not have an off-season, the only way to enjoy reduced rates in the city's higher-priced hotels is to cram your visit into a weekend. Most leading hotels offer weekend rates, often with sightseeing tours and theater/concert tickets thrown in. A weekend is, of course, much too short for Berlin, but one way of spinning out your stay at minimal cost is to make sure it encompasses a Saturday and Sunday.

Climate The climate of Berlin and environs is temperate, although winter temperatures can often plunge to Siberian lows and some summer days can be swelteringly hot. Snowfalls are often heavy, and the eastern part of both the city and the country are rarely prepared for them. So, if you're traveling in the east during a winter snowstorm, prepare for delays on the roads, railways, and at airports.

The following are the average daily maximum and minimum temperatures for Berlin.

Jan.	36F	2C	May	67F	19C	Sept.	68F	20C
	27	− 3		47	8		50	10
Feb.	38F	3C	June	72F	22C	Oct.	56F	13C
	27	− 3		54	12		43	6
Mar.	47F	8C	July	76F	24C	Nov.	45F	7C
	32	0		58	14		36	2
Apr.	56F	13C	Aug.	74F	23C	Dec.	38F	3C
	40	4		56	13		31	− 1

For current weather conditions for cities in the United States and abroad, plus the local time and helpful travel tips, call the **Weather Channel Connection** (tel. 900/WEATHER; 95¢ per minute) from a touch-tone phone.

Festivals and Seasonal Events

Berlin is a premier—some would say *the* premier—German festival city. Scarcely a week passes without at least one major event getting under way. What follows are the city's most notable festivals:

January–February The museums are open throughout the year, of course, but during the **Berliner Museumstage** special exhibitions and concerts are held.
Internationale Grüne Woche, Berlin's annual agricultural and produce fair, is held at the Messegelände, the fairgrounds at the radio and the Funkturm (television tower).
Internationale Filmfestspiele is the world-famous Berlin Film Festival.

March **Internationale Tourismus-Börse** is Europe's biggest travel and tourism fair. Berliners say farewell to winter at the **Frühlingsfest,** a popular spring fair on the central Lützowplatz.

April–May Berlin galleries join in presenting a giant fine arts fair during the **Berliner Kunsttage.**
Freie Berliner Kunstaustellung is another major fine arts festival open to all Berlin artists.
Whitsun: During **Frühkonzerte im Freien,** music is in the air everywhere, with bands, pop groups, and small ensembles touring Berlin's parks, open-air cafés, pubs, and restaurants.

May–June All Berlin becomes a stage for **Theatertreffen** when scores of theater groups perform anywhere they can find an audience—in tents, tavern taprooms, parks, marketplaces, and even on the pavements of downtown Berlin.
The garden setting for **Jazz in the Garden**, held Fridays in June, is the sculpture-strewn grounds of the Neue Nationalgalerie.
Held in Spandau's old town center, **Kiezfest** is one of Berlin's most popular summer festivals.
Horizonte, Festival der Weltkulturen is an international culture exchange presented in the Kongresshalle, Tiergarten, and other venues.

June–July **Bläser-Serenaden** is a series of brass ensemble concerts performed in the courtyard of the Grunewald Jagdschloss, a Renaissance hunting lodge.
Barrel-organ enthusiasts of the world turn their handles in one of Berlin's most unusual musical get-togethers, the **Internationales Drehorgelfest,** held outside the Gedächtniskirche.
Berliner Bachtage is a week-long festival celebrating the great German composer.

Jugglers do their thing on Los-Angeles-Platz in the **Gauklerfest.**

Insiders say that **Jazz in July** at the Quasimodo Club is Berlin's leading international jazz festival.

July–August **Deutsch-Amerikanisches Volksfest** in Dahlem celebrates German-American friendship.

Glienicker Schlosskonzerte are chamber-music concerts presented in the enchanting open-air courtyard setting of the Remisenhof of the Glienicker Schloss.

Sommerkonzerte are organ recitals in the Eosander chapel of Schloss Charlottenburg.

August–September Kreuzberg's summer festival, **Kreuzberger Festliche Tage,** celebrated on and around the Kreuzberg hill in Victoria Park, is a huge party.

Turmstrassenfest is the Moabit district's attempt to outdo Kreuzberg.

September– **Berliner Festwochen** is Berlin's major music and theater festi-
October val.

Allgemeine Auto-Ausstellung Berlin, the annual motor show, is held at the fairgrounds.

Dozens of Berlin groups blow the dust off the Music Instrument Museum exhibition in a three-day jazz festival, the **Jazztreffen im Musikinstrumenten-Museum.**

Berlin's 20th annual **International Marathon** is set for September 26, 1993.

November The German national contest of young songwriters, the **Treffen Junger Liedermacher,** takes place in various venues.

December **Weihnachtsmärkte,** the Christmas markets, spring up all over Berlin, the best of them around the Gedächtniskirche, by the Staatsoper on Unter den Linden, and in Spandau's old town.

What to Pack

What you pack depends more on the time of year than on any particular dress code. Winters can be bitterly cold; summers are warm but with days that suddenly turn cool and rainy.

For Berlin, pack as you would for an American city: dressy outfits for formal restaurants and nightclubs, casual clothes elsewhere. Jeans are as popular in Germany as anywhere else and are perfectly acceptable for sightseeing and informal dining. In the evening, men will probably feel more comfortable wearing a jacket and tie in more expensive restaurants. Many German women are extremely fashion-conscious and wear stylish outfits to restaurants and the theater, especially in the larger cities.

Miscellaneous If you plan to swim in a pool, take a bathing cap. They're obligatory in Germany, for men and women. For stays in budget hotels, take your own soap. Many do not provide soap or provide only one small bar. Bring an extra pair of eyeglasses or contact lenses. If you have a health problem that requires you to take a prescription drug, pack enough to last the duration of the trip, or have your doctor write a prescription using the drug's generic name, since brand names vary from country to country. And don't forget to pack a list of the addresses of offices that supply refunds for lost or stolen traveler's checks.

Electricity The electrical current in Germany is 220 volts, 50 cycles alternating current (AC); the United States runs on 110-volt, 60-cycle AC current. Unlike wall outlets in the United States, which accept plugs with two flat prongs, outlets in Germany take Continental-type plugs, with two round prongs.

Adapters, To plug in U.S.-made appliances abroad, you'll need an adapter
Converters, plug. To reduce the voltage entering the appliance from 220 to
Transformers 110 volts, you'll also need a converter, unless it is a dual-voltage appliance, made for travel. There are converters for high-wattage appliances (such as hair dryers), low-wattage items (such as electric toothbrushes and razors), and combination models. Hotels sometimes have outlets marked "For Shavers Only" near the sink; these are 110-volt outlets for low-wattage appliances; don't use them for a high-wattage appliance. If you're traveling with a laptop computer, especially an older one, you may need a transformer—a type of converter used with electronic-circuitry products. Newer laptop computers are autosensing, operating equally well on 110 and 220 volts (so you need only the appropriate adapter plug). When in doubt, consult your appliance's owner's manual or the manufacturer. Or get a copy of the free brochure "Foreign Electricity is No Deep Dark Secret," published by adapter-converter manufacturer Franzus (Murtha Industrial Park, Box 142, Beacon Falls, CT 06403, tel. 203/723–6664; send a stamped, self-addressed envelope when ordering).

Luggage Free baggage allowances on an airline depend on the airline,
Regulations the route, and the class of your ticket. In general, on domestic flights and on international flights between the United States and foreign destinations, you are entitled to check two bags—neither exceeding 62 inches, or 158 centimeters (length + width + height), or weighing more than 70 pounds (32 kilograms). A third piece may be brought aboard as a carryon; its total dimensions are generally limited to less than 45 inches (114 centimeters), so it will fit easily under the seat in front of you or in the overhead compartment. There are variations, so ask in advance. The only rule, a Federal Aviation Administration safety regulation that pertains to carry-on baggage on U.S. airlines, requires only that carryons be properly stowed and allows the airline to limit allowances and tailor them to different aircraft and operational conditions. Charges for excess, oversize, or overweight pieces vary, so inquire before you pack.

If you are flying between two foreign destinations, note that baggage allowances may be determined not by the piece method but by the weight method, which generally allows 88 pounds (40 kilograms) of luggage in first class, 66 pounds (30 kilograms) in business class, and 44 pounds (20 kilograms) in economy. If your flight between two cities abroad *connects* with your transatlantic or transpacific flight, the piece method still applies.

Safeguarding Your Before leaving home, itemize your bags' contents and their
Luggage worth; this list will help you estimate the extent of your loss if your bags go astray. To minimize that risk, tag them inside and out with your name, address, and phone number. (If you use your home address, cover it so that potential thieves can't see it.) At check-in, make sure that the tag attached by baggage handlers bears the correct three-letter code for your destination. If your bags do not arrive with you, or if you detect dam-

age, do not leave the airport until you've filed a written report with the airline.

Taking Money Abroad

Traveler's Checks Although you will want plenty of cash when visiting small cities or rural areas, traveler's checks are usually preferable. The most widely recognized are **American Express, Barclay's, Thomas Cook,** and those issued by major commercial banks such as **Citibank** and **Bank of America.** American Express also issues *Traveler's Cheques for Two*, which can be signed and used by you or your traveling companion. Some checks are free; usually the issuing company or the bank at which you make your purchase charges 1% of the checks' face value as a fee. Be sure to buy a few checks in small denominations to cash toward the end of your trip, when you don't want to be left with more foreign currency than you can spend. Always record the numbers of checks as you spend them, and keep this list separate from the checks.

Currency Exchange Banks and bank-operated exchange booths at airports and railroad stations are usually the best places to change money. Hotels, stores, and privately run exchange firms typically offer less favorable rates.

Before your trip, pay attention to how the dollar is doing vis-à-vis Germany's currency. If the dollar is losing strength, try to pay as many travel bills as possible in advance, especially the big ones. If it is getting stronger, pay for costly items overseas, and use your credit card whenever possible—you'll come out ahead, whether the exchange rate at which your purchase is calculated is the one in effect the day the vendor's bank abroad processes the charge, or the one prevailing on the day the charge company's service center processes it at home.

To avoid lines at airport currency-exchange booths, arrive in a foreign country with a small amount of the local currency already in your pocket—a so-called tip pack. **Thomas Cook Currency Services** (630 5th Ave., New York, NY 10111, tel. 212/757–6915) supplies foreign currency by mail.

Getting Money from Home

Cash Machines Automated-teller machines (ATMs) are proliferating; many are tied to international networks such as **Cirrus** and **Plus.** You can use your bank card at ATMs away from home to withdraw money from your account and get cash advances on a credit-card account (providing your card has been programmed with a personal identification number, or PIN). Check in advance on limits on withdrawals and cash advances within specified periods. Ask whether your bank-card or credit-card PIN number will need to be reprogrammed for use in the area you'll be visiting—a possibility if the number has more than four digits. If you know your PIN number as a word, learn the numerical equivalent before you leave, since some ATM keypads show no letters, only numbers. Remember that on cash advances you are charged interest from the day you get the money from an ATM or teller. And note that, although transaction fees for ATM withdrawals abroad will probably be higher than fees for withdrawals at home, Cirrus and Plus exchange rates tend to be good.

Be sure to plan ahead: Obtain ATM locations and the names of affiliated cash-machine networks before departure. For specific foreign Cirrus locations, call 800/4–CIRRUS; for foreign Plus locations, consult the Plus directory at your local bank.

American Express Cardholder Services The company's **Express Cash** system lets you withdraw cash and/or traveler's checks from a worldwide network of 57,000 American Express dispensers and participating bank ATMs. You must *enroll first* (call 800/CASH–NOW for a form and allow two weeks for processing). Withdrawals are charged not to your card but to a designated bank account. You can withdraw up to $1,000 per seven-day period on the basic card, more if your card is gold or platinum. There is a 2% fee (minimum $2.50, maximum $10) for each cash transaction, and a 1% fee for traveler's checks (except for the platinum card), which are available only from American Express dispensers.

At AmEx offices, cardholders can also cash personal checks abroad for up to $1,000 in any 21-day period; of this $200 can be in cash, more if available, with the balance paid in traveler's checks, for which all but platinum cardholders pay a 1% fee. Higher limits apply to the gold and platinum cards.

Wiring Money You don't have to be a cardholder to send or receive an **American Express MoneyGram** for up to $10,000. To send one, go to an American Express MoneyGram agent, pay up to $1,000 with a credit card and anything over that in cash, and phone a transaction reference number to your intended recipient, who needs only present identification and the reference number to the nearest MoneyGram agent to pick up the cash. There are MoneyGram agents in more than 60 countries (call 800/543–4080 for locations). Fees range from 5% to 10%, depending on the amount and how you pay. You can't use American Express, which is really a convenience card—only Discover, Master-Card, and Visa credit cards.

You can also use **Western Union.** To wire money, take either cash or a check to the nearest office. (Or you can order money sent by phone, using a credit card.) Fees are roughly 5%–10%. Money sent from the United States or Canada will be available for pick up at agent locations in Germany within minutes. (Note that once the money is in the system it can be picked up at *any* location. You don't have to miss your train waiting for it to arrive in City A, because if there's an agent in City B, where you're headed, you can pick it up there, too.) There are approximately 20,000 agents worldwide (call 800/325–6000 for locations).

German Currency

The unit of currency in Germany is the Deutschemark (DM), divided into 100 pfennings (pf). Bills are DM 1,000, 500, 200, 100, 50, 20, and 10. Coins are DM 5, 2, and 1, and 50, 10, 5, 2, and 1 pf. At press time, the mark stood at DM 1.57 to the U.S. dollar, DM 1.24 to the Canadian dollar, and DM 2.48 to the pound sterling.

The Deutschemark became the official currency of united Germany in July 1990. However, great discrepancies still exist in the standard of living between western and eastern Germany.

What It Will Cost

Germany has an admirably high standard of living—perhaps the highest in Europe—which inevitably makes it an expensive country to visit, particularly if you spend time in the cities. Many items—gas, food, hotels, and trains, to name but a few—are often more expensive than in the United States.

Although Germany's largest city, Berlin is not its most expensive. Restaurant bills are generally lower (particularly in the eastern half of the city), hotel package-deals are more numerous, and theater/concert ticket prices tend to be lower than in, say, Hamburg or Munich. Until unification, East Berlin and eastern German excursion cities such as Potsdam and Magdeburg were a budget-traveler's dream. Currency reform and political union rapidly changed that, and today the former communist-ruled areas that attract tourists are at a rough price parity with western German areas.

Passports and Visas

If your passport is lost or stolen abroad, report it immediately to the nearest embassy or consulate and to the local police. If you can provide the consular officer with the information contained in the passport, they will usually be able to issue you a new passport. For this reason, it is a good idea to keep a copy of the data page of your passport in a separate place, or to leave the passport number, date, and place of issuance with a relative or friend at home.

U.S. Citizens All U.S. citizens, even infants, need a valid passport to enter Germany for stays of up to three months. You can pick up new and renewal passport application forms at any of the 13 U.S. Passport Agency offices and at some post offices and courthouses. Although passports are usually mailed within two weeks of your application's receipt, it's best to allow three weeks for delivery in low season, five weeks or more from April through summer. Call the Department of State Office of Passport Services' information line (1425 K St. NW, Washington, DC 20522, tel. 202/647–0518) for fees, documentation requirements, and other details.

A tourist/business visa is not required for U.S. citizens staying up to three months in Germany, but longer stays generally require a visa. Check with the German Embassy, 4645 Reservoir Rd. NW, Washington, DC 20007, tel. 202/298–4000.

Canadian Citizens Canadian citizens need a valid passport to enter Germany for stays of up to three months. Passport application forms are available at 23 regional passport offices as well as post offices and travel agencies. Whether applying for a first or subsequent passport, you must apply in person. Children under 16 may be included on a parent's passport but must have their own passport to travel alone. Passports are valid for five years and are usually mailed within two weeks of an application's receipt. For fees, documentation requirements, and other information in English or French, call the passport office (tel. 514/283–2152).

Visas are not required for Canadian citizens to enter Germany for stays of up to three months.

U.K. Citizens Citizens of the United Kingdom need a valid passport or British Visitor's Passport to enter Germany. Applications for new and renewal passports are available from main post offices as well as at the six passport offices, located in Belfast, Glasgow, Liverpool, London, Newport, and Peterborough. You may apply in person at all passport offices, or by mail to all except the London office. Children under 16 may travel on a parent's passport when accompanying them. All passports are valid for 10 years. Allow a month for processing.

A British Visitor's Passport is valid for holidays and some business trips of up to three months to Germany. It can include both partners of a married couple. Valid for one year, it will be issued on the same day that you apply. You must apply in person at a main post office.

Visas are not required for British citizens to enter Germany.

Customs and Duties

On Arrival Since a single, unrestricted market took effect within the European Community (EC) early in 1993, there are no longer restrictions for citizens of the 12 member countries traveling between EC countries. For citizens of non-EC countries and anyone entering Germany from outside the Community, the following limitations apply.

On goods obtained (duty- and tax-paid) within another EC country, you are allowed (1) 300 cigarettes or 150 cigarillos or 75 cigars or 400 grams of tobacco; (2) 5 liters of still table wine plus (3) 1.5 liters of spirits over 22% volume or 3 liters of spirits under 22% volume (fortified or sparkling wines) or 3 more liters of table wine; (4) 90 milliliters of perfume and 375 milliliters of toilet water; (5) other goods to the value of DM 780.

On goods obtained anywhere outside the EC or for goods purchased in a duty-free shop within an EC country, you are allowed (1) 200 cigarettes or 100 cigarillos or 50 cigars or 250 grams of tobacco (twice that if you live outside of Europe); (2) 2 liters of still table wine plus (3) 1 liter of spirits over 22% volume or 2 liters of spirits under 22% volume (fortified and sparkling wines) or 2 more liters of table wine; (4) 60 milliliters of perfume and 250 milliliters of toilet water; (5) other goods to the value of DM 115.

Tobacco and alcohol allowances are for visitors ages 17 and over. Other items intended for personal use can be imported and exported freely. There are no restrictions on the import and export of German currency.

U.S. Customs Provided you've been out of the country for at least 48 hours and haven't already used the exemption, or any part of it, in the past 30 days, you may bring home $400 worth of foreign goods duty-free. So can each member of your family, regardless of age; and your exemptions may be pooled, so one of you can bring in more if another brings in less. A flat 10% duty applies to the next $1,000 of goods; above $1,400, the rate varies with the merchandise. (If the 48-hour or 30-day limits apply, your duty-free allowance drops to $25, which may not be pooled.) Please note that these are the *general* rules, applicable to most countries, including Germany.

Travelers 21 or older may bring back 1 liter of alcohol duty-free, provided the beverage laws of the state through which they reenter the United States allow it. In addition, 100 non-

Cuban cigars and 200 cigarettes are allowed, regardless of your age. Antiques and works of art more than 100 years old are duty-free.

Gifts valued at less than $50 may be mailed duty-free to stateside friends and relatives, with a limit of one package per day per addressee (do not send alcohol or tobacco products, nor perfume valued at more than $5). These gifts do not count as part of your exemption, unless you bring them home with you. Mark the package "Unsolicited Gift" and include the nature of the gift and its retail value.

For a copy of "Know Before You Go," a free brochure detailing what you may and may not bring back to the United States, rates of duty, and other pointers, contact the **U.S. Customs Service** (Box 7407, Washington, DC 20044, tel. 202/927–6724).

Canadian Customs Once per calendar year, when you've been out of Canada for at least seven days, you may bring in $300 worth of goods duty-free. If you've been away less than seven days but more than 48 hours, the duty-free exemption drops to $100 but can be claimed any number of times (as can a $20 duty-free exemption for absences of 24 hours or more). You cannot combine the yearly and 48-hour exemptions, use the $300 exemption only partially (to save the balance for a later trip), or pool exemptions with family members. Goods claimed under the $300 exemption may follow you by mail; those claimed under the lesser exemptions must accompany you on your return.

Alcohol and tobacco products may be included in the yearly and 48-hour exemptions but not in the 24-hour exemption. If you meet the age requirements of the province through which you reenter Canada, you may bring in, duty-free, 1.14 liters (40 imperial ounces) of wine or liquor *or* two dozen 12-ounce cans or bottles of beer or ale. If you are 16 or older, you may bring in, duty-free, 200 cigarettes, 50 cigars or cigarillos, and 400 tobacco sticks or 400 grams of manufactured tobacco. Alcohol and tobacco must accompany you on your return.

Gifts may be mailed to friends in Canada duty-free. These do not count as part of your exemption. Each gift may be worth up to $60—label the package "Unsolicited Gift—Value under $60." There are no limits on the number of gifts that may be sent per day or per addressee, but you can't mail alcohol or tobacco.

For more information, including details of duties on items that exceed your duty-free limit, ask the Revenue Canada Customs and Excise Department (Connaught Bldg., MacKenzie Ave., Ottawa, Ont., K1A OL5, tel. 613/957–0275) for a copy of the free brochure "I Declare/Je Déclare."

U.K. Customs If your journey was wholly within EC countries, you no longer need to pass through customs when you return to the United Kingdom. According to EC guidelines, you may bring in 800 cigarettes, 400 cigarillos, 200 cigars, and 1 kilogram of smoking tobacco, plus 10 liters of spirits, 20 liters of fortified wine, 90 liters of wine, and 110 liters of beer. If you exceed these limits, you may be required to prove that the goods are for your personal use or are gifts.

For further information or a copy of "A Guide for Travellers," which details standard customs procedures as well as what you may bring into the United Kingdom from abroad, contact HM

Customs and Excise (New King's Beam House, 22 Upper Ground, London SE1 9PJ, tel. 071/620–1313).

Traveling with Cameras, Camcorders, and Laptops

About Film and Cameras If your camera is new or if you haven't used it for a while, shoot and develop a few rolls of film before leaving home. Pack some lens tissue and an extra battery for your built-in light meter, and invest in an inexpensive skylight filter, to both protect your lens and provide some definition in hazy shots. Store film in a cool, dry place—never in the car's glove compartment or on the shelf under the rear window.

Films above ISO 400 are more sensitive to damage from airport security X-rays than others; very high speed films, ISO 1,000 and above, are exceedingly vulnerable. To protect your film, don't put it in checked luggage; carry it with you in a plastic bag and ask for a hand inspection. Such requests are up to the inspector abroad. Don't depend on a lead-lined bag to protect film in checked luggage—the airline may very well turn up the dosage of radiation to see what you've got in there. Airport metal detectors do not harm film, although you'll set off the alarm if you walk through one with a roll in your pocket. Call the Kodak Information Center (tel. 800/242–2424) for details.

About Camcorders Before your trip, put new or long-unused camcorders through their paces, and practice panning and zooming. Invest in a skylight filter to protect the lens, and check the lithium battery that lights up the LCD (liquid crystal display) modes. As for the rechargeable nickel-cadmium batteries that are the camera's power source, take along an extra pair, so while you're using your camcorder you'll have one battery ready and another recharging. Most newer camcorders are equipped with the battery (which generally slides or clicks onto the camera body) and, to recharge it, with what's known as a universal or worldwide AC adapter charger (or multivoltage converter) that can be used whether the voltage is 110 or 220. All that's needed is the appropriate plug.

About Videotape Unlike still-camera film, videotape is not damaged by X-rays. However, it may well be harmed by the magnetic field of a walk-through metal detector. Airport security personnel may want you to turn the camcorder on to prove that that's what it is, so make sure the battery is charged when you get to the airport.

About Laptops Security X-rays do not harm hard-disk or floppy-disk storage. Most airlines allow you to use your laptop aloft but request that you turn it off during takeoff and landing so as not to interfere with navigation equipment. Make sure the battery is charged when you arrive at the airport, because you may be asked to turn on the computer at security checkpoints to prove that it is what it appears to be. If you're a heavy computer user, consider traveling with a backup battery. For international travel, register your laptop with U.S. Customs as you leave the country, providing it's manufactured abroad (U.S.-origin items cannot be registered at U.S. Customs); when you do so, you'll get a certificate, good for as long as you own the item, containing your name and address, a description of the laptop, and its serial number, that will quash any questions that may arise on your return. If your laptop is U.S.-made, call the consulate of the country you'll be visiting to find out whether it should be registered with customs in that country upon arrival. Some travelers do this as a matter of course and ask customs officers to sign a document that specifies the total configuration of the system, computer and peripherals, and its value. In addition, before leaving home, find out about repair facilities at your destination, and don't forget any transformer or adapter plug you may need (*see* Electricity in What to Pack, *above*).

Language

The Germans are great linguists, and you'll find that English is spoken in virtually all hotels, restaurants, airports, stations, museums, and other places of interest. Berliners are particularly cosmopolitan and enjoy the opportunity to show off their ability to speak English.

Staying Healthy

Sanitation and health standards in Germany are as high as those anywhere in the world, and there are no serious health risks associated with travel there. No inoculations are required.

Finding a Doctor The **International Association for Medical Assistance to Travellers** (IAMAT, 417 Center St., Lewiston, NY 14092, tel. 716/754–4883; 40 Regal Rd., Guelph, Ontario N1K 1B5; 57 Voirets, 1212 Grand-Lancy, Geneva, Switzerland) publishes a worldwide directory of English-speaking physicians whose qualifications meet IAMAT standards and who have agreed to treat members for a set fee. Membership is free.

Assistance Companies Pretrip medical referrals, emergency evacuation or repatriation, 24-hour telephone hot lines for medical consultation, dispatch of medical personnel, relay of medical records, up-front cash for emergencies, and other personal and legal assistance are among the services provided by several membership organizations specializing in medical assistance to travelers. Among them are **International SOS Assistance** (Box 11568, Philadelphia, PA 19116, tel. 215/244–1500 or 800/523–8930; Box 466, Pl. Bonaventure, Montréal, Qué. H5A 1C1, tel. 514/874–7674 or 800/363–0263), **Near Services** (450 Prairie Ave., Suite 101, Calumet City, IL 60409, tel. 708/868–6700 or 800/654–6700), and **Travel Assistance International** (1133 15th St. NW, Suite 400, Washington, DC 20005, tel. 202/331–1609 or 800/821–2828), part of Europ Assistance Worldwide Services, Inc. Because these companies will also sell you death-and-dismemberment, trip-cancellation, and other insurance coverage, there is some overlap with the travel-insurance policies discussed below, which may include the services of an assistance company among the insurance options or reimburse travelers for such services without providing them.

Insurance

For U.S. Residents Most tour operators, travel agents, and insurance agents sell specialized health-and-accident, flight, trip-cancellation, and luggage insurance as well as comprehensive policies with some or all of these features. But before you make any purchase, review your existing health and homeowner policies to find out whether they cover expenses incurred while traveling.

Health and Supplemental health-and-accident insurance for travelers is
Accident Insurance usually a part of comprehensive policies. Specific policy provisions vary, but they tend to address three general areas, beginning with reimbursement for medical expenses caused by illness or an accident during a trip. Such policies may reimburse anywhere from $1,000 to $150,000 worth of medical expenses; dental benefits may also be included. A second common feature is the personal-accident, or death-and-dismemberment, provision, which pays a lump sum to your beneficiaries if you die or to you if you lose one or both limbs or your eyesight. This is similar to the flight insurance described below, although it is not necessarily limited to accidents involving airplanes or even other "common carriers" (buses, trains, and ships) and can be in effect 24 hours a day. The lump sum awarded can range from $15,000 to $500,000. A third area generally addressed by these policies is medical assistance (referrals, evacuation, or repatriation and other services). Some policies reimburse travelers for the cost of such services; others may automatically enroll you as a member of a particular medical-assistance company.

Flight Insurance This insurance, often bought as a last-minute impulse at the airport, pays a lump sum to a beneficiary when a plane crashes and the insured dies (and sometimes to a surviving passenger who loses eyesight or a limb); thus it supplements the airlines' own coverage as described in the limits-of-liability paragraphs on your ticket (up to $75,000 on international flights, $20,000 on domestic ones—and that is generally subject to litigation). Charging an airline ticket to a major credit card often automatically signs you up for flight insurance; in this case, the coverage may also embrace travel by bus, train, and ship.

Baggage Insurance In the event of loss, damage, or theft on international flights, airlines limit their liability to $20 per kilogram for checked baggage (roughly about $640 per 70-pound bag) and $400 per passenger for unchecked baggage. On domestic flights, the ceiling is $1,250 per passenger. Excess-valuation insurance can be bought directly from the airline at check-in but leaves your bags vulnerable on the ground.

Trip Insurance There are two sides to this coin. **Trip-cancellation-and-interruption insurance** protects you in the event you are unable to undertake or finish your trip. **Default** or **bankruptcy insurance** protects you against a supplier's failure to deliver. Consider the former if your airline ticket, cruise, or package tour does not allow changes or cancellations. The amount of coverage to buy should equal the cost of your trip should you, a traveling companion, or a family member get sick, forcing you to stay home, plus the nondiscounted one-way airline ticket you would need to buy if you had to return home early. Read the fine print carefully; pay attention to sections defining "family member" and "preexisting medical conditions." A characteristic quirk of default policies is that they often do not cover default by travel agencies or default by a tour operator, airline, or cruise line if you bought your tour and the coverage directly from the firm in question. To reduce your need for default insurance, give preference to tours packaged by members of the United States Tour Operators Association (USTOA), which maintains a fund to reimburse clients in the event of member defaults. Even better, pay for travel arrangements with a major credit card, so that you can refuse to pay the bill if services have not been rendered—and let the card company fight your battles.

Comprehensive Policies Companies supplying comprehensive policies with some or all of the above features include **Access America, Inc.,** underwritten by BCS Insurance Company (Box 11188, Richmond, VA 23230, tel. 800/284–8300); **Carefree Travel Insurance,** underwritten by The Hartford (Box 310, 120 Mineola Blvd., Mineola, NY 11501, tel. 516/294–0220 or 800/323–3149); **Tele-Trip** (Mutual of Omaha Plaza, Box 31762, Omaha, NE 68131, tel. 800/228–9792), a subsidiary of Mutual of Omaha; **The Travelers Companies** (1 Tower Sq., Hartford, CT 06183, tel. 203/277–0111 or 800/243–3174); **Travel Guard International,** underwritten by Transamerica Occidental Life Companies (1145 Clark St., Stevens Point, WI 54481, tel. 715/345–0505 or 800/782–5151); and **Wallach and Company, Inc.** (107 W. Federal St., Box 480, Middleburg, VA 22117, tel. 703/687–3166 or 800/237–6615), underwritten by Lloyds, London. These companies may also offer the above types of insurance separately.

U.K. Residents Most tour operators, travel agents, and insurance agents sell specialized policies covering accident, medical expenses, personal liability, trip cancellation, and loss or theft of personal property. Some policies include coverage for delayed departure and legal expenses, winter-sports, accidents, or motoring abroad. You can also purchase an annual travel-insurance policy valid for every trip you make during the year in which it's purchased (usually only trips of less than 90 days). Before you leave, make sure you will be covered if you have a preexisting medical condition or are pregnant; your insurers may not pay for routine or continuing treatment, or may require a note from your doctor certifying your fitness to travel.

For advice by phone or a free booklet, "Holiday Insurance," that sets out what to expect from a holiday-insurance policy and gives price guidelines, contact the Association of British Insurers (51 Gresham St., London EC2V 7HQ, tel. 071/600–3333; 30 Gordon St., Glasgow G1 3PU, tel. 041/226–3905; Scottish Provincial Bldg., Donegall Sq. W, Belfast BT1 6JE, tel. 0232/249176; call for other locations).

Car Rentals

Some major car-rental companies are represented in Germany, including **Avis** (tel. 800/331–1212; in Canada, 800/879–2847); **Hertz** (tel. 800/654–3131; in Canada, 800/263–0600); **National** (tel. 800/227–7368), known internationally as InterRent and Europcar (tel. 800/227–7368). Rental rates vary widely, depending on size and model; most rates include unlimited mileage but not European value added taxes (VAT), which is 15% in Germany.

Requirements Your own U.S., Canadian, or U.K. driver's license is acceptable. An International Driver's Permit, available from the American Automobile Association, is a good idea.

Extra Charges Picking up the car in one city or country and leaving it in another may entail drop-off charges or one-way service fees, which can be substantial. The cost of a collision or loss-damage waiver (*see below*) can be high, also. Automatic transmissions and air-conditioning are not universally available; ask for them when you book if you want them, and check the cost before you commit yourself to the rental.

Cutting Costs If you know you will want a car for more than a day or two, you can save by planning ahead. Major international companies have programs that discount their standard rates by 15%–30% if you make the reservation before departure (anywhere from two to 14 days), rent for a minimum number of days (typically three or four), and prepay the rental. Ask about these advance-purchase schemes when you call for information. More economical rentals are those that come as part of fly/drive or other packages, even those as bare-bones as the rental plus an airline ticket (*see* Tours and Packages, *above*).

Other sources of savings are the several companies that operate as wholesalers—companies that do not own their own fleets but rent in bulk from those that do and offer advantageous rates to their customers. Rentals through such companies must be arranged and paid for before you leave the United States. Among them are **Auto Europe** (Box 1097, Camden, ME 04843, tel. 207/236–8235, 800/223–5555, or 800/458–9503), **Connex International** (23 N. Division St., Peekskill, NY 10566, tel. 914/739–0066 or 800/333–3949; in Canada, 800/843–5416), **Europe by Car** (mailing address, 1 Rockefeller Plaza, New York, NY 10020; walk-in address, 14 W. 49th St, New York, NY 10020, tel. 212/581–3040 or 212/245–1713; 9000 Sunset Blvd., Los Angeles, CA 90069, tel. 213/252–9401; in CA, 800/223–1516), **Foremost Euro-Car** (5430 Van Nuys Blvd., Suite 306, Van Nuys, CA 91401, tel. 818/786–1960 or 800/272–3299), and **Kemwel** (106 Calvert St., Harrison, NY 10528, tel. 914/835–5555 or 800/678–0678). You won't see these wholesalers' deals advertised; they're even better in summer, when business travel is down. Always ask whether the prices are guaranteed in U.S. dollars or foreign currency and if unlimited mileage is available. Find out about any required deposits, cancellation penalties, and drop-off charges, and confirm the cost of the CDW.

One last tip: Remember to fill the tank when you turn in the vehicle, to avoid being charged for refueling at what you'll swear is the most expensive pump in town.

Insurance and Collision Damage Waiver The standard rental contract includes liability coverage (for damage to public property, injury to pedestrians, etc.) and coverage for the car against fire, theft (not included in certain countries), and collision damage with a deductible—most commonly $2,000–$3,000, occasionally more. In the case of an accident, you are responsible for the deductible amount unless you've purchased the collision damage waiver (CDW), which costs an average of $12 a day, although this varies depending on what you've rented, where, and from whom.

Because this adds up quickly, you may be inclined to say "no thanks"—and that's certainly your option, although the rental agent may not tell you so. Planning ahead will help you make the right decision. By all means, find out if your own insurance covers damage to a rental car while traveling (not simply a car to drive when yours is in for repairs). And check whether charging car rentals to any of your credit cards will get you a CDW at no charge. Note before you decline that deductibles are occasionally high enough that totaling a car would make you responsible for its full value.

Rail Passes

The German Flexipass, not available to Germans, allows you to travel over the entire German rail network for five, 10, or 15 days within a single month; cost is $250, $390, and $498 in first-class, and $170, $268, and $348 in second class. A German Twin Pass discounts these rates for two people traveling together; cost is $450, $698, and $898 for first-class, and $300, $468, and $598 for second-class. A Youthpass, sold to those ages 12–25 for second-class travel costs $110–$180. All of these passes can be used on buses operated by the DB, meaning Deutsche Bundesbahn (the German Federal Railways), as well as on tour routes along the Romantic and Castle roads served by Deutsche Touring (*see* Getting Around by Bus in Staying in Germany, *below*), and Rhine, Main, and Mosel river cruises operated by the Köln-Düsseldorfer (KD) Line. Passes are sold by **DER Tours** (Box 1606, Des Plains, IL 60017, tel. 800/782–2424).

Still other passes can be purchased in Germany; *see* Staying in Germany, Getting Around by Rail, *below*.

Germany is also one of 17 countries in which you can use **EurailPasses,** which provide unlimited first-class rail travel during their period of validity. If you plan to rack up the miles, they can be an excellent value. Standard passes are available for 15 days ($460), 21 days ($598), one month ($728), two months ($998), and three months ($1,260). **Eurail Saverpasses,** valid for 15 days, cost $390 per person; you must do all your traveling with at least one companion (two companions from April through September). **Eurail Youthpasses,** which cover second-class travel, cost $508 for one month, $698 for two; you must be under 26 on the first day you travel. Flexipasses allow you to travel for five, 10, or 15 days within any two-month period. You pay $298, $496, and $676 for the **Eurail Flexipass,** sold for first-class travel; and $220, $348, $474 for the **Eurail Youth Flexipass,** available to those under 26 on their first travel day, sold for second-class travel. Apply through your travel agent, or **Rail Europe** (226–230 Westchester Ave., White Plains, NY 10604, tel. 914/682–5172; in eastern U.S., 800/848–7245; in western U.S., 800/438–7245).

Don't make the mistake of assuming that your rail pass guarantees you seats on the trains you want to ride. Seat reservations are required on some trains, particularly high-speed trains, and are a good idea on trains that may be crowded. You will also need reservations for overnight sleeping accommodations. Rail Europe can help you determine if you need reservations and can make them for you (about $10 each, less if you purchase them in Europe at the time of travel).

Student and Youth Travel

Students qualify for a wide range of price reductions in Germany, from opera tickets to rail passes, so be sure to carry some official student identification. Even if you aren't a student or can't produce an ID, if you're under 28 years old, don't be too shy to find out if you can receive a reduced price.

Travel Agencies The foremost U.S. student travel agency is **Council Travel**, a subsidiary of the nonprofit Council on International Educational Exchange. It specializes in low-cost travel arrangements, is the exclusive U.S. agent for several discount cards, and, with its sister CIEE subsidiary, **Council Charter,** is a source of airfare bargains. The Council Charter brochure and CIEE's twice-yearly *Student Travels* magazine, which details its programs, are available at the Council Travel office at CIEE headquarters (205 E. 42nd Street, New York, NY 10017, tel. 212/661–1450) and at 37 branches in college towns nationwide (free in person, $1 by mail). The **Educational Travel Center** (ETC, 438 N. Francis St., Madison, WI 53703, tel. 608/256–5551) also offers low-cost rail passes, domestic and international airline tickets (mostly for flights departing from Chicago), and other budgetwise travel arrangements. Other travel agencies catering to students include **Travel Management International** (TMI, 18 Prescott St., Suite 4, Cambridge, MA 02138, tel. 617/661–8187) and **Travel Cuts** (187 College St., Toronto, Ont. M5T 1P7, tel. 416/979–2406).

Discount Cards For discounts on transportation and on museum and attractions admissions, buy the **International Student Identity Card** (ISIC) if you're a bona fide student, or the **International Youth Card** (IYC) if you're under 26. In the United States the ISIC and IYC cards cost $15 each and include basic travel accident and sickness coverage. Apply to **CIEE** (*see* address *above*, tel. 212/661–1414; the application is in *Student Travels*). In Canada the cards are available for $15 each from **Travel Cuts** (*see above*). In the United Kingdom they cost £5 and £4 respectively at student unions and student travel companies, including Council Travel's London office (28A Poland St., London W1V 3DB, tel. 071/437–7767).

Hosteling An **International Youth Hostel Federation** (IYHF) membership card is the key to more than 5,300 hostel locations in 59 countries; the sex-segregated, dormitory-style sleeping quarters, including some for families, go for $7–$20 a night per person. Membership is available in the United States through **American Youth Hostels** (AYH, 733 15th St. NW, Washington, DC 20005, tel. 202/783–6161), the American link in the worldwide chain, and costs $25 for adults 18–54, $10 for those under 18, $15 for those 55 and over, and $35 for families. Volume 1 of the two-volume *Guide to Budget Accommodation* lists hostels in Europe and the Mediterranean ($13.95, including postage). IYHF membership is available in Canada through the **Canadian Hostelling Association** (CHA, 1600 James Naismith Dr., Suite 608, Gloucester, Ont. K1B 5N4, tel. 613/748–5638) for $26.75, and in the United Kingdom through the **Youth Hostel Association of England and Wales** (Trevelyan House, 8 St. Stephen's Hill, St. Albans, Herts. AL1 2DY, tel. 0727/55215) for £9.

Traveling with Children

Publications
Local Guides Ask the German National Tourist Board for the booklet **"Berlin Loves Children,"** filled with information about family restaurants and accommodations, children's museums, puppet theaters, and other child-friendly activities in Berlin. Although it is written in German, it offers an excellent starting point.

Newsletter ***Family Travel Times,*** published 10 times a year by **Travel With Your Children** (TWYCH, 45 W. 18th St., 7th Floor Tower, New York, NY 10011, tel. 212/206–0688; annual subscription $55), covers destinations, types of vacations, and modes of travel.

Books *Great Vacations with Your Kids,* by Dorothy Jordon and
Marjorie Cohen ($13; Penguin USA, 120 Woodbine St., Ber-
genfield, NJ 07621, tel. 800/253–6476) and *Traveling with Children—And Enjoying It,* by Arlene K. Butler ($11.95 plus $3
shipping per book; Globe Pequot Press, Box 833, Old Saybrook,
CT 06475, tel. 800/243–0495; in CT, 800/962–0973), both help
plan your trip with children, from toddlers to teens. *Innocents
Abroad: Traveling with Kids in Europe,* by Valerie Wolf
Deutsch and Laura Sutherland ($15.95 or $4.95 paperback,
Penguin USA, *see above*), covers child- and teen-friendly activities, food, and transportation.

Tour Operators **GrandTravel** (6900 Wisconsin Ave., Suite 706, Chevy Chase,
MD 20815, tel. 301/986–0790 or 800/247–7651) offers international and domestic tours for grandparents traveling with their
grandchildren. The catalogue, as charmingly written and illustrated as a children's book, positively invites armchair traveling with lap-sitters aboard. **Families Welcome!** (21 W. Colony
Pl., Suite 140, Durham, NC 27705, tel. 919/489–2555 or 800/
326–0724) packages and sells family tours to Europe. **Rascals
in Paradise** (650 5th St., Suite 505, San Francisco, CA 94107,
tel. 415/978–9800 or 800/872–7225) specializes in programs for
families.

Getting There On international flights, the fare for infants under 2 not occupy-
Air Fares ing a seat is generally 10% of the accompanying adult's fare;
children ages 2–11 usually pay half to two-thirds of the adult
fare. On domestic flights, children under 2 not occupying a seat
travel free, and older children currently travel on the "lowest
applicable" adult fare.

Baggage In general, infants paying 10% of the adult fare are allowed one
carry-on bag, not to exceed 70 pounds or 45 inches (length +
width + height). The adult baggage allowance applies for children paying half or more of the adult fare. Check with the airline for particulars, especially regarding flights between two
foreign destinations, where allowances for infants may be less
generous than those above.

Safety Seats The FAA recommends the use of safety seats aloft and details
approved models in the free leaflet "**Child/Infant Safety Seats
Recommended for Use in Aircraft**" (available from the Federal
Aviation Administration, APA–200, 800 Independence Ave.
SW, Washington, DC 20591, tel. 202/267–3479). Airline policy
varies. U.S. carriers must allow FAA-approved models, but
because these seats are strapped into a regular passenger seat,
they may require that parents buy a ticket even for an infant
under 2 who would otherwise ride free. Foreign carriers may
not allow infant seats, may charge the child's rather than the
infant's fare for their use, or may require you to hold your baby
during takeoff and landing, thus defeating the seat's purpose.

Facilities Aloft Airlines do provide other facilities and services for children,
such as children's meals and freestanding bassinets (to those
sitting in seats on the bulkhead, where there's enough legroom
to accommodate them). Make your request when reserving.
The annual February/March issue of *Family Travel Times*
gives details of the children's services of dozens of airlines (*see
below*). "Kids and Teens in Flight" (free from the U.S. Department of Transportation, tel. 202/366–2220) offers tips for children flying alone.

Lodging Although few hotels in Berlin have extensive facilities or programs for children, **Hotel Berlin,** part of the **Dial Berlin Consortium** (tel. 800/237–5469 for reservations) has several L-shaped rooms with dividing curtains for family use. They also offer children's menus. At both the **Intercontinental Berlin** and **Intercontinental's Schweizerhoss** hotels (tel. 800/327–0200), one child under 14 can stay free in his or her parents' room.

Baby-Sitting You can get recommendations from your hotel desk, and up-
Services dated lists of well-screened baby-sitters from most local tourist offices. Rates are usually about DM 25 per hour.

Hints for Travelers with Disabilities

Nearly 100 German cities and towns issue special guides for disabled visitors, which offer information, usually in German, about how to get around destinations and suggestions for places to visit. Recent changes in eastern Germany and Berlin mean that many organizations are combining, changing names, or disappearing. For the time being, you should contact the Berlin Tourist Office for all information concerning accessibility and special services for travelers with disabilities.

Hotels Most Berlin hotels offer some wheelchair-accessible rooms. The totally accessible **Hotel Mondial** (Kurfürstendamm 47, D-1000, Berlin 15, tel. 030/884–110), sponsored by an association of injured war veterans, is a must for all disabled visitors planning an extended stay. Situated in the heart of western Berlin, the Hotel Mondial has no steps or revolving doors and offers specially designed rooms and bathrooms and a physical therapy center. As there are only 75 rooms, reservations are advised. Other hotels with wheelchair-accessible facilities include the **Berlin Penta** (tel. 800/223–8585), **Hotel Berlin** (tel. 800/237–5469), and **Novotel Berlin** (tel. 800/221–4542).

All the major hotel chains in Germany (Hilton, Sheraton, Marriott, Holiday Inn, Steigenberger, and Kempinski) have special facilities for guests with disabilities, including specially equipped and furnished rooms.

The **Deutsche Bundesbahn** (German Railways) provide a complete range of services and facilities for disabled travelers. All InterCityExpress (ICE) and InterRegio trains and most EuroCity and InterCity trains have special areas for wheelchair users. Seat and wheelchair-space reservations are free of charge for wheelchair users. The **German Red Cross** and a welfare service called the **Bahnhofs Mission** (Railway Station Mission) have support facilities at all major and many smaller, regional stations. They organize assistance in boarding, leaving, and changing trains and also help with reservations. The Bundesbahn issues a booklet dealing with its services for disabled travelers, with an English-language section. It can be obtained by contacting **Deutsche Bundesbahn Zentrale** (Zentralstelle Absatz, 6550 Mainz 1, tel. 06131/25800).

Organizations Several organizations provide travel information for people with disabilities, usually for a membership fee, and some publish newsletters and bulletins. Among them are the **Information Center for Individuals with Disabilities** (Fort Point Pl., 27–43 Wormwood St., Boston, MA 02210, tel. 617/727–5540 or in MA 800/462–5015 between 11 and 4, or leave message; TDD/TTY, 617/345–9743); **Mobility International USA** (Box 3551,

Eugene, OR 97403, voice and TDD tel. 503/343–1284), the U.S. branch of an international organization based in Britain (*see below*) and present in 30 countries; **MossRehab Hospital Travel Information Service** (1200 W. Tabor Rd., Philadelphia, PA 19141, tel. 215/456–9603; TDD, 215/456–9602); the **Society for the Advancement of Travel for the Handicapped** (SATH, 347 5th Ave., Suite 610, New York, NY 10016, tel. 212/447–7284, fax 212/725–8253); the **Travel Industry and Disabled Exchange** (TIDE, 5435 Donna Ave., Tarzana, CA 91356, tel. 818/368–5648); and **Travelin' Talk** (Box 3534, Clarksville, TN 37043, tel. 615/552–6670).

In the United Kingdom Main information sources include the **Royal Association for Disability and Rehabilitation** (RADAR, 25 Mortimer St., London W1N 8AB, tel. 071/637–5400), which publishes travel information for the disabled in Britain, and **Mobility International** (228 Borough High St., London SE1 1JX, tel. 071/403–5688), the headquarters of an international membership organization that serves as a clearinghouse of travel information for people with disabilities.

Travel Agencies and Tour Operators **Directions Unlimited** (720 N. Bedford Rd., Bedford Hills, NY 10507, tel. 914/241–1700), a travel agency, has expertise in tours and cruises for the disabled. **Evergreen Travel Service** (4114 198th St. SW, Suite 13, Lynnwood, WA 98036, tel. 206/776–1184 or 800/435–2288) operates Wings on Wheels Tours for those in wheelchairs, White Cane Tours for the blind, and tours for the deaf and makes group and independent arrangements for travelers with any disability. **Flying Wheels Travel** (143 W. Bridge St., Box 382, Owatonna, MN 55060, tel. 800/535–6790; in MN, 800/722–9351), a tour operator and travel agency, arranges international tours, cruises, and independent travel itineraries for people with mobility disabilities. **Nautilus**, at the same address as TIDE (*see above*), packages tours for the disabled internationally.

Publications In addition to the fact sheets, newsletters, and books mentioned above are several free publications available from the Consumer Information Center (Pueblo, CO 81009): "New Horizons for the Air Traveler with a Disability," a U.S. Department of Transportation booklet describing changes resulting from the 1986 Air Carrier Access Act and those still to come from the 1990 Americans with Disabilities Act (include Department 608Y in the address), and the Airport Operators Council's *Access Travel: Airports* (Dept. 5804), which describes facilities and services for the disabled at more than 500 airports worldwide.

Twin Peaks Press (Box 129, Vancouver, WA 98666, tel. 206/694–2462 or 800/637–2256) publishes the *Directory of Travel Agencies for the Disabled* ($19.95), listing more than 370 agencies worldwide; *Travel for the Disabled* ($19.95), listing some 500 access guides and accessible places worldwide; the *Directory of Accessible Van Rentals* ($9.95) for campers and RV travelers worldwide; and *Wheelchair Vagabond* ($14.95), a collection of personal travel tips. Add $2 per book for shipping. GI/US BOOKS/The Sierra Club publishes *Easy Access to National Parks* ($16 plus $3 shipping; 730 Polk St., San Francisco, CA 94109, tel. 415/776–2211).

Hints for Older Travelers

Organizations   The **American Association of Retired Persons** (AARP, 601 E St. NW, Washington, DC 20049, tel. 202/434–2277) provides independent travelers the Purchase Privilege Program, which offers discounts on hotels, car rentals, and sightseeing, and the AARP Motoring Plan, provided by Amoco, which furnishes domestic trip-routing information and emergency road-service aid for an annual fee of $39.95 per person or couple ($59.95 for a premium version). AARP also arranges group tours, cruises, and apartment living through AARP Travel Experience from American Express (400 Pinnacle Way, Suite 450, Norcross, GA 30071, tel. 800/927–0111); these can be booked through travel agents, except for the cruises, which must be booked directly (tel. 800/745–4567). AARP membership is open to those 50 and over; annual dues are $8 per person or couple.

Two other membership organizations offer discounts on lodgings, car rentals, and other travel products, along with such nontravel perks as magazines and newsletters. The **National Council of Senior Citizens** (1331 F St. NW, Washington, DC 20004, tel. 202/347–8800) is a nonprofit advocacy group with some 5,000 local clubs across the United States; membership costs $12 per person or couple annually. **Mature Outlook** (6001 N. Clark St., Chicago, IL 60660, tel. 800/336–6330), a Sears Roebuck & Co. subsidiary with 800,000 members, charges $9.95 for an annual membership.

Note: When using any senior-citizen identification card for reduced hotel rates, mention it when booking, not when checking out. At restaurants, show your card before you're seated; discounts may be limited to certain menus, days, or hours. If you are renting a car, ask about promotional rates that might improve on your senior-citizen discount.

Educational Travel   **Elderhostel** (75 Federal St., 3rd floor, Boston, MA 02110, tel. 617/426–7788) is a nonprofit organization that has inexpensive study programs for people 60 and older since 1975. Programs take place at more than 1,800 educational institutions in the United States, Canada, and 45 countries overseas, and courses cover everything from marine science to Greek myths and cowboy poetry. Participants generally attend lectures in the morning and spend the afternoon sightseeing or on field trips; they live in dorms on the host campuses. Fees for two- to three-week international trips—including room, board, and transportation from the United States—range from $1,800 to $4,500.

Interhostel (University of New Hampshire, 6 Garrison Ave., Durham, NH 03824, tel. 800/733–9753), a slightly younger enterprise than Elderhostel, caters to a slightly younger clientele—that is, 50 and over—and runs programs overseas in some 25 countries. But the idea is similar: Lectures and field trips mix with sightseeing, and participants stay in dormitories at cooperating educational institutions or in modest hotels. Programs are usually two weeks in length and cost $1,500–$2,100, not including airfare from the United States.

Tour Operators   **Saga International Holidays** (222 Berkeley St., Boston, MA 02116, tel. 800/343–0273), which specializes in group travel for people over 60, offers a selection of variously priced tours and cruises covering five continents. If you want to take your grandchildren, look into **GrandTravel** (*see* Traveling with Children, *above*).

Further Reading

Berlin is the setting for many good spy novels, including Len Deighton's *Funeral in Berlin* and *Berlin Game*, John Le Carré's *The Spy Who Came in from the Cold*, Ken Follett's *Key to Rebecca*, Adam Hall's *Berlin Memorandum*, Fredrick Knebel's *Crossing in Berlin*, and Ian McEwan's *The Innocent*.

For fiction about Berlin in the days of the Weimar Republic, pick up Vicki Baum's *Grand Hotel*, Alfred Döblin's *Berlin-Alexanderplatz*, and Christopher Isherwood's *Goodbye to Berlin*. Leon Uris's *Armageddon: A Novel of Berlin* is set at the end of World War II. Contemporary novels about Berlin include Peter Schneider's *The Wall Jumper* and Philip Kerr's *March Violets*.

Notable memoirs include *Zoo Station*, by Ian Walker, a British journalist who lived in the city in the mid-1980s, *Berlin Diaries*, the secret journals of a Russian emigré living in Nazi Berlin, and Lillian Hellman's *Pentimento*, about the author's friend who was active in the Nazi resistance.

Walter Hubatsch's *Frederick the Great: Absolutism and Administration* and Christopher Duffy's *Frederick the Great: A Military Life* examine the life of the man who was largely responsible for transforming Berlin and Prussia into dominant forces in Germany and Europe. Histories of the Weimar era include John Willett's *Weimar Years* and Alex de Jonge's *The Weimar Chronicle*. For excellent accounts of the war years, read William Shirer's *The Rise and Fall of the Third Reich*, George Clare's *Berlin Days 1946–1947*, and Hugh Trevor-Roper's *The Last Days of Hitler*.

For a look at life in the city after the fall of the Wall, try *After the Wall: East Meets West in New Berlin*, by John Borneman and *The German Comedy* by Peter Schneider. *Portrait of a City* features photographs by Stéphane Duroy that chronicle the divided city over the last decade and includes images of the smashing of the Wall. The most recent studies of the Germans available in English include *Germany and the Germans* by John Ardagh, *Germany, the Empire Within* by Amity Shlaes, and *The New Germany* by David Marsh.

Arriving and Departing

From North America by Plane

Since the air routes between North America and Germany are heavily traveled, you have a choice of many airlines and fares.

Flights are either nonstop, direct, or connecting. A **nonstop** flight requires no change of plane and makes no stops. A **direct** flight stops at least once and can involve a change of plane, although the flight number remains the same; if the first leg is late, the second waits. This is not the case with a **connecting** flight, which involves a different plane and a different flight number.

Airlines All scheduled and charter flights arrive at Berlin's Tegel Airport. Among U.S. airlines serving Berlin, **Delta** (tel. 800/241–4141), offers a nonstop flight from New York and a direct flight from Atlanta, and **American Airlines** (tel. 800/433–7300) has a nonstop flight from Chicago. Other U.S. airlines serving Berlin with connecting flights include **Northwest Airlines** (tel. 800/447–4747), **United** (tel. 800/555–1212), and **TWA** (tel. 800/892–4141). **Lufthansa** (tel. 800/645–3880), the German national airline, only has connecting flights between the United States and Berlin, requiring changes in Frankfurt, Düsseldorf, and other German cities.

Flying Time The flying time to Berlin from New York is 8.25 hours.

Cutting Flight Costs The Sunday travel section of most newspapers is a good source of deals. When booking, particularly through an unfamiliar company, call the Better Business Bureau to find out whether any complaints have been registered against the company, pay with a credit card if you can, and consider trip-cancellation and default insurance (*see* Insurance, *above*). *The Airline Passenger's Guerrilla Handbook*, by George Albert Brown (\$14.95; Slawson Communications, Inc., 165 Vallecitos de Oro, San Marcos, CA 92069, tel. 619/744–2299 or 800/752–9766), may be out of date in a few areas but remains a solid source of information on every aspect of air travel, including finding the cheapest fares; it can turn a neophyte into a veteran in short order.

Promotional Airfares All the less expensive fares, called promotional or discount fares, are round-trip and involve restrictions. The exact nature of the restrictions depends on the airline, the route, and the season and on whether travel is domestic or international, but you must usually buy the ticket—commonly called an APEX (advance purchase excursion) when it's for international travel—in advance (seven, 14, or 21 days are usual). You must also respect certain minimum- and maximum-stay requirements (for instance, over a Saturday night or at least seven and no more than 30, 45, or 90 days), and you must be willing to pay penalties for changes. Airlines generally allow some changes for a fee. But the cheaper the fare, the more likely the ticket is nonrefundable; it would take a death in the family for the airline to give you any of your money back if you had to cancel. The cheapest fares are also subject to availability; because only a certain percentage of the plane's total seats will be sold at that price, they may go quickly.

Consolidators Consolidators or bulk-fare operators—also known as bucket shops—buy blocks of seats on scheduled flights that airlines anticipate they won't be able to sell. They pay wholesale prices, add a markup, and resell the seats to travel agents or directly to the public at prices that still undercut the airline's promotional or discount fares. You pay more than on a charter but ordinarily less than for an APEX ticket, and, even when there is not much of a price difference, the ticket usually comes without the advance-purchase restriction. Moreover, although tickets are marked nonrefundable so you can't turn them in to the airline for a full-fare refund, some consolidators sometimes give you your money back. Carefully read the fine print detailing penalties for changes and cancellations. If you doubt the reliability of a company, call the airline once you've made your booking and confirm that you do, indeed, have a reservation on the flight.

The biggest U.S. consolidator, C.L. Thomson Express, sells only to travel agents. Well-established consolidators selling to the public include **UniTravel** (Box 12485, St. Louis, MO 63132, tel. 314/569–0900 or 800/325–2222); **Council Charter** (205 E. 42nd St., New York, NY 10017, tel. 212/661–0311 or 800/800–8222), a division of the Council on International Educational Exchange and a longtime charter operator now functioning more as a consolidator; and **Travac** (989 6th Ave., New York, NY 10018, tel. 212/563–3303 or 800/872–8800), also a former charterer.

Charter Flights Charters usually have the lowest fares and the most restrictions. Departures are limited and seldom on time, and you can lose all or most of your money if you cancel. (Generally, the closer to departure you cancel, the more you lose, although sometimes you will be charged only a small fee if you supply a substitute passenger.) The charterer, on the other hand, may legally cancel the flight for any reason up to 10 days before departure; within 10 days of departure, the flight may be canceled only if it becomes physically impossible to operate it. The charterer may also revise the itinerary or increase the price after you have bought the ticket, but if the new arrangement constitutes a "major change," you have the right to a refund. Before buying a charter ticket, read the fine print for the company's refund policy and details on major changes. Money for charter flights is usually paid into a bank escrow account, the name of which should be on the contract. If you don't pay by credit card, make your check payable to the escrow account (unless you're dealing with a travel agent, in which case, his or her check should be payable to the escrow account). The Department of Transportation's Consumer Affairs Office (I–25, Washington, DC 20590, tel. 202/366–2220) can answer questions on charters and send you its "Plane Talk: Public Charter Flights" information sheet.

Charter operators may offer flights alone or with ground arrangements that constitute a charter package. Well-established charter operators include **Council Charter** (205 E. 42nd St., New York, NY 10017, tel. 212/661–0311 or 800/800–8222), now largely a consolidator, despite its name, and **Travel Charter** (1120 E. Long Lake Rd., Troy, MI 48098, tel. 313/528–3570 or 800/521–5267), with Midwestern departures. **DER Tours** (Box 1606, Des Plains, IL 60017, tel. 800/782–2424), a charterer and consolidator, sells through travel agents.

Discount Travel Travel clubs offer their members unsold space on airplanes,
Clubs cruise ships, and package tours at nearly the last minute and at well below the original cost. Suppliers thus receive some revenue for their "leftovers," and members get a bargain. Membership generally includes a regular bulletin or access to a toll-free telephone hot line giving details of available trips departing anywhere from three or four days to several months in the future. Packages tend to be more common than flights alone, so if airfares are your only interest, read the literature before joining. Reductions on hotels are also available. Clubs include **Discount Travel International** (114 Forrest Ave., Suite 203, Narberth, PA 19072, tel. 215/668–7184; $45 annually, single or family), **Moment's Notice** (425 Madison Ave., New York, NY 10017, tel. 212/486–0503; $45 annually, single or family), **Travelers Advantage** (CUC Travel Service, 49 Music Sq. W, Nashville, TN 37203, tel. 800/548–1116; $49 annually, single or

family), and **Worldwide Discount Travel Club** (1674 Meridian Ave., Miami Beach, FL 33139, tel. 305/534–2082; $50 annually for family, $40 single).

Flying as a Courier A courier is someone who accompanies a shipment between designated points so it can clear customs quickly as personal baggage. Because the courier company actually purchases a seat for the package, which uses the seat's checked-baggage allowance, it can allow you to occupy the paid seat at a vastly reduced rate. You must have a flexible schedule, however, as well as the ability to travel light, because you usually must make do with only carry-on baggage. *The Insiders Guide to Air Courier Bargains*, by Kelly Monaghan, gives more information ($16.95, including postage; Intrepid Traveler, Box 438, New York, NY 10034, tel. 800/356–9315). If you're really serious, you might want to join a membership organization such as the International Association of Air Travel Couriers (Box 1349, Lake Worth, FL 33460, tel. 407/582–8320), which publishes six newsletters and six bulletins yearly listing courier opportunities worldwide. In general, couriers get their assignments from a booking agent, not directly from the courier company. One such agent is **Now Voyager** (74 Varick St., Suite 307, New York, NY 10013, tel. 212/431–1616), which places couriers on flights to various destinations.

Enjoying the Flight Fly at night if you're able to sleep on a plane. Because the air aloft is dry, drink plenty of beverages while on board; remember that drinking alcohol contributes to jet lag, as do heavy meals. Sleepers usually prefer window seats to curl up against; restless passengers ask to be on the aisle. Bulkhead seats, in the front row of each cabin, have more legroom, but since there's no seat ahead, trays attach awkwardly to the arms of your seat, and you must stow all possessions overhead. Bulkhead seats are usually reserved for the disabled, the elderly, and people traveling with babies.

Smoking Since February 1990, smoking has been banned on all domestic flights of less than six hours duration; the ban also applies to domestic segments of international flights aboard U.S. and foreign carriers. On U.S. carriers flying overseas, a seat in a no-smoking section must be provided for every passenger who requests one, and the section must be enlarged to accommodate such passengers if necessary as long as they have complied with the airline's deadline for check-in and seat assignment. If smoking bothers you, request a seat far from the smoking section.

Foreign airlines are exempt from these rules but do provide no-smoking sections, and some nations, including Canada as of July 1, 1993, have gone as far as to ban smoking on all domestic flights; other countries may ban smoking on flights of less than a specified duration. The International Civil Aviation Organization has set July 1, 1996, as the date to ban smoking aboard airlines worldwide, but the body has no power to enforce its decisions.

From the United Kingdom by Plane

British Airways and **Lufthansa** are the main airlines flying from London to Berlin's Tegel Airport. **British Airways** (tel. 081/897–4000) flies four times a day from Heathrow. **Lufthansa** (tel. 081/750–3300) has a daily flight from both Heathrow and

Gatwick. Dan Air (tel. 0293/567955), better known as a charter company, has a daily flight from Gatwick to Berlin.

From the United Kingdom by Train

British Rail operates up to 10 services a day to Germany. Eight of the departures are from Victoria (via the Dover–Ostend ferry or jetfoil) with the other two from Liverpool Street (via Harwich–Hook of Holland).

Berlin is reached via Hannover in about 20 hours, with up to four departures a day—two from Victoria, two from Liverpool Street.

From the United Kingdom by Bus

Europabus service runs three times weekly from London to Berlin. The buses leave London's Victoria Coach Station Wednesday, Thursday, and Friday at 7 PM and arrive in Berlin the next evening at 7:30. Buses leave Berlin's central bus station (at the Funkturm in West Berlin) Wednesday, Saturday, and Sunday at 10 AM and arrive in London at 10 AM. For reservations call 071/730–3499.

From the United Kingdom by Car and Boat

Berlin is 476 miles from the closest Channel port, the Hook of Holland (Ostend, in Belgium, is 45 miles farther along the coast).

For the Hook of Holland, ferries depart from Harwich—the east coast port reached from London via A12 (about 2½ hours' drive). **Sealink** (tel. 0233/646801) operates one ferry daily and one overnight; both sail year-round. It is an eight-hour crossing, and round-trip fares start from £60 for a foot passenger; from £146 for a car with up to five passengers. You must buy a cabin (£8 per person) for night voyages.

Like Sealink, **Olau Line** (tel. 0795/666666) operates newer, high-quality ships on its Netherlands route. There is one daily and one overnight departure from the north Kent port of Sheerness (two hours from London via A-2/M-2) to Vlissingen. The round-trip fares start from £55; from £170 for a car with up to five passengers.

From the Hook, take the A12 to Apeldoorn and then the A1 to Osnabrück and Hannover. There you can pick up E30 to Berlin. From Vlissingen, take the A67 to Venlo and then the A2 to Dortmund. Just east of Dortmund, take E37 north, then E30 to Berlin.

P&O European Ferries (tel. 081/575–8555) operates services from Dover to both Zeebrugge (up to six a day) and Ostend, 19 miles southwest down the coast. Crossing time to Ostend is four hours, half an hour longer to Zeebrugge. Round-trip passengers' fares to both Belgian ports start from £48; from £135 for a car with up to five passengers.

P&O also operates a ferry service into Zeebrugge from Felixstowe (another English east coast port just north of Harwich); while **North Sea Ferries** operates from much farther north at Hull to Zeebrugge and Rotterdam Europoort, two miles south of the Hook.

It is recommended that motorists acquire a green card from their insurance companies, which extends insurance coverage to Europe. Extra breakdown insurance and vehicle and personal security is also advisable.

Staying in Germany

Getting Around

By Plane Germany's internal air network is excellent, with frequent flights linking all major cities. Services are operated by **Lufthansa** and by Germany's other leading airline, **LTU.** In addition, three small airlines operate services between a limited number of northern cities and the East and North Frisian islands, though many of these flights operate only in the summer. Details of all internal services are available from travel agents; otherwise, contact Lufthansa at Frankfurt Airport (tel. 069/690–3050–9).

Lufthansa also runs an excellent train, the "Lufthansa Express," linking Düsseldorf, Köln, Bonn, and Frankfurt airports and acting as a supplement to existing air services. Only passengers holding air tickets may use the train, but there is no extra charge for it. Service is first class. Luggage is automatically transferred to your plane on arrival at the airport. German Railways operates a similar service called "Rail and Fly" (*see below*), and trains on the Hamburg–Köln–Munich line stop at Frankfurt airport instead of at Wiesbaden for connections with flights to and from Frankfurt.

By Train German Federal Railways—or **DB,** meaning Deutsche Bundesbahn, as it is usually referred to—operates one of the most comprehensive and fastest rail systems in Europe. DB runs trains in what was formerly West Germany, while train service in eastern Germany is still operated by the Reichsbahn. The two systems are expected to merge in the near future but in the meantime are increasingly integrating their networks. For instance, there are many more trains now linking the eastern cities of Leipzig, Dresden, Halle, Magdeburg, Potsdam, Rostock, and Schwerin—as well as Berlin—with western cities. DB offers a range of discounted fares and inclusive tickets.

All major cities in western Germany are linked by fast InterCity (IC) hourly service. A DM 6 (DM 10 first class) surcharge is made regardless of distance on all InterCity journeys. (Holders of German Rail passes pay no supplements.) IC provides excellent connections at the main nodal points—Hannover, Dortmund, Köln, Mannheim, Würzburg, Munich, and Frankfurt—and changing trains couldn't be easier. You only have to cross to the other side of the platform. Special train maps on platform notice boards give details of the layout of each IC train arriving on that line, showing where first- and second-class cars and the restaurant car are situated, as well as where they will stop along the length of the platform. If you have a reservation, it will give the number of the car with your seats; locate this car on the map so that you can stand on the platform exactly where your car will stop when the train pulls in. It is possible to check your baggage for Frankfurt Airport from any of 52 Intercity stations throughout Germany. Except on weekends, there is guaranteed overnight delivery.

Super high-speed InterCity Express (ICE) trains, capable of speeds of up to 165 miles per hour, were introduced in 1991 on the Hamburg–Munich and Hamburg–Frankfurt lines. Travel times have been cut by as much as 30% on these comfortable trains, allowing passengers to cross Germany from the north coast to southern Bavaria in six hours.

Although the eastern German Reichsbahn has train classifications similar to the DB, their trains remain much slower because of the poor condition of tracks and bridges. Many trains have first- and second-class cars, and longer-distance routes provide dining cars or buffet facilities. Since fewer people have cars in the east, trains are more heavily used and seat reservations are strongly advised for long journeys.

Rail passengers in possession of a valid round-trip air ticket can buy a heavily discounted "Rail and Fly" ticket for DB trains connecting with 14 German airports: Berlin's Schonefeld and Tegelairports, Bremen, Dresden, Düsseldorf, Franfurt/Main, Hamburg, Hanover, Köln-Bonn, Leipzig/Halle, Munich, Münster/Osnabrück, Nürnberg, and Stuttgart.

The IC network is complemented by fast regional trains (*Inter-Regio*), while E-trains provide slower local services. A DM 6 (DM 10 first class) surcharge is made regardless of distance on all IC trains, but seat reservations on IC services are free when tickets are bought 24 hours or more in advance. Bikes are not carried on IC or ICE trains.

Note that in high season you will frequently encounter lines at ticket offices for seat reservations. Unless you are prepared to board the train without a reserved seat, taking the chance of a seat being available, the only way to avoid these lines is to make an advance reservation by phone. Call the ticket office (*Fahrkarten Schalter*) of the rail station from which you plan to depart. Here again, you will probably have to make several attempts before you get through to the reservations section (*Reservierungen-Platzkarten*), but you will then be able to collect your seat ticket from a special counter without having to wait in line.

Tourist Rail Cards Holders of British Rail Senior Citizens' Rail Cards can buy an "add-on" **European Senior Citizens' Rail Card** that permits half-price train travel in most European countries, including Germany.

Travelers under 26 who have not invested in a Eurail Youthpass, or in any of the other rail passes, should inquire about discount travel fares under a **Billet International Jeune** (BIJ) scheme. The special one-trip tariff is offered by EuroTrain International, with offices in London, Dublin, Paris, Madrid, Lisbon, Rome, Zurich, Athens, Brussels, Budapest, Hannover, Leiden, Vienna, and Tangier. You can purchase a Eurotrain ticket at one of these offices or at travel-agent networks, mainline rail stations, and specialist youth-travel operators.

A German Rail Pass allows up to 15 days unlimited travel throughout Germany for DM (US$300) and DM (US$450) for first class. Children up to 12 years old pay half-price, and visitors under the age of 25 years old may buy a German Rail Youthpass for DM (US$180) for 15 days of second-class travel. The passes can be purchased at railway stations and travel agents in Germany with German currency. Spar (Savings) and

Super-Spar tickets allow travel from any two points within Germany–from the far north to the deep south, for example–for as little as DM 140. Accompanying travelers pay only DM 70. In many holiday regions of Germany, special travel deals are also offered by the DB. In the southeast corner of Bavaria, for instance, 10 days of unlimited travel costs only DM 49 (or DM 75 for a whole family). Prices vary widely around the country; if you're staying in one area for any length of time, ask the local train station if any specially priced tickets are available.

By Bus Germany has good local bus services, but no proper nationwide network like Greyhound. A large proportion of services are operated by the railways (**Bahnbus**) and are closely integrated with train services, while on less busy rail lines, services are run by buses in off-peak periods—normally midday and weekends. Rail tickets are valid on these services. The railways, in the guise of **Deutsche Touring**, also operate the German sections of the Europabus network. Contact them at Am Römerhof 17,6000-Frankfurt/Main 90, tel. 069/79030, for details about a range of two- to seven-day package tours.

One of the best services is provided by the Romantic Road bus between Würzburg (with connections to and from Frankfurt and Wiesbaden) and Füssen (with connections to and from Munich, Augsburg, and Garmisch-Partenkirchen). This is an all-reserved-seats bus with a stewardess, offering one- or two-day tours in each direction in summer, leaving in the morning and arriving in the evening. Details and reservations are available from Deutsche Touring (*see above*) or big city tourist offices.

All towns of any size operate their own local buses. For the most part, those link up with local trams (streetcars), electric railways services (S-bahn), and subways (U-bahn). Fares vary according to distance, but a ticket usually allows you to transfer freely between the various forms of transportation. Some cities issue 24-hour tickets at special rates.

By Bike Information on all aspects of cycling in Germany is available from the Allgmeiner Deutscher Fahrrad-Club (The German Cycle Club; Am Dobben 91, 2800 Bremen 1). There are no formalities governing the importation of bikes into Germany, and no duty is required. Bikes can also be carried on trains—though *not* on IC or ICE trains—if you buy a *Fahrradkarte*, or bicycle ticket. These cost DM 6.50 per journey and can be bought at any train station. Those under 23 (or 27, if you're a student) with a "Tramper Ticket"—a monthly rover that costs DM 335—can take bikes free of charge. Full details are given in the German railway's brochure *Fahrrad am Bahnhof*.

Bicycles are also available for rental at more than 300 train stations throughout the country, most of them in south Germany. The cost is DM 10–DM 12 per day, DM 6–DM 8 if you have a valid rail ticket. They can be returned at any other station.

By Boat River and lake trips are among the greatest delights of a vacation in Germany, especially along the Rhine, Germany's longest river. The Rhine may be viewed at a variety of paces: by fast hydrofoil, by express boat, by sedate motorship, or by romantic paddle steamer. For those in a hurry, there is a daily hydrofoil service from Düsseldorf right through to Mainz. It is advisable to book in advance for this. For gentler souls, there is a wide range of more leisurely cruises. German cruise ships also operate on the Upper Rhine as far as Basel, Switzerland; on the

Main between Frankfurt and Mainz; on the Danube to Linz and on to Vienna; on the Europe Canal joining the Main and the Danube; on the Elbe and Weser and their estuaries; on the Inn and Ilz; and on the Ammersee, Chiemsee, Königsee, Bodensee, and many other smaller German lakes.

EurailPasses are valid on all services of the KD German Rhine Line and on the Mosel between Trier and Koblenz. (If you use the fast hydrofoil, a supplementary fee has to be paid.) DB Tourist Card holders are given a 50% reduction on KD ships. Regular rail tickets are also accepted, meaning that you can go one way by ship and return by train. All you have to do is pay a small surcharge to KD Rhine Line and get the ticket endorsed at one of the landing-stage offices. But note that you have to buy the rail ticket first and *then* get it changed.

KD Rhine Line also offers a program of luxury cruises along the Rhine, Main, Mosel, Elbe, and Danube rivers. The cruises include two-day trips from Köln to Trier (from DM 408), five-day journeys from Amsterdam to Basel in Switzerland, and seven-day holidays from Passau to Budapest (from DM 3,410). Prices include all meals. The cruises are supplemented by trips of one day or less on the Rhine and Mosel. During the summer there are good services between Bonn and Koblenz and between Koblenz and Birgen; both trips take around five hours.

The cruises, especially for the newer Elbe routes, are in great demand, so reservations are necessary several months in advance.

KD has several money-saving deals each year; for example, in 1993 traveling couples celebrating silver, golden, or diamond wedding aniversaries during the year were offered one ticket free of charge. For details of all KD services, contact the company in the United States at 170 Hamilton Avenue, White Plains, NY 10601–1788 (tel. 914/948–3600) or at 323 Geary Street, San Francisco, CA 94102–1860 (tel. 415/392–8817); in Germany contact Köln-Düsseldorfer Deutsche Rheinschiffahrt AG, Frankenwerft 15, 5000–Köln 1 (tel. 0221/20880).

By Car Entry formalities for motorists are few: All you need is proof of insurance, an international car-registration document, and an international driver's license. If you or your car are from an EC country, or from Austria, Norway, Switzerland, Sweden, or Portugal, all you need is your domestic license and proof of insurance. *All* foreign cars must have a country sticker.

Roads in the western part of the country are generally excellent, but many surfaces in eastern Germany, where an urgent improvement program is under way, are in poor condition.

There are three principal automobile clubs: **ADAC** (Allegmeiner Deutscher Automobil-Club, Am Westpark 8, 8000-Munich 70), **AvD** (Lyonerstr. 16, Frankfurt/Niederrad), and **DTC** (Amalienburgstr. 23, Munich 60).

ADAC and AvD operate tow trucks on all Autobahns; they also have emergency telephones every 1½ miles. On minor roads, go to the nearest call box and dial 19211. Ask, in English, for "road service assistance," if you have to use the service. Help is free, but all materials must be paid for.

Scenic Routes Germany boasts many specially designated tourist roads, all covering areas of particular scenic and/or historic interest. The longest is the **Deutsche Ferienstrasse,** the German Holiday Road, which runs from the Baltic to the Alps, a distance of around 1,070 miles. The most famous, however, and also the oldest, is the **Romantische Strasse,** the Romantic Road, which runs from Würzburg in Franconia to Füssen in the Alps, covering around 220 miles and passing some of the most historic cities and towns in Germany. (*See* Chapter 8 for full details.)

Among other notable touring routes—all with expressive and descriptive names—are the **Grüne Küstenstrasse** (Green Coast Road), running along the North Sea coast from Denmark to Emden; the **Burgenstrasse** (Castle Road), running from Mannheim to Nürnberg; the **Deutsche Weinstrasse** (German Wine Road), running through the heartland of German wine country; and the **Deutsche Alpenstrasse** (German Alpine Road), running the length of the country's south border. In addition, there are many other equally delightful, if less well-known, routes, such as the **Märchenstrasse** (the Fairy-tale Road); the **Schwarwald Hochstrasse** (the Black Forest Mountain Road); and the **Deutsche Edelsteinstrasse** (German Gem Road).

Rules of the Road As elsewhere in Western Europe, in Germany you drive on the right, and road signs give distances in kilometers. There is no speed limit on autobahns, although motorists are advised to keep below 120 kph (70 mph). Speed limits on non-autobahn country roads vary from 80 to 100 kph (50 to 60 mph). Alcohol limits on drivers are equivalent to two small beers or a quarter of a liter of wine. Note that seat belts must be worn at all times by front- *and* back-seat passengers.

Gasoline Gasoline (petrol) costs are between DM 1.35 and DM 1.60 per liter. As part of antipollution efforts, most German cars now run on lead-free fuel. Some models use diesel fuel, so that if you are renting a car, establish beforehand which form of fuel the car takes. Some older vehicles cannot take unleaded fuel. German filling stations are highly competitive and bargains are often available if you shop around, but *not* at autobahn filling stations. Self-service, or *SB-Tanken*, stations are cheapest. Pumps marked *Bleifrei* contain unleaded gas.

Telephones

Apart from the more remote rural corners of eastern Germany, telephone links between western and eastern areas of the country were completely upgraded in 1992. When the system was improved, all area codes in the five new states acquired the prefix 03, replacing the previous 0037.

Local Calls Local public phones charge a minimum 30 pfennigs per call (for six minutes). All public phones take 10 pf, DM 1, and DM 5 coins. If you're anticipating making a lot of phone calls, purchase a phone card at the local German post office—a DM 50 card allows you DM 60 worth of calls. Most phone booths have instructions in English as well as German; if yours doesn't, simply lift the receiver, put the money in, and dial.

International Calls These can be made from public phones bearing the sign "Inlands and Auslandsgespräche." Using DM 5 coins is best for long-distance dialing; a four-minute call to the United States costs DM 15. To avoid weighing yourself down with coins, however, make international calls from post offices; even those in small country towns will have a special booth for international calls. You pay the clerk at the end of your call. Never make international calls from your hotel room; rates will be at least double the regular charge.

Operators and Information The German telephone system is fully automatic, and it's unlikely that you'll have to employ the services of an operator. If you do, dial 010, or 0010 for international calls. If the operator doesn't speak English (also unlikely), you'll be passed to one who does.

Mail

Postal Rates Airmail letters to the United States and Canada cost DM 1.40; postcards cost DM 1.05. All letters to the United Kingdom cost DM 1; postcards cost 60 pfennigs.

Receiving Mail You can arrange to have mail sent to you in care of any German post office; have the envelope marked "Postlagernd." This service is free. Alternatively, have mail sent to any American Express office in Germany. There's no charge to cardholders, holders of American Express traveler's checks, or anyone who has booked a vacation with American Express. Otherwise, you pay DM 2 per collection (not per item).

Tipping

The service charges on hotel bills suffice for most tips in your hotel, though you should tip bellhops and porters; DM 2 per bag or service is ample. It's also customary to leave a small tip (a couple of marks per night) for the room cleaning staff. Whether you tip the desk clerk depends on whether he or she has given you any special service.

Service charges are included in all restaurant bills (listed as *Bedienung*), as is tax (listed as *MWST*). Nonetheless, it is customary to round out the bill to the nearest mark or to leave about 5% (give it to the waiter or waitress as you pay the bill; don't leave it on the table).

In taxis, round out the fare to the nearest full mark as a tip. Only give more if you have particularly cumbersome or heavy luggage (though you will be charged 50 pfennigs for each piece of luggage anyway).

Opening and Closing Times

Banks Banks in Berlin are generally open 9–1:30 (until 5:30 on Tuesday and Thursday). Branches at airports and main train stations open as early as 6:30 AM and close as late as 10:30 PM.

Museums Most museums are open from Tuesday to Sunday 9–6. Some close for an hour or more at lunch, and some are open on Monday.

Shops Times vary slightly, but generally shops are open 9 or 9:15–6:30 Monday through Friday and until 2 PM on Saturday, except for the first Saturday in the month, when the bigger stores stay open until 4. Many shops also now remain open on Thursday evenings until 8:30.

National Holidays January 1; January 6 (Epiphany), April 1 (Easter Friday), April 4 (Easter Monday), May 1, May 12 (Ascension), May 23 (Whit Monday), June 23 (Corpus Christi), October 3 (German

Unity Day), November 1 (All Saints' Day), November 16 (Repentance Day), Christmas, December 24–26 (Germany shuts down at midday on the 24th).

Sports and Outdoor Activities

The Germans are nothing if not sports-crazy, and there is practically no sport, however arcane, that cannot easily be arranged almost anywhere in the country. A good number of sports packages—for sailboats, tennis, climbing, walking, horseback riding, to name only a few—are also available. Below, we give details of some of the more popular participant sports. Details of important sporting events are also published every month by regional and local tourist offices.

Fishing Fishing is available at many locations in Germany, but a permit, valid for one year and costing from DM 10 to DM 20, available from local tourist offices, is required, as is a local permit to fish in a particular spot. The local permits are available from the owner of the stretch of water in which you plan to fish. Further details are available from local tourist offices or from **Verband der Deutschen Sportfischer** (Bahnhofstr. 35, 6050 Offenbach).

A number of hotels offer fishing for guests, but you will normally be expected to deliver your catch—if any—to the hotel.

Golf Golf in Germany is rapidly increasing in popularity, and the number of courses is increasing. Clubs will usually allow nonmembers to play if they are not too busy; charges will be about DM 30 during the week and up to DM 60 on weekends and on public holidays. For information, write the **Deutscher Golf-Verband** (German Golf Association; Leberberg 25, 6200 Wiesbaden).

Hiking and Mountaineering Germany's hill and mountain regions have thousands of miles of marked hiking and mountain-walking tracks. They are administered by regional hiking clubs and, where appropriate, mountaineering groups, all of which are affiliated with the **Verband Deutscher Gebirgs- und Wandervereine e.V.** (Reichs str. 4, 6600 Saarbrücken 3). It can provide information on routes, hiking paths, overnight accommodations, and mountain huts.

For Alpine walking, contact the **Deutsche Alpenverein** (Praterinsel 5, D–8000 Munich 22). It administers more than 50 mountain huts and about 9,500 miles of Alpine paths. In addition, it can provide courses in mountaineering and touring suggestions for routes in both winter and summer. Foreign members are admitted.

Various mountaineering schools offer week-long courses ranging from basic techniques for beginners to advanced mountaineering. Contact the **Verband Deutscher Ski und Bergführer** (Lindenstr. 16, D–8980 Oberstdorf).

Local tourist offices and sports shops can usually supply details of mountain guides.

Horseback Riding Riding schools and clubs can be found throughout Germany. Rates are generally high, and most schools will insist on a minimum standard of competence before allowing novices to venture out. Alternatively, pony treks are available in many parts of the country.

Sailing   A wide variety of sailing vacations and opportunities to rent sailboats is available throughout Germany. Most North Sea and Baltic resorts and harbors have either sailing schools or sailboats of varying types to rent. Lake sailing is equally popular, particularly on the Chiemsee in Bavaria and on the Bodensee. For details, write **Verband Deutscher Segelschulen** (Graelstr. 45, 44 Münster).

Swimming   Almost all larger towns and resorts have open-air and indoor pools, the former frequently heated, the latter often with wave or whirlpool machines. In addition, practically all coastal resorts have indoor seawater pools, as well as good, if bracing, beaches. Similarly, all German spas have thermal or mineral-water indoor pools. Finally, Bavaria's Alpine lakes and a large number of artificial lakes elsewhere have marked-off swimming and sunbathing areas.

Note that swimming in rivers, especially the larger ones, is not recommended and in some cases is positively forbidden—look for the "Baden Verboten" signs—either because of shipping, pollution, or both.

Bathing caps are obligatory at all indoor and outdoor pools; if you don't have your own, you can buy one cheaply at the cash desk. It's hard not to notice that the Germans are keen on nudism. Many pools will have special days for nude bathing only, and on certain beaches nude bathing is also allowed. Signs that read "FKK" mean nudity is allowed.

Tennis   In the home country of champions Steffi Graf and Boris Becker, courts are available practically everywhere, summer and winter. Local tourist offices will supply details of where to play, charges, and how to book, the latter being essential in most areas. Charges vary from DM 20 to DM 30 for outdoor courts and DM 25 to DM 35 for indoor courts.

Windsurfing   This has become so popular, particularly on the Bavarian lakes, that it has had to be restricted on some beaches as a result of collisions between Windsurfers and swimmers. Nonetheless, there are still many places where you can windsurf and where Windsurfers can easily be rented. Lessons, at around DM 25 per hour, are also generally available. For further information, contact the German National Tourist Office or **VDWS** (Fasserstr. 30, 8120 Weilheim, Oberbayern).

Winter Sports   South Bavaria is the big winter-sports region, with Garmisch-Partenkirchen the best-known center. There are also winter-sports resorts in the Black Forest, the Harz region, the Bavarian Forest, the Rhön Mountains, the Fichtelgebirge, the Sauerland, and the Swabian mountains. The season generally runs from the middle of December to the end of March, but at higher altitudes, such as the Zugspitze (near Garmisch), you can usually ski from as early as the end of November to as late as the middle of May. There's no need to bring skis with you—you can rent or buy them on the spot. Look for the special winter off-season rates (*Weisse Wochen*) offered by most winter sports-resorts for cross-country and downhill skiing vacations. Prices include seven days' bed and breakfast (or half-board) plus ski lessons.

For cross-country (or *Langlauf*) skiing, which is becoming increasingly popular, there are stretches of prepared tracks (or *Loipen*) to be found in the valleys and foothills of most winter-sports centers, as well as in the suburbs of larger towns in south Bavaria.

Ski-bobbing is on the increase. There are runs and schools at Bayrischzell, Berchtesgaden, Garmisch-Partenkirchen, Füssen, and Oberstdorf in the Alps, as well as at Altglashütten, Bernau, and Felberg in the Black Forest. Ice rinks, many open all year, can be found everywhere.

Dining

Berlin has an enormous variety of eating places, ranging from street-corner hamburger stands to international-class restaurants, from traditional German taverns to exotic establishments offering every kind of ethnic food. Virtually every street corner in Berlin has its *Gaststätte*, a sort of combination diner and pub. There are 6,000 of them in Berlin, one for every 400 inhabitants. Here the emphasis is on the characteristic German preference for *gut bürgerliche Küche*, or good home cooking, with simple food, wholesome rather than sophisticated, at reasonable prices. These are also places where people meet in the evening for a chat, a beer, and a game of cards, so you needn't feel compelled to leave as soon as you've eaten. They normally serve hot meals from around 11 AM to 9 PM or later; many places stop serving hot meals between 2 and 6 PM, although you can still order cold dishes. Lunch rather than dinner is the main meal of the day, accounting for the general practice of offering a *Tageskarte*, or suggested lunchtime menu. For less than DM 20 you can tuck into a soup and main course and perhaps a dessert. Some, although not all, expensive restaurants also offer a table d'hote (suggested or special) daily menu. Prices will be much higher than in a Gaststätte but considerably cheaper than à la carte.

A specialty of the Berlin dining scene is the abundance of "breakfast cafés," where you can order a filling breakfast and unlimited coffee virtually all day. On Sunday mornings they are the scene of *Frühschoppen*, when live jazz is played as the breakfast buffet is served. In eastern Berlin, the variety of fare is smaller but this is changing as new businesses find their footing.

Budget Eating Tips
Foreign Restaurants

Berlin has a vast selection of moderately priced Italian, Greek, Chinese, and—largely as a result of the number of Turkish workers in Germany—Turkish restaurants. All are good value. Italian restaurants are about the most popular of all specialty restaurants in Berlin. One restaurant in ten in Berlin is Italian—the pizza-to-go is as much a part of the average German's diet as *Bratwurst* or a hamburger. You'll find that Chinese restaurants in particular offer special tourist and lunch menus.

Stand-Up
Snack Bars

Often located in pedestrian zones, *Imbiss* stands can be found in almost every busy shopping street, in parking lots, train stations, and near markets. They serve *Wurst* (sausages), grilled, roasted, or boiled, of every shape and size, and rolls filled with cheese, cold meat, or fish. Prices range from DM 3 to DM 6 per portion.

Department Stores

For lunch, restaurants in local department stores (*Kaufhäuser*) are especially recommended for wholesome, appetizing, and inexpensive food. **Karstadt, Wertheim,** and **KaDeWe** have particularly good restaurants.

Fast Food A number of fast-food chains exist all over the country. The fast-food chains such as **McDonald's** and **Burger King** are well established in the area that was West Berlin and are now extending into the eastern part of the city.

Picnics Buy some wine or beer and some cold cuts and rolls (*Brötchen*) from a department store, supermarket, or delicatessen and turn lunchtimes into picnics. You'll not only save money, but you'll also be able to enjoy Berlin's beautiful parks and riverside greenery. Be aware, however, that picnics are not typically German and you might be examined by many with amusement.

Ratings The restaurants in our listings are divided by price into four categories: Very Expensive; Expensive; Moderate; and Inexpensive. *See* Dining in individual chapters for specific prices. Nearly all restaurants display their menus, with prices, outside; all prices shown will include tax and service charge. Prices for wine also include tax and service charge.

Lodging

Berlin has the wide range of hotel accommodations you'd expect to find in such a metropolis, although eastern Berlin is desperately short of medium-priced and inexpensive rooms. The luxury hotels in the eastern part of the city are just as modern and well appointed as those in the west—and equally pricey. Unification has been followed by a building boom in the east, and the number of hotels there is expected to double in the next five years. Eastern Berlin's top hotels are all situated around the historic city center, while western Berlin's tend to be grouped within a few steps of the Kurfürstendamm. For reasonably priced accommodations try outlying areas such as Charlottenburg or Schöneberg. The tourist offices in both parts of Berlin will make reservations for a nominal fee, but to be sure of securing a room, use their services before 4 PM.

The standard of German hotels—from sophisticated luxury spots (of which the country has more than its fair share) to the humblest country inn—is excellent. Rates vary enormously, though not disproportionately so in comparison with other north European countries. You can nearly always expect courteous and polite service and clean and comfortable rooms.

In addition to hotels proper, the country also has numerous Gasthöfe or *Gasthäuser*, which are country inns that serve food and also have rooms; pensions, or *Fremdenheime* (guest houses); and, at the lowest end of the scale, *Zimmer*, meaning simply "rooms," normally in private houses (look for the sign reading *Zimmer frei* or *zu vermieten* on a green background, meaning "to rent"; a red sign reading *besetzt* means that there are no vacancies).

Lists of German hotels are available from the German National Tourist Office and all regional and local tourist offices. (Most hotels have restaurants, but those listed as *Garni* will provide breakfast only.) Tourist offices will also make bookings for you at a nominal fee, but they may have difficulty doing so after 4 PM in high season and on weekends, so don't wait until too late in the day to begin looking for your accommodations. (If you do get stuck, ask someone who looks local—a postman, policeman, or waitress, for example—for a Zimmer zu vermieten or

Gasthof; in rural areas especially you'll find that people are genuinely helpful). An excellent nationwide hotel reservation service is also operated by **ADZ** (Corneliusstr. 34, W-6000 Frankfurt/Main, tel. 069/740767, fax 069/751056). The service is free of charge.

Many major American hotel chains—Hilton, Sheraton, Holiday Inn, Arabella, Canadian Pacific, Ramada, Preferred—have hotels in the larger German cities. Similarly, European chains are well represented.

Romantik Hotels Among the most delightful places to stay—and eat—in Germany are the aptly named Romantik Hotels and Restaurants. The Romantik group now has establishments throughout north Europe (and even a few in the United States), with more than 60 in Germany itself. All are in atmospheric and historic buildings—an essential prerequisite for membership—and are personally run by the owners, with the emphasis on excellent food and service. Prices vary considerably from Very Expensive to Moderate (*see* Ratings, *below*), but in general represent good value, particularly the special-weekends and short-holiday rates. A three- or four-day stay, for example, with one main meal, is available at about DM 300 to DM 400 per person.

In addition, German Railways offers a special "Romantik Hotel Rail" program, which, in conjunction with a GermanRail Tourist Ticket, gives nine days' unlimited travel. You don't need to plan your route in advance—only your first night's accommodation needs to be reserved before you leave. The remaining nights can be reserved as you go. The package also includes sightseeing trips, a Rhine/Mosel cruise, bicycle rentals, and the like.

A detailed brochure listing all Romantik Hotels and Restaurants, which costs $7.50 (including mailing), and a free miniguide are available from **Romantik Hotels Reservations** (Box 1278, Woodinville, WA 98072, tel. 206/486–9394; reservations, 800/826–0015).

Castle Hotels Of comparable interest and value are Germany's castle, or *Schloss*, hotels, all privately owned and run and all long on atmosphere. A number of the simpler ones may lack some amenities, but the majority combine four-star luxury with valuable antique furnishings, four-poster beds, stone passageways, and a baronial atmosphere. Some offer full resort facilities, too (tennis, swimming pools, horseback riding, hunting, and fishing). Nearly all are located away from cities and towns.

For a brochure listing 60 such castle hotels, write to **Gast im Schloss,** D-3526 Trendelburg 1, Germany. They, and your travel agent, can also advise on a number of packages available for castle hotels, including four- to six-night tours.

Spas Taking the waters in Germany, whether for curing the body or merely beautifying it, has been popular since Roman times. There are about 250 health resorts and mineral springs in the country—the word *Bad* before the name of a place usually means it's a spa—offering treatments, normally at fairly high prices. Beauty farms are normally found only in Very Expensive spa hotels. Although spas exist in eastern Germany, most are rundown and not highly recommended.

There are four main groups of spas and health resorts: (1) the mineral and moorland spas, where treatments are based on natural warm-water springs; (2) those by the sea on the Baltic and North Sea coasts; (3) hydropathic spas, which use an invigorating process developed in the 19th century; and (4) climatic health resorts, which depend on their climates—usually mountainous—for their health-giving properties.

The average cost for three weeks of treatment is from DM 1,800 to DM 4,000; for four weeks, DM 2,400 to DM 5,000. This includes board and lodging, doctor's fees, treatments, and tax. A complete list of spas, giving full details of their springs and treatments, is available from the German National Tourist Office, or from **Deutsche Bäderverband,** the German Health Resort and Spa Association (Schumannstr. 111, 5300 Bonn 1).

Apartment and Villa Rentals If you want a home base that's roomy enough for a family and comes with cooking facilities, a furnished rental may be the solution. Bungalows or apartments (*Ferienwohungen* or *Ferienapartments*), usually accommodating two to eight people, can be rented throughout Germany. Rates are low, with reductions for longer stays. There is usually an extra charge for gas and electricity, and sometimes water. There is also normally a charge for linen, though you may also bring your own.

Details on rentals in all regions are available from local and regional tourist offices. In addition, the German Automobile Association issues listings of family holiday apartments; write **ADAC Reisen** (Am Westpark 8, 8000 Munich 70).

There are also services that can not only look for a house or apartment for you (even a castle if that's your fancy) but also handle the paperwork. Some send an illustrated catalogue and others send photographs of specific properties, sometimes at a charge; up-front registration fees may apply. Among the companies are **At Home Abroad** (405 E. 56th St., Suite 6H, New York, NY 10022, tel. 212/421–9165), **Interhome Inc.** (124 Little Falls Rd., Fairfield, NJ 07004, tel. 201/882–6864), **Overseas Connection** (31 North Harbor Dr., Sag Harbor, NY 11963, tel. 516/725–9308), **Rent a Home International** (7200 34th Ave. NW, Seattle, WA 98117, tel. 206/789–9377 or 800/488–7368), **Vacation Home Rentals Worldwide** (235 Kensington Ave., Norwood, NJ 07648, tel. 201/767–9393 or 800/633–3284), **Villa Leisure** (Box 209, Westport, CT 06881, tel. 407/624–9000 or 800/526–4244), and **Villas International** (605 Market St., Suite 510, San Francisco, CA 94105, tel. 415/281–0910 or 800/221–2260). **Hideaways International** (15 Goldsmith St., Box 1270, Littleton, MA 01460, tel. 508/486–8955 or 800/843–4433), functions as a travel club. Membership ($79 yearly per person or family at the same address) includes two annual guides plus quarterly newsletters; rentals are arranged directly between members, not by the club staff.

Home Exchange This is obviously an inexpensive solution to the lodging problem, because house-swapping means living rent-free. You find a house, apartment, or other vacation property to exchange for your own by becoming a member of a home-exchange organization, which then sends you its annual directories listing available exchanges and includes your own listing in at least one of them. Arrangements for the actual exchange are made by the two parties to it, not by the organization. Principal clearinghouses include **Intervac U.S./International Home Exchange** (Box 590504, San Francisco, CA 94159, tel. 415/435–3497), the oldest, with thousands of foreign and domestic homes for exchange in its three annual directories; membership is $62, or $72 if you want to receive the directories but remain unlisted. The **Vacation Exchange Club** (Box 650, Key West, FL 33041, tel. 800/638–3841), also with thousands of foreign and domestic listings, publishes four annual directories plus updates; the $50 membership includes your listing in one book. **Loan-a-Home** (2 Park La., Apt. 6E, Mount Vernon, NY 10552, tel. 914/664–7640) specializes in long-term exchanges; there is no charge to list your home, but the directories cost $35 or $45 depending on the number you receive.

Farm Vacations   *Urlaub auf dem Bauernhof,* or vacations down on the farm, have increased dramatically in popularity throughout Germany over the past five years, and almost every regional tourist office now produces a brochure listing farms in its area that offer bed-and-breakfasts, apartments, and entire farmhouses to rent. In addition, the German Agricultural Association (DLG) produces an illustrated brochure listing over 1,500 farms, all inspected and graded, from the Alps to the North Sea, that offer accommodations. It costs DM 7.50 (send an international reply coupon if writing from the United States) and is available from **DLG Reisedienst, Agratour** (Zimmerweg 16, D–6000 Frankfurt/Main 1) or the National Tourist Office.

Camping   Campsites—some 2,000 in all—are scattered the length and breadth of Germany. The **DCC,** or German Camping Club (Mandlstr. 28, D–8000 Munich 40) produces an annual listing of 1,600 sites; it also details sites where trailers and mobile homes can be rented. Similarly, the German Automobile Association (*see* Rentals, *above,* for address) publishes a listing of all campsites located at autobahn exits. In addition, the German National Tourist Office publishes a comprehensive and graded listing of campsites.

Sites are generally open from May to September, though about 400 are open year-round for the very rugged. Most sites get crowded during high season, however. Prices range from around DM 10 to DM 15 for a car, trailer, and two adults; less for tents. If you want to camp elsewhere, you must get permission from the landowner beforehand; ask the police if you can't track him or her down. Drivers of mobile homes may park for one night only on roadsides and in autobahn parking-lot areas, but may not set up camping equipment there.

Youth Hostels   Germany's youth hostels—*Jugendherbergen*—are probably the most efficient, up-to-date, and proportionally numerous of any country's in the world. There are more than 600 in all, many located in castles that add a touch of romance to otherwise utilitarian accommodations. Since unification, many eastern German youth hostels have closed down. An effort is being made, however, to keep as many open as possible, and renovations are currently under way to bring eastern hostels up to the standards of their western counterparts.

Apart from Bavaria, where there is an age limit of 26, there are no restrictions on age, though those under 20 take preference when space is limited. Accommodation is available only to those members of the International Youth Hostel Association; membership costs DM 18 annually in Germany (DM 30 for adults and their families). Accommodation charges range from about DM 12 to DM 18 for youth under 27 and DM 13.50 to DM 22 for adults (breakfast included). Cards are available from the

American Youth Hostels Association, the **Canadian Hostelling Association,** and the United Kingdom's **Youth Hostels Association** (*see* Student and Youth Travel, *above*). For listings of German youth hostels, contact the **Deutsches Jugendherbergswerk Hauptverband** (Bismarckstr. 8, D–4930 Detmold, tel. 05231/74010).

Ratings The hotels in our listings are divided by price into four categories: Very Expensive; Expensive; Moderate; and Inexpensive. *See* Lodging in individual chapters for specific prices. Note that there is no official grading system for hotels in Germany. Rates are by no means inflexible, and depend very much on supply and demand; you can save money by inquiring about reductions. Many resort hotels offer substantial reductions in winter, except in the Alps, where rates often rise. Likewise, many Very Expensive and Expensive hotels in cities cut their prices on weekends and when business is quiet. Always be careful about trying to book late in the day at peak times. During trade fairs (most commonly held in the spring and fall), rates in city hotels can rise appreciably. Breakfast is usually but not always included. Inexpensive rooms may have neither shower nor tub. Ask about both breakfast and bathing facilities when booking. Usually you pay more for the tub. When you arrive, if you don't like the room you're offered, ask to see another.

Credit Cards

The following credit card abbreviations are used: AE, American Express; DC, Diners Club; MC, Mastercard; V, Visa.

2 Portrait of Berlin

Seeing Is Believing

By Christopher Hope

South African–born novelist Christopher Hope happened to be visiting West Berlin when the Wall fell; his eyewitness account appeared in The New Republic *one month later, in December 1989. His new novel,* Serenity House, *was published in 1992, as was a collection of short stories,* Swirsky Aloft.

You know that things are serious when the TV news stations start flying in their anchor men and women. Chattering groups of them thronged Berlin Airport when I arrived on November 12, father figures and mother confessors from the news desks of the American networks, the British Broadcasting Corp., Japanese TV, and the European pop and sports satellite channels. They were eager to present the news in situ, beside the Berlin Wall, in front of the Brandenburg Gate. They were attended by baggage bearers, drones, and soldiers who formed a kind of protective scrimmage, easing their costly charges through passport control, incredulous that mere officials should obstruct the faces welcomed into millions of homes each night.

Berliners have always displayed disrespect when faced with power or privilege. And household names become very parochial the moment they leave the house. The famous faces, it must be said, are paler than expected, the eyes flutter restlessly as if searching for makeup and the auto-cue. As the Berliners well knew, these were people who a few weeks ago could not have picked out their divided city on a map. Berlin flickered in the memory, if at all, mixed with images of Liza Minnelli belting out her stuff in *Cabaret*. Indeed, for most people Berlin was an improbable oasis in the East German wilderness, cut in two by the Wall, surrounded by Russian troops, a stump of a city crowded with allied soldiers, spiked with missiles, lined with steak houses.

Berlin was last in the news in a big way during the Berlin airlift, and during the building of the Wall in 1961. It was featured vividly when President Kennedy gazed out across the Wall and proclaimed: "I am a Berliner." But thereafter it was simply a schizophrenic city. A remnant of a vanished metropolis, occupied by its conquerors—in the West a prosperous fortress of 2 million people; in the East a prison house its masters called paradise, a place of outer darkness. Berlin was not a place—it was an issue. It never quite seemed to be part of modern Germany. When people thought of West Germany they tended to think of Bonn, the apologetic federal capital, of Mercedes and BMW, and of the strength of the deutsche mark. It was devoutly to be hoped that the two Germanys would one day be reunited, but outside the circles of the devout, no one was putting any money on it.

Since the erection of the Wall 30 years ago, Berlin has become a kind of distant theater of the cold war. A fine place for spy stories, the scene of memorable exchanges of secret agents; daring escapes by hugely brave men and women hidden in the cunning compartments of trucks and automobiles; flights by hot-air balloon; midnight dashes through the sewers beneath the city. And of abortive escapes that ended in gunfire and bleeding bodies. Along the length of the Wall small tabernacles remember with a name or a photograph those who did not get away.

Then suddenly the world was stood on its head. The night of Friday, November 10, the East Germans began smashing through the Wall. By November 14 there were 22 new crossing points, with promises of more to come. And through these gaps poured the grateful tens of thousands. The invasion so long predicted was coming true. Even the direction was right—the invaders came from the East. But they carried not rifles but shopping bags, and they arrived not in tanks but on foot, or in tiny two-stroke motorcars called Trabants, belching fumes, their fiberglass frames shivering on their uncertain chassis. To watch the tiny Trabant cross the Wall and go chugging along the broad West Berlin boulevards, impatiently followed by a gas-guzzling, absurdly fast turbo triumph of German automotive engineering, is to be present at a motorized street theater. The way into the future might be summed up by a single stage direction: "Exit a Trabant, pursued by a Porsche."

West Berliners, usually so laconic, acerbic, irreverent, melted in the face of this invasion. The Opera House offered free performances of Mozart's *Magic Flute*. The city fathers allowed free travel on the subway, the U-Bahn. They gave each new arrival 100 marks to spend. The department stores hung out welcome signs and exchanged the visitors' dud currency at the rate of 10 East German marks for one West German mark. Around the square at the top of the Kurfürstendamm, beside the ruins of the Kaiser Wilhelm Memorial Church commemorating the destruction of Berlin, sausage stalls appeared, trestle tables, beakers of beer, mobile toilets, street musicians, and unbounded conviviality. The visitors were quickly dubbed the "*Ossies*" to distinguish them from the West Berliners, who became, naturally, the "*Wessies*." When Ossies met Wessies, there took place in West Berlin the biggest damn family reunion Europe has seen since the War.

True, there were also a few party poopers about. Taxi drivers worried aloud about the cost of it all. After all, there were at least 1.2 million East Berliners (or were the last time any had been brave enough or foolhardy enough to count them), and at 100 marks a head, the overall subsidy for this invasion, in every sense, was not small beer. Similarly, guest workers employed to do the work that West Berliners disdain took a rather dim view. "What will happen to me?" the Turkish cleaning attendant of a block of flats asked her employer, "when the Ossies undercut me?"

Her employer appeared happily unconcerned. "I know, I've had three offers already."

And what of the thousands of troops that the Western allies and the Russians have kept massed along this crucial border? More worrying still, to the Poles and others—with sad memories of the last united Germany—where were the borders of Germany itself? Why had the West German chancellor, on a visit to Poland, declined to state that the postwar boundaries were immovable? And what on earth was one to make of a German people who, it seemed, were no longer preparing for the war but mounting shopping expeditions instead?

I t was all very confusing and very euphoric and vaguely troubling all at once. Anyone who imagined that things would settle down did not, as they say in Berlin, have all his cups in the cupboard. Such people also mistook the significance of symbols. A Wall had once stood between East and West, built of stone and stained with blood. One night, without warning, it fell down. And only the rich bird life, thriving along its empty, eerie length, would mourn its passing. No one was surprised by the news that three Communist mayors from the East had committed suicide. It was the opinion of otherwise pacific matrons taking coffee in the Kempinski Eck, the famous plush, glass-fronted observatory on the Kurfürstedamm, that the disgraced former leader of East Germany, Erich Honecker, should "do the decent thing" and follow suit.

West Berliners have always detested the Wall, but they learned to live with it. They have jogged along its length and have daubed it with graffiti from end to end, but except on rare occasions when it thrust itself into view with a spectacular escape, or some important politician came to call and made a speech, they forgot about it. What West Berlin has never allowed anybody to forget is the War itself. Bullet holes are still to be seen, spattering the sides of buildings. Fragments of the portals of the old Berlin synagogue are cemented into the porch of the Jewish Community Center in Fasanenstrasse. West Berlin is a city loud with ghosts.

The area around the Wall added to the sense of war-torn desolation. Once it was the site of the Potsdamer Platz, among the busiest intersections in Europe, the very heart of Berlin. Since the War ended it has been a muddy, disconsolate slum. Taxi drivers assured visitors with laconic understatement that it was not "a development area." The deserted embassies look like the victims of some below-stairs revolt by the lower vegetable orders. Creepers spread across their facades and reach through open windows into empty rooms.

Reminders of the cataclysms are everywhere: the Hitler bunker; the site of the Gestapo torture chambers in Wilhelmstrasse; the fragmentary remains of the old Anhalter station, a crumbling facade and a few headless statues on a roof out of which trees have sprouted. Before the War the Anhalter dispatched 60 trains a day to Dresden, Rome, Vienna. Nearby is Friedrichstrasse, now a gray shadow of its prewar, tinselly self. It sputters out in a pizzeria and a rash of bars, ending abruptly when it runs up against Checkpoint Charlie. The graffiti on the Wall reveals the genial derision in which West Berliners hold the foreigner's tender fascination with this monstrous monument: "What are you staring at? Have you never seen a wall before?"

There has always been something inconsolably sad in the air of West Berlin. East Berlin, by contrast, has always pretended otherwise. East Berliners never spoke of their city as "East Berlin," but always and only as Berlin, the capital of the only legitimate Germany. They preferred to ignore the existence of the impostor stuck away in the middle of 110 miles of East German territory. East German soldiers were to be seen regularly changing the guard on Unter Den Linden, still doing the goose step, wearing helmets like soup plates.

Naturally I crossed the Wall into the East for the simple pleasure of witnessing East Germans moving the other way. They waited patiently in long lines, helped by the border guards to fill in their travel forms. It must be strange to ask directions from a man who a week earlier would have shot you for trying to leave the country. It must have been even stranger for the guards themselves, trained to snarl, shoot, and inspect the undersides of tourist buses with giant dentist mirrors. Overnight they had become part of the courtesy staff, obliging, efficient, seemingly delighted that most of the population planned a trip abroad.

I traveled to the East with a British novelist who had never made the crossing before. She had a theory that you could tell you were getting older when the popes started looking younger. But in Berlin, that test seemed really to apply to border guards. They appeared to have shed years overnight. "Please step this way to exchange your money," a smiling fellow invited toothily, holding the door. Only those used to making this dreary crossing would understand the novelty of his demeanor. I exchanged good West German marks for bad, an obligatory transfer, a tax on curiosity. One day East German banknotes will, like the Wall itself, become collector's items. On the face of the 20-mark note Goethe stares back quietly, as if disturbed to find himself so framed.

There has never been much to see in the streets of East Berlin, or in the shops. A smart new coffeehouse adorns the corner of Friedrichstrasse, in its continuation on the other side of the Wall. It is always packed to capacity. Most of the customers appear to have taken up their seats soon after the building was completed and show no signs of leaving. In a nearby supermarket, food is more plentiful than it is, say, in Moscow. But a German economy, *any* German economy, must be in deep trouble if it cannot make even bottles of sauerkraut look attractive. But what lightens everything in a lovely, astonishing fashion are the chattering crowds of East Berliners at the crossing points, waiting to leave as if it were the most natural thing in the world. Most are going for the day, complete with bags, babies, and beaming smiles, heading for the bright lights of West Berlin.

And for citizens of a regime known for its prim moralizing, its political piety, and it claims to be untainted by the lures of Western junk, the Ossies show themselves to be endearingly human. They crowd the nonstop strip shows on Kant Strasse. The unexpected connection between vice and philosophy is a feature of West Berlin. After all, the crown (if that is the word) of Martin Luther Strasse happens to be an emporium known as Big Sexy Land. The clip joints reduced their entry fee and offered two free beers to our "Eastern guests" and reported that the crowds were "good-humored."

And so they were. They were also "different," a word that kept cropping up among West Berliners who observed the visitors closely. The Ossies manifest that special sort of raging docility that distinguishes Eastern European crowds, people accustomed to standing in line and monitoring their expectations every wish of the way. The Wessies looked upon the Ossies with a benign complexity attended by gentle satisfaction. They were, quite simply, as pleased as punch to see them in West Berlin—though not quite sure what to do with them.

And thus it was with a certain relief that the Wessies sought refuge in their bars, restaurants, and watering holes where the Ossies could not follow and sat talking excitedly over meals that only they could afford. And the Ossies would press their noses to the windows of the Paris Bar like gentle ghosts. Yet there was no discernible resentment in their stares. Ossies were to be seen striding through the most distant suburbs, stopping to stare at children playing in the park, or a man washing his car, or gathering in great crowds outside the windows of the BMW showrooms. After all, what qualitative difference is there among the objects of your fascination when you are seeing it all for the first time? It is all very natural, and not a little sad.

At the entrance to a large department store I watched a family of East Berliners, freshly arrived, wide-eyed and eerily silent. Father, mother, and a boy of about six were passing the chocolate counter. Suddenly the little boy stopped dead. He had seen the chocolates, homemade and gleaming darkly under the lights, perfection behind the glass, a costly pyramid, profligate, tempting, untouchable. His adoration passed like an electric current into his mother and father and rooted them to the spot. No one spoke. After a while, like sleepers awakening, they shook themselves and went on their way. Seeing is believing. It's not the same as having, but it will do, for a while at least.

3 Berlin

Since autumn 1989 Berlin had been in the headlines as the focal point and touchstone of a reuniting Germany, culminating in the historic vote on June 20, 1991, by the German Parliament to make the city once again the full-time seat of the German government. Thus ends one of the great geographic and political anomalies of the 20th century: a city split in two by a 10-foot-high concrete wall, with its larger western half an island of capitalist democracy, surrounded by an East Germany run by hard-line Stalinist Communists. Built in 1961 at the height of the cold war, the Berlin Wall symbolized the separation of two distinctly different political and economic systems. Ironically, though, it also became a major tourist attraction, where viewing platforms along the western side enabled visitors to see the battlefrontlike no-man's-land, guarded by soldiers and peppered with deadly mines and booby traps. The Wall's demolition cast it once more as a symbol: this time, though, a symbol of the change sweeping over former Iron Curtain countries. Two large chunks of the Wall have been left standing as reminders of the grim past.

Berlin actually began as two cities more than 750 years ago. Museum Island, on the Spree River, was once called Cölln, while the mainland city was always known as Berlin. As early as the 1300s, Berlin prospered from its location at the crossroads of important trade routes, and it became filled with merchants and artisans of every description. After the ravages of the Thirty Years' War (1618–48), Berlin rose to power as the seat of the Brandenburg dynasty, and 200 years later when the Brandenburgian and Prussian realms united under the Hohenzollerns, Berlin was the chosen capital. The 1701 coronation of the enlightened ruler King Friedrich II—also known as Frederick the Great—set off a renaissance in the city, especially in the construction of academic institutions such as the Academy of Arts and the Academy of Sciences.

The Prussian Empire, especially under Count Bismarck in the late 19th century, proved to be the dominant force in unifying the many independent German principalities. Berlin maintained its status as the German capital throughout the German Empire (1871–1918), the post–World War I Weimar Republic (1919–33), and Hitler's Third Reich (1933–45). During the 1920s and early 1930s the city also served as an important European social and cultural capital, tinged with a reputation for decadence. But during World War II, acting as the Nazi headquarters, it was bombed to smithereens—at the end of hostilities there was more rubble in Berlin than in all other German cities combined. Most of what you see there today has been built, or rebuilt, since 1945.

With the division of Germany after World War II, Berlin was also partitioned, with American, British, and French troops in the districts to the west, the Soviet Union's forces to the east. After the Potsdam Agreement in 1945, the three western zones of occupation gradually merged into one, becoming West Berlin, while the Soviet-controlled eastern zone defiantly remained separate. In 1948, in an attempt to force the Western Allies to relinquish their stake in the city, the U.S.S.R. set up a blockade cutting off all overland supply routes from the West. The Western Allies countered by mounting the Berlin Airlift, during which some 750,000 flights delivering 2 million tons of goods kept Berlin alive for most of a fateful year, until the

Soviets finally lifted the blockade. As peace conferences repeatedly failed to resolve the question of Germany's division, the Soviets in 1949 established East Berlin as the capital of its new puppet state in East Germany. West Berlin was not technically part of the West Germany republic, though it was clearly tied to its legal and economic system. The division of the city was emphasized even more in 1961 when the East Germans constructed the infamous Berlin Wall.

Reunited Berlin is much more than two halves of a large city stitched together again after decades of painful separation. With surprising speed this amazing metropolis has grown together to reemerge as the largest city on the continent. You can now walk with ease across a former fortified frontier without realizing it, and you have to look hard to find the ugly traces of the Wall that divided the city for so long. Berlin really is one city again, and there's not much point now in clinging to the old comparisons between east and west. Gone, too, is the cheap, first-time thrill of venturing through the Wall and into the forbidden territory of the East. Those who did it have their memories; those who visit Berlin for the first time in these post-unification years are deprived of a frisson or two—but they are rewarded with the sight of a city in the exciting phase of renewal and self-recognition. The visible signs of this are almost all to be found in eastern Berlin, much of which in 1992 resembled one huge construction site, with entire blocks either being razed to make way for dazzling new department stores, hotels, and commercial centers or returned to their long-neglected historical appearance.

With the Wall now on the junk pile of history, visitors can at last appreciate the qualities that mark the city as a whole. Its particular charm always lay in its spaciousness, its trees and greenery, its racy atmosphere, and the ease with which you could reach the lakes and forests within its perimeter. It is a vast city, laid out on an epic scale—western Berlin alone is four times the size of Paris. Entire towns and villages are inlaid into the countryside beyond the downtown area. The really stunning parts of the prewar capital are in the eastern sector, with its grand boulevards and monumental buildings, the classical Brandenburg Gate, and the stately tree-lined avenue of Unter den Linden.

What really makes Berlin special, however, are the intangibles—the spirit and bounce of the city. Here is life in a pressure cooker, life on the edge—literally and figuratively. Berliners of whatever age are survivors; they have lived with adversity all their lives, and have managed to do so with a mordant wit and cynical acceptance of life as it is rather than the way one hopes it might be.

Berliners are brash, no-nonsense types, who speak German with their own racy dialect. Their high-voltage energy is invariably attributed to the bracing Berlin air, the renowned *Berliner Luft*. Crisis has been a way of life here for as long as anyone can remember. "To survive with a measure of style and humor" could serve as the city's theme.

Essential Information

More than three years after the official unification of the two Germanys, the nuts-and-bolts work of joining up the two halves is by no means complete, and uncertainties still abound. We have given addresses, telephone numbers, and other logistical details based on the best available information, but please understand that changes are taking place at a furious pace in everything from postal codes and telephone numbers to street names. Eastern Berlin's separate telephone code (02) has been phased out; the code for the entire city is now 030 (formerly only western Berlin's code). Public museums in western Berlin, once free, are starting to charge admission.

Important Addresses and Numbers

Tourist Information
The **Verkehrsamt Berlin** (main tourist office) is located in the heart of the city in the Europa Center (tel. 030/262–6031). If you want materials on the city before your trip, write **Verkehrsamt Berlin** (Martin-Luther-Strasse 105, D–1000 Berlin 62). For information on the spot, the office is open daily 8 AM–10:30 PM. There are also offices at **Tegel Airport** (tel. 030/410–13145; open daily 8 AM–11 PM) and the **Bahnhof Zoo** train station (tel. 030/313–9063; open daily 8 AM–11 PM). Berlin has an information center especially for women, offering help with accommodations and information on upcoming events. Contact **Fraueninfothek Berlin,** c/o Frauennetzwerk (Potsdamerstr. 139, tel. 030/282–3930; open Tues.–Sat. 9–9, Sun. and public holidays 9–3).

For information on all aspects of the city, pick up a copy of *Berlin Turns On*, free from any tourist office. Also, the listings in *Berlin Programm* (DM 2.80), a monthly guide to Berlin arts, provide the latest information about concerts, opera, and theater.

Embassies and Consulates
United States Consulate (Clayallee 170, tel. 030/832–4087).

Following the unification of the city, the American and British embassies in former East Berlin have taken on the character of information centers. The **American** office is still at Neustädtische Kirchstrasse 4–5 (tel. 030/220–2741) and the **British** office remains at Unter den Linden 32–34 (tel. 030/220–2431). **Canada** has a Consulate-General at the International Trade Center Friedrich Str. 95, tel. 030/261–1161.

Emergencies
Police: tel. 030/110. **Ambulance and emergency medical attention:** tel. 030/310–031. **Dentist:** tel. 030/1141 or after 9 PM, tel. 030/892–0379. **Pharmacies:** Berlin pharmacies offer late-night service on a rotation basis. Every pharmacy displays a notice indicating the location of the nearest shop with evening hours. For emergency pharmaceutical assistance, call 030/1141.

Changing Money
Berlin banks are open Monday, Wednesday, and Friday 9–1:30, Tuesday and Thursday 3:30–5:30. You can change money or cash checks at the Wechselstube at the Bahnhof Zoo (Mon.–Sat. 8 AM–9 PM, Sun. and public holidays 10–6) and at the Berlin Bank City Service's Tegel Airport office (open daily 8 AM–10 PM).

English-Language Bookstores
Marga Schoeller, Knesebeckstr. 33, tel. 030/881–1112. **Buchhandlung Kiepert,** Hardenbergstr. 4–5, tel. 030/311–0090. **The**

British Book Shop, Mauerstr. 83–84, tel. 030/238–4680 or Herder Tauntzienstr. 13, tel. 030/212–440. **Buchexpress,** Habelschwerdter Allee 4, tel. 030/831–4004.

Travel Agencies **American Express,** Friedrichstr. 172, tel. 030/238–4102. **American Express Reisebüro,** Kurfürstendamm 11, tel. 030/882–7575.

American Lloyd, Kurfürstendamm 36, tel. 030/883–7081.

Car Rental **Avis:** Tegel Airport, tel. 030/410–13148; Budapesterstr. 43, Europa Center, tel. 030/261–1881; Haus der Reise, Alexander-pl. 5, tel. 030/214–1239.
Europcar: Kurfürstenstr. 101, tel. 030/213–7097.
Hertz: Tegel Airport, tel. 030/410–13315; Budapesterstr. 39, tel. 030/261–1053.
Sixt-Budget: Tegel Airport, tel. 030/41012886; Budapesterstr. 16, tel. 030/261–1357.

Luxury Cars For chauffeured limousines and luxury sports cars, try **Autohansa** (Bundesallee, tel. 030/851–4061), **Both Rent a Car** (Stralauer Platz, tel. 030/279–1412; Karl-Marx-Str. 36, tel. 030/623–5066, **First Class Car** (in the Hotel Steigenberger, Los-Angeles-Platz, tel. 030/213–9634 or 030/213–9600), **Chauffeur & Limousine Service** (Kaisderdamm 28, tel. 030/301–7027), and **Janisch Limousinen Service** (Uhlandstr. 185, tel. 030/883–3079). **Sixt-Budget** (*see above*) has Berlin's biggest fleet of Mercedes and Porsches.

Arriving and Departing by Plane

Airlines flying to western Berlin's **Tegel Airport** from major U.S. and European cities include Delta, TWA, United, Iberia, Alitalia, SwissAir, Air France, British Airways, Lufthansa, Euro-Berlin, and some charter companies. Because of increased air traffic following unification, the former military airfield at **Tempelhof** is being used increasingly. Despite substantial government subsidies, domestic fares are low. Tegel Airport is only 6 kilometers (4 miles) from the downtown area, and Tempelhof is even closer. For information on arrival and departure times for Tegel, call 030/41011.

Eastern Berlin's **Schönefeld Airport** is about 24 kilometers (15 miles) outside the downtown area. It is used principally by Soviet and eastern European airlines, although with the increase in flights to Tegel, it's been taking more and more charter traffic. For information on arrival and departure times, call 030/67–870.

Between the Blue airport bus No. 109 runs at 10-minute intervals between
Airport and Tegel and downtown via Kurfürstendamm (the main avenue),
Downtown Bahnhof Zoologischer (the main train station), and Budapesterstrasse. The total trip is 30 minutes; the fare is DM 3.20. Expect to pay about DM 25 for the same trip by taxi. If you rent a car at the airport, take the Stadtautobahn (there are signs), the highway into Berlin. The Halensee exit leads to Kurfürstendamm (Ku'damm for short).

From Schönefeld, a shuttle bus leaves every 10–15 minutes for the nearby S-bahn station; S-bahn trains leave every 20 minutes for the Friedrichstrasse station downtown. A taxi ride from the airport takes about 40 minutes. By car, follow the signs for "Stadtzentrum Berlin."

Arriving and Departing by Train, Bus, and Car

By Train There are five major rail routes to Berlin from the western half of the country (from Hamburg, Hannover, Köln, Frankfurt, and Nürnberg), and the network is set to expand to make eastern German territory more accessible. At press time, trains were jointly being run by the former East German Deutsche Reichsbahn (DR) and former West Germany's Deutsche Bundesbahn (DB), and reduced-price DB tickets were accepted. Check out the 10-day "Berlin Saver Ticket," sold at western German stations; it offers reductions of 33%. Trains from western Germany arrive at Berlin's main terminus, Bahnhof Zoologischer Garten (Bahnhof Zoo). The U-bahn (subway) and S-bahn (suburban railroad) stop here, too. Eastern Berlin's chief stations are at Friedrichstrasse or the Ostbanhof. For details, call **Deutsche Bundesbahn Information** (tel. 030/19419) or **Deutsche Reichsbahn** (tel. 030/311–02–111); **reservations** (tel. 030/311–02–112).

By Bus Buses are slightly cheaper than trains; Berlin is linked by bus to 170 European cities. The main station is at the corner of Masurenallee 4–6 and Messedam. Reserve through DER (state), commercial travel agencies, or the station itself. For information, call 030/301–8028, daily 9–5:30.

By Car The "transit corridor" roads linking former West Germany with western Berlin are still there, but the strict restrictions that once confined foreign motorists driving through East Germany have vanished, and today you can travel at will through the country. Expressways link Berlin with the eastern German cities of Magdeburg, Leipzig, Rostock, Dresden, and Frankfurt an der Oder. At press time, speed restrictions of 130 kph (80 mph) still applied, and you must carry your driver's license, car registration, and insurance documents.

Getting Around

By Public Transportation Berlin is too large to be explored on foot. To compensate, the city has one of the most efficient public transportation systems in Europe, a smoothly integrated network of subway (U-bahn) and elevated (S-bahn) train lines, buses, trams (in eastern Berlin only), and even a ferry (across the Wannsee Lake), making every part of the city easily accessible. There's also an all-night bus service, indicated by the letter "N" next to route numbers. In summer, there are excursion buses linking the downtown area with the most popular recreational areas.

A DM 3.20 ticket (DM 2.10 for children) covers the entire system for two hours and allows you to make an unlimited number of changes between trains and buses. The best deal for visitors who plan to travel extensively around the city is the **Berlin Ticket,** valid for 24 hours and good for all trains and buses; it costs DM 12 (DM 6 for children). A seven-day **Tourist Pass** is also available; it costs DM 32 and allows unlimited travel on all city buses and trains. If you plan to visit the Wannsee Lake, buy the **combined day ticket,** good for the entire network and the excursion boats of the Stern- und Kreisschiffahrt line; it costs DM 25 (DM 12.50 for children). If you are just making a short trip, buy a Kurzstreckentarif. It allows you to ride six bus stops or three U-bahn or S-bahn stops for DM 2.10 (DM 1.60 for children). Buy it in packs of four for the best value (DM

Berlin Public Transit System

U1 U-Bahn
S1 S-Bahn

Oranienburg **S1**
Lehnitz
Borgsdorf
S10 **Birkenwerder** Schönfli
Hohen Neuendorf
Bergfelde

Frohnau
Hermsdorf
Waidmannslust
Wittenau
Wilhelmsruh

Alt-Tegel **U6**
Borsigwerke
Hotzhauser Str. **Paracelsus-Bad** **U8** **Schönhol:**
Seidelstr. **S2**
Residenzstr.
Scharnweberstr.
Franz-Neumann-Pl.
Kurt-Schumacher-Pl.
Nauener Pl.
Afrikanische Str. Pank
Rehberge
Seestr. Gesu
Leopoldpl. Humbold
Amrumer Str. Wedding
Westhafen ReinickendorferStr.
Birkenstr. Schwartzkopffstr.
Turmstr. Zinnowitzer Str
Oranienbu

BUS 9 **BUS 8**

Berlin-Tegel
Airport

Jakob-Kaiser-Pl.
Jungfernheide
Mierendorffpl.
Rich.-Wagner-Pl.

Altstadt Spandau
Zitadelle
Haselhorst
Paulsternstr.
Rohrdamm
Siemensdamm
Halemweg

U7
Rathaus
Spandau

Ruhleben
U1

Olympia-Stadion
Neu-Westend
Theodor-Heuss-Pl.
Kaiserdamm
Sophie-Charlotte-Pl.
Deutsche Oper
Bismarckstr.
Ernst-Reuter-Pl.
Wilmersdorfer Str. **S5** Savignypl.

Hansapl.
Tier-garten
Bellevue
Lehrter
Stadtbahnhof
U.d. Linden
Mohrenstr.
U2
Zoologischer Garten

Wittenbergpl.
Nollendorfpl.

Charlottenburg
Kurfürstendamm
U2 **U3**
U3 **U4**
Uhlandstr.

Kurfürstenstr.
Anhalter Bhf.
Möcke
brü
Gleisdreieck

Westkreuz **S9**
S6

Adenauerpl.
Konstanzer Str.
Hohenzollernpl.
Augsburger Str.
Spichernstr.
Güntzelstr.
Viktoria-Luise-Pl.
Grossgörschenstr.
Yorckst
Kleistpark
Bayerischer Pl.
Eisenacher Str.
Papestr

Grunewald

Fehrbelliner Pl.
Blissestr.
Berliner Str.
Rath. Schöneberg
Bundespl.
Innsbrucker
Pl. **U4**
Schöneberg

Heidelberger Pl.
Rüdesheimer Pl.
Breitenbachpl.
Friedr. Wilhelm-Pl.
Walther-Schreiber-Pl.
Friedenau
Priesterweg

Dahlem-Dorf Podbielskiallee
Attilastr.
Oskar-Helene-Heim Thielplatz
Schlosstr.
Feuerbachstr.
Marienfelde

Krumme
Lanke **U2**
Onkel Toms Hütte
U9 **Rathaus**
Steglitz
Buckower
Chaussee

S3
Bobelsberg
Griebnitzsee
Nikolassee
Lichtenrade

Potsdam
Stadt **S1** Wannsee
Schlachtensee
Mexikoplatz
Zehlendorf
Sundgauer Str.
Lichterfelde-West
Botanischer Garten
Mahlow

Former location of Berlin Wall

Blankenfelde **S2**
(Kr. Zossen)

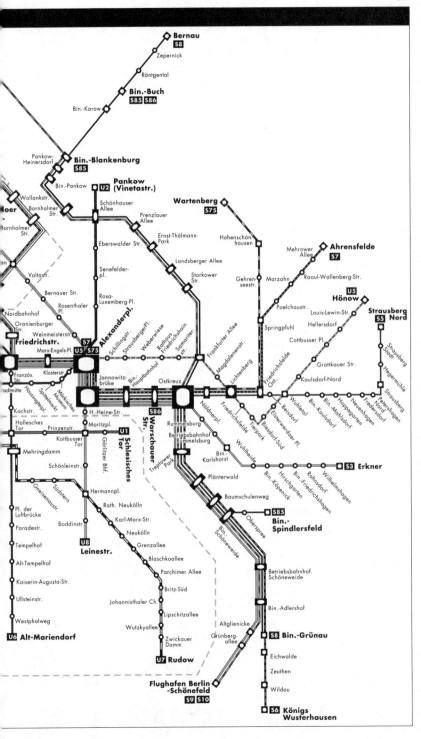

6.70 adults, DM 5.10 children). Finally, there's a ticket good only for rides along the Ku'damm on bus Nos. 119 and 129: it costs DM 1. The fare structure now covers transportation systems for both parts of Berlin.

All regular tickets are available from vending machines at U-bahn and S-bahn stations. Punch your ticket into the red machine on the platform. The Berlin ticket and the combined day ticket can only be bought from the main BVG ticket offices at the Bahnhof Zoo station and at the Kleistpark U-bahn station. For information, either call the **BVG** (Berliner Verkehrsbetriebe, tel. 030/752–7020) or go to the information office on Hardenbergplatz, directly in front of the Bahnhof Zoo train station.

By Taxi Fares start at DM 3.60 and increase by DM 1.79 per kilometer (DM 1.99 after midnight). There's an additional charge of 50 pfennigs per piece of luggage. Figure on paying around DM 15 for a ride the length of Ku'damm. Hail cabs in the street or order one by calling tel. 030/6902, 030/210–101, 030/261–026, 030/210–102, or 030/6944 in eastern Berlin.

By Bike Bicycling is popular in Berlin. While it's not recommended in the downtown area, it's ideal in outlying areas. Bike paths are generally marked by red bricks on the walkways. Many stores that rent or sell bikes carry the Berlin biker's atlas to help you find the paths. Call **Harry's Bike Shop** (Grolmanstr. 46, tel. 030/883–3942) Mon.–Sat. for information and rental locations, or rent your bikes at most major hotels for approximately DM 30 for 24 hours. Bicycles can travel with you on the U-Bahn system for an additional DM 2 fare. For bike rental in the Grunewald forest, go to the S-bahn station Grunewald, tel. 030/8115829.

Guided Tours

Orientation Tours There's no shortage of companies offering orientation tours (in English) covering all major sights in both eastern and western Berlin. They range in length from two and a half hours to four hours, with fares from DM 30 to DM 45. All operators also offer excursions to Potsdam (DM 50–DM 70) and Dresden (DM 50–DM 100), and tours of Berlin by night (the DM 95 fare includes two or three drinks at nightclubs). These general tours are more or less identical in program and price.

Tour Operators **Berliner Bären Stadtrundfahrten** (BBS, Rankestr. 35, tel. 030/213–4077). Groups depart from the corner of Rankestrasse and Kurfürstdendamm.

Berolina Stadtrundfahrten (Meinekestr. 3, tel. 030/882–2091). Groups depart from the corner of Kurfürstendamm and Meinekestrasse, and, in eastern Berlin, from the corner of Unter den Linden and Universitätstrasse.

Bus-Verkehr-Berlin (BVB, Kurfürstendamm 225, tel. 030/885–9880). Tours leave from Kurfürstendamm 225.

Severin & Kühn (BVB, Kurfürstendamm 216, tel. 030/883–1015). Groups leave from clearly marked stops along the Kurfürstendamm, and in eastern Berlin, at the corner of Unter den Linden and Universitätstrasse.

Special-Interest Sightseeing tours with a cultural/historical bias are offered on
Tours various weekends for approximately DM 20 by **Kultur Kontor**

(Savignypl. 9–10, tel. 030/310–888). Tours include "Berlin Becoming Berlin," "Berlin 1933–45," and "The Roaring '20s." Departures are from the corner of Savignyplatz and Kantstrasse. **Berliner Geschichtswerkstatt** (Goltzstr. 49, tel. 030/215–4450) also offers historical tours and tours on foot, starting from the Naturkundemuseum, at Invalidenstrasse 43. Bus excursions into the countryside around Berlin and as far as Magdeburg are offered by **Pluspunkt e.V.** (Hohenzollerndamm 188, tel. 030/862–1260).

Boat Trips Berlin not only has more water than any other inland European city but also Europe's biggest inland resort lake, so a tour by boat is as good a way of seeing the city as one by bus. There are several operators offering cruises ranging from a pleasure trip around the Wannsee to a cultural tour of the canals of the inner city.

A tour of the **Havel lakes** is the thing to do in summer. Trips begin at Wannsee (S-bahn: Wannsee) and at the Greenwich Promenade in Tegel (U-bahn: Tegel). You'll sail on either the whale-shaped vessel *Moby Dick* or the *Havel Queen*, a Mississippi-style boat, and cruise 17 miles through the lakes and past forests. Tours last 4½ hours and cost between DM 15 and DM 20. There are 20 operators. *See below* for the leading ones.

Tours of downtown Berlin's **canals** take in sights such as the Charlottenburg Palace and the Congress Hall. Tours depart from Kottbusser Bridge in Kreuzberg and cost around DM 10.

Two companies concentrate on cultural tours in which Berlin's history and architectural development can be followed from the deck of a boat. They are: **Kultur-Kontor** (Savignyplatz 9–10, tel. 030/310–888) and **Berliner Geschichtswerkstatt** (Goltzstr. 49, tel. 030/215–4450).

Tour Operators **Stern- und Kreisschiffahrt** (Sachtlebenstr. 60, tel. 030/810–0040).

Reederei Bruno Winkler (Levetzowstr. 16, tel. 030/391–7010).

Reederei Heinz Riedel (Planufer 78, tel. 030/691–3782 or 030/693–4646). Included in its large itinerary of lake and river cruises is a tour of the central city canals, starting from the Kottbusser Bridge near the Kottbusser Tor U-bahn station.

Die Weisse Flotte (Haupthafen Treptow, tel. 030/271–2327 or 030/271–2328). This is former East Germany's state-run pleasure-boat company, and no line knows the eastern Berlin waters better. Boats depart from the Haupthafen Treptow (Treptow S-bahn station).

Personal Guides The Verkehrsamt Berlin (tel. 030/262–6031) at Europa Center can provide you with a list of reputable guides who are fluent in English.

Walking Tours Walking tours of Berlin are organized by several companies and walking clubs, among them:

Berliner Wanderclub (Geschäftsstelle Berliner Strasse 40–41, tel. 030/875–175). This club also conducts hiking, cycling, and skiing tours in the Berlin and Brandenburg areas.

Historische Statt Reisen Berlin (Stephanstr. 24, tel. 030/395–3078).

Wanderkreis Berlin (Marschnerstr. 12, tel. 030/834–9977) features different tours that emphasize culture, history, architecture, and politics.

Exploring Berlin

The Berlin familiar to Western visitors was already a huge city before reunification. After the Wall fell and the two halves of the long-divided city joined up, Berlin became an enormous metropolis. By the year 2005 it's expected to become the biggest European continental city between the Atlantic and the Urals. It's already the largest in area. Paris, with twice the population, could fit six times within its borders, which enclose an urban area of nearly 900 square kilometers.

Berlin is a remarkably green city, with forests, rivers, lakes, 60 parks, and even large tracts of farmland covering more than 30% of its surface. It has Europe's largest inland stretch of recreational lakeland and the Continent's biggest inland beach; a boat tour of its canals and Havel lakes covers a greater distance than the Middle Rhine between Koblenz and Rüdesheim. You can walk 70 kilometers from the inner-city zoo to Berlin's outermost community, Lübars, without touching more than a few hundred yards of main road. And Lübars really is a community, one of 59 villages and 27 estates and farms that were absorbed to create Greater Berlin in 1920.

Seventy years later, Berlin still has the character of a collection of disparate parts, more like a country than a metropolis. The bells of no fewer than 55 village parish churches ring out on Sunday mornings. Visit Spandau, Schöneberg, or Köpenick on market day and you'll be excused for checking your map to make sure you're still in Berlin. Go on an outing to the Wannsee or Müggelsee lakes on a summer day and you'll think the Baltic coast has moved overnight.

This sense of a multifaceted city-state has its fascination—but also its frustrations. Berlin is a very difficult city for the visitor to get to know comfortably. You can't walk around it in a day, and even if you have the luxury of a week's stay you'll still return home with the nagging certainty that you've only just touched the surface. You'll also find a city again united but with its old prejudices still lingering like a Trabbi's poisonous exhaust fumes hanging in the air. You'll still sense the divide as you cross the largely invisible but still emotionally perceptible line that was once the Wall. The only really visible division now is the River Spree, which winds an east–west course between green banks and gray wharves and warehouses. In the eastern section of the city, the Spree is identified with the only part of Berlin that could be described as its "old town," the picturesque Nikolaiviertel. In the west, it skirts the city's biggest park, the Tiergarten, which means "Zoological Garden." (Don't be alarmed—the only wild animals you'll find there are safe behind bars and deep ditches in the Zoo, which slots into the park's southwestern corner.) The chances are that you'll be staying in this area, for this is Berlin's premier hotel territory, the point where the celebrated Kurfürstendamm starts on its arrow-straight journey westward to Berlin's other great, green playground, the Grunewald Forest. Here you'll find Berlin's other river, the Havel, and its lakes. Eastern Berlin claims the city's largest lake, the Müggelsee, and if you're seeking a swim on a hot day, that's the one to head for; the Grunewald lakes can get very crowded. You can escape the crowds just about anywhere in eastern Berlin, for much of that part of the city is still off-the-beaten-track territory. You'll find few tourists in areas such as Prenzlauerberg and Köpenick, although Berlin is changing with such speed that they could soon be rivaling the "in" suburbs of the western half. And who knows—by the time you visit you may really discover a truly united city. You'll certainly discover a fascinating one.

Highlights for First-Time Visitors

Ägyptisches Museum (*see* Tour 7)
Alexanderplatz (*see* Tour 3)
Brandenburger Tor (*see* Tour 2)
Gemäldegalerie, Dahlem (*see* Outlying Sights and Attractions)
Haus am Checkpoint Charlie (*see* Tour 3)
Kaiser-Wilhelm-Gedächtniskirche (*see* Tour 1)
Kaufhaus des Westens (Ka De We) department store (*see* Tour 1)
Pergamon Museum (*see* Tour 4)
Reichstag (*see* Tour 2)
Schloss Charlottenberg (*see* Tour 7)
Zoologischer Garten (*see* Tour 1)

Tour 1: Kurfürstendamm to Zoologischer Garten

Numbers in the margin correspond to points of interest on the Inner Berlin map.

Every city has its "main street," and sometimes the thoroughfare acquires such a central place in its history, tradition, and everyday life that the two become almost interchangeable. Mention western Berlin and the name "Ku'damm" springs automatically to mind. Newly unified Berlin has two such streets now, of course, with Unter den Linden doing for eastern Berlin what the Ku'damm performs for the western part of the city (*see* Tour 4, *below*). That was an additional bonus bestowed by unification, and who can begrudge the long-beleaguered Berliners the pleasure?

The odd name is short for **Kurfürstendamm,** meaning the "Elector's Causeway." The elector Joachim II of Brandenburg laid it out in the 16th century as his personal highway to connect his riverside palace in central Berlin to his hunting lodge in the Grunewald (*see* Excursions, *below*). Bismarck, the "Iron Chancellor" and the force behind Germany's 19th-century unification, widened it to a stately 55 yards in order to give Berlin a boulevard to compare with the grand avenues of Paris, but it was still some years before the Ku'damm developed into anything like the glittering avenue you see today. In fact, during Berlin's heydays of the turn of the century and the Roaring Twenties, the Ku'damm was outshone by Unter den Linden and other streets of what was to become drab postwar East Berlin. That was where the real heart of Berlin lay, and the Ku'damm was off the beaten track for many society types. The Ku'damm's prewar fame was based on its sometimes sordid nighttime scene, dominated by bars, dance halls, prostitutes, and all the gaudy ragtag and bobtail of the city's "alternative" lifestyle.

The Ku'damm shared the wartime fate of the rest of Berlin and suffered severe bomb damage. Nearly half of the 245 Bismarck-era buildings were destroyed and the rest were damaged in varying degrees. What you see today (as in most of Berlin) is either restored or was constructed since the war. The result is a garish clash of styles, with fin-de-siècle mansions rubbing fine shoulders with cheap department stores and exclusive cafés sharing the sidewalk with seedy clubs. Some Berliners hate the street and try to avoid it at any hour. But there can't be many of them, because the Ku'damm throbs with life 24 hours a day—and certainly not all who pack its wide pavements are visitors. Whatever you think about the street, you'll admit that it would be difficult to imagine Berlin without it.

The Ku'damm is 3 kilometers (2 miles) long and every block offers a contrast of one kind or another, so you can begin your tour at any point. If you stroll the length of it on one side and return on the other, you will have covered a literally blistering distance, but if you tire there are several bus lines traveling the route and a specially reduced Ku'damm ticket.

The Ku'damm is at its most impressive at its eastern end. ❶ Starting out at **Breitscheidplatz,** a large, untidy square partly ruined by high rises (including the Europa-Center), you'll find this stretch redeemed by the presence of western Berlin's most famous memorial, the bombed-out church tower of the ❷ **Kaiser-Wilhelm-Gedächtniskirche.** The church was built in a curious neo-Romanesque style and dedicated not to a saint but to Kaiser Wilhelm I, who attended the consecration in 1895. Allied bombers destroyed all but the bell tower, which was kept in its war-scarred state as a memorial. A permanent exhibit inside the base of the tower includes a collection of photographs and documents tracing the history of the church and items stressing the theme of forgiveness and reconciliation, including a cross of four medieval nails recovered from the ruins of Coventry Cathedral in England after German bombers destroyed that historic church. On the ceiling of the tower's interior you'll see 19th-century mosaics portraying not only religious scenes but also German imperial pageantry. The imperial character of the church is musically underscored by a carillon that peals from the tower on the hour, playing a jaunty tune composed by Kaiser Wilhelm's grandson, Prinz Ludwig Ferdinand von Hohenzollern. *Admission free. Open Tues.–Sat. 10–6, Sun. 11–6.*

A new church was built in 1961–63, next to the Gedächtniskirche ruins. Paired with a hexagonal bell tower, it's a modern, octagonal structure with honeycomb walls of vivid stained glass (imported from Chartres in France), which burst magically into life after dark with an indigo light that acts as a beacon in the night sky of central Berlin. (The two have been dubbed the "Lipstick" and "Compact.") Inside, you'll find a very moving representation of Mary and the infant Jesus—the *Stalingrad Madonna*—drawn in charcoal by a German army doctor shortly before Christmas, 1942, at the height of the siege of Stalingrad. Next to it is a 13th-century Spanish crucifix that forms the centerpiece of a memorial to the men and women of the July 1944 plot to overthrow Hitler. *Open Tues.– Sat. 10–6, Sun. 11–6.*

Time Out Set some time aside for coffee in the nearby **Einstein Stadtcafe** (Kurfürstendamm 67), where you can choose from an array of exotic coffees. There's also an interesting art gallery on the first floor of this fine 19th-century mansion.

Vying with the Gedächtniskirche for attention on Breitscheid-
❸ platz is the 22-story **Europa Center,** a vast complex that makes up in variety what it lacks in surface beauty. This 1960s eye-sore—nicknamed "Pepper's Manhattan" after its architect, K. H. Pepper—houses more than 100 shops, restaurants and cafés, a hotel, casino, thermal spa, two cinemas, and a central office of the Berlin Tourist Office, the Verkehrsamt. For a spec-tacular view of the city, take the elevator to the i-Punkt restau-rant and observation terrace on the top floor.

At its eastern end, the Ku'damm leads into another major Ber-lin shopping street, Tauentzienstrasse, where on the right you'll find the city's largest department store, the **Kaufhaus**
❹ **des Westens,** universally known as **KaDeWe** (Tauentzienstr. 21, tel. 030/2121–0). It's claimed that KaDeWe is the largest de-partment store not just in Berlin but in all Europe, although that boast is challenged by at least three London and Paris con-cerns. Try placing an outlandish order and waiting for a batted eyelid by the management, which assures customers it can pro-vide anything from a rare aspidistra to a zebra. The top floor is unquestionably tops: a culinary cornucopia of display cases proferring, among other delicacies, more than 150 sausages, myriad variations of herring, and hundreds of salads. If all this sets you salivating, you can pull up a stool at one of the many counters and sample much of what you see displayed, accompa-nied by wine, champagne, and beer. It's a great place for lunch or even an early dinner (KaDeWe closes at 6:30 PM weekdays).

Across the road from KaDeWe you'll see the neoclassical outline of the beautifully restored turn-of-the-century subway station **Wittenbergplatz.** Walk to Nürnburgerstrasse and pass the Penta Hotel (next door to Reuters and Merrill Lynch) and get
❺ onto Budapesterstrasse, where you'll see **Zoologischer Garten,** Berlin's extraordinary zoo. It's one of the world's oldest, founded in 1841, and it has the largest number of individual spe-cies of all the world's zoos. Less than 50 years ago, however, it had to start practically from zero. Only 91 animals survived the war; now there are more than 13,000. The public's favorite is Bao-Bao, a panda given to the people of Berlin by the Republic of China. But Bao-Bao isn't the only crowd pleaser, and scarce-ly a week goes by without the zoo announcing an attractive new addition to its animal population. The zoo has the world's larg-est birdhouse, a terrarium renowned for crocodiles, and an aquarium with thousands of fish, reptiles, and amphibians. *En-trances at Hardenbergpl. and Budapesterstr. Tel. 030/254010. Zoo admission: DM 8 adults, DM 4 children. Aquarium and zoo admission: DM 12.50 adults, DM 6 children. Zoo open dai-ly 9 AM–dusk. Aquarium open daily 9 AM–9 PM.*

Tour 2: Tiergarten, Brandenburger Tor, Kulturforum

Considering it is such a central Berlin attraction, the Branden-burger Tor (Brandenburg Gate) is not so easy to reach by public transport, and only a handful of hotels in eastern Berlin (and none in western Berlin) are within walking distance. If you're staying in the western part of the city, and anywhere near the Ku'damm, jump onto a No. 129 bus, claim an upstairs seat, and travel to the Tor in style. You'll take in some sights on the way

Inner Berlin

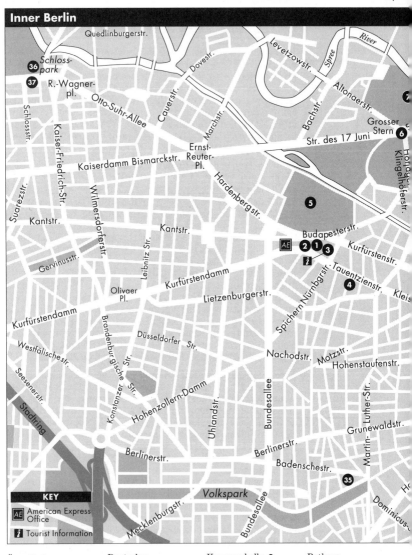

KEY

AE American Express Office

𝒊 Tourist Information

Ägyptisches Museum, **37**

Alexanderplatz, **20**

Bebelplatz, **22**

Berlin Cathedral, **27**

Brandenburger Tor, **10**

Brecht-Haus, **28**

Breitscheidplatz, **1**

Checkpoint Charlie, **14**

Deutsches Historisches Museum, **25**

Europa Center, **3**

Fischerinsel, **31**

Friedrichswerdersche Kirche, **16**

Gendarmenmarkt, **15**

Kaiser-Wilhelm-Gedächtniskirche, **2**

Kaufhaus des Westens (KaDeWe), **4**

Kongresshalle, **8**

Kottbusser Tor, **33**

Kreuzberg, **34**

Kulturforum, **13**

Märkisches Museum, **32**

Marx-Engels-Platz, **17**

Museumsinsel, **26**

Neue Wache, **24**

Nikolaiviertel, **30**

Potsdamerplatz, **12**

Rathaus Schöneberg, **35**

Reichstag, **9**

Ribbeckhaus, **18**

Rotes Rathaus, **19**

St. Hedwig's Cathedral, **23**

Schloss Bellevue, **7**

Schloss Charlottenburg, **36**

Siegessäule, **6**

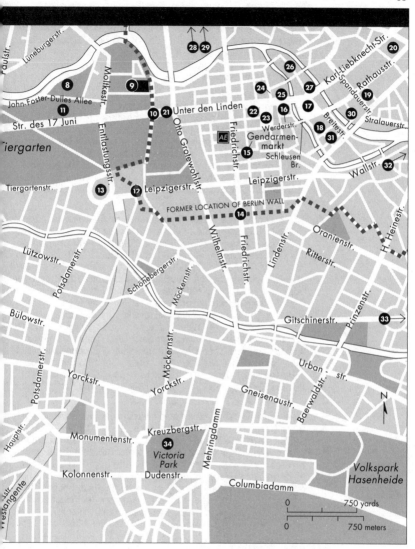

Soviet Victory
Memorial, **11**
Synagogue, **29**
Unter den Linden, **21**
Zoologischer
Garten, **5**

6 and be tempted to break your journey—at the **Siegessäule,** for instance, the victory column in the middle of the traffic circle known as the Grosser Stern (Big Star). Several main roads meet here, including Strasse des 17 Juni, the east–west axis of the park, named for the date of the unsuccessful 1953 uprising of East Berlin workers against the Soviets.

The 69-meter-high (227 feet) granite, sandstone, and bronze monument, built in 1873 to celebrate three illustrious Prussian military campaigns, originally stood before the Reichstag, on the former Königsplatz (King's Square), today's vast, grassy Platz der Republik (Republic Square). It was moved to its present position in 1938 during Hitler's ill-fated efforts to remodel Berlin to his own megalomaniacal plans. There's an observation platform at the top, reached by a giddy climb of 285 steps. *Admission: DM 1.50 adults, DM 1 children. Open Mon. 3–6, Tues.–Sun. 9–6.*

7 The next stop on the No. 129 is the **Schloss Bellevue,** an exquisite palace built on the banks of the Spree for Frederick the Great's youngest brother, Prince Augustus-Ferdinand. Today the palace serves as the German president's official Berlin residence, but there is talk of relocating him. The stately gray-and-cream-colored building is set in 50-acre grounds containing a small park called the English Garden, which was dedicated by Britain's prime minister Anthony Eden, who followed up the gesture shortly afterward by declaring war on Germany. Most of the trees there were later chopped down to provide fuel in the hard wartime winters. There are no hard feelings now on either side: Britain's Queen Elizabeth donated some of the park's new trees, and the Berliners refer affectionately to one of their favorite parks as the "Garden of Eden." *Schloss Bellevue Park: open daily 8–dusk. Closed when president is in residence.*

8 Soon you'll be passing the weirdest assembly hall you'll encounter in Berlin, the **Kongresshalle,** (John-Foster-Dulles-Allee 10, tel. 030/3970050), a conference center built in 1957 as the American contribution to the International Building Exhibition, Interbau. It was designed by Hugh Stubbins. The shock effect of its modernistic architectural style—it resembles an open oyster shell (or a giant, toothy grin—Berliners dubbed it "Jimmy Carter's Smile" when the American president came to Berlin on an official visit)—was increased when the roof fell in in 1980. The building has since reopened. You don't have to attend a meeting to inspect this oddity; temporary exhibitions there are open to the public.

9 The massive bulk of the **Reichstag** (Imperial Parliament) will then loom into sight. The bus stops right next to it. This imposing example of Prussian architectural grandeur was built in the 1890s to house the Prussian Parliament, and 30 years later it performed a similar function for the ill-fated Weimar Republic. The Reichstag was burned to a shell under mysterious circumstances on the night of February 28, 1933. The Nazis blamed the communists and thus found a convenient pretext for suspending the constitution and outlawing all opposition parties. After reconstruction, the Reichstag was again badly damaged in 1945 in the last Allied offensive of the war. The Reichstag will once again house the Bundestag, the German Parliament, but at press time the timetable for the move from Bonn to Berlin had not yet been set. Some Bonn politicians would prefer to stay within the cozy confines of the Rhine and are trying to delay the move for as long as possible. As a result, it could be 8 to 10 years before the move occurs. (What *is* certain is that the area around the Reichstag will become one huge construction site, as new offices are built for parliamentary members and their staffs.) Currently, the west wing of the building houses a comprehensive and very interesting exhibition entitled "Questions on German History," covering German history since 1800. The sections dealing with the Third Reich are especially fascinating. The exhibition is likely to remain in the Reichstag until Parliament moves in, but visitors should contact the Berlin Tourist Office for the latest information. *Pl. der Republik. Admission free. Open Tues.–Sun. 10–5.*

Time Out You can break your tour at this point (and still catch the next bus, using your current ticket) with a refresher at the Reichstag café. It's light, airy, and the prices are not ceiling-high.

Before moving on, stroll to the nearby Spree River bank for a sad reminder of the most recent painful phase of German history. You'll see several crosses on the riverbank, each commemorating someone who died while trying to cross the river frontier to the West. The closely guarded frontier between East and West, which ran down the center of the river, skirted the back of the Reichstag and around the next monument in your tour, the nearby Brandenburger Tor.

Just south of the Reichstag, where Strasse des 17 Juni meets Unter den Linden, is a monumental symbol of German unity ❿ and of the long division of Berlin—the mighty **Brandenburger Tor.** Ever since the Wall was built the Brandenburger Tor, once the pride of imperial Berlin, remained stranded in the eerie no-man's-land. When the Wall came down, it was the focal point of much celebrating, for this evocative symbol of Berlin was finally restored to all the people of the newly united city. The Brandenburger Tor is the only remaining gate of an original group of 14 gates built by Carl Gotthard Langhans in 1788–91, in virile classical style, as a triumphal arch for King Frederick Wilhelm II. The Quadriga, a chariot drawn by four horses and driven by the Goddess of Peace, was added in 1793. The goddess was originally naked, but puritanical protesters persuaded the city fathers to clothe her in a sheath of sheet copper. Troops paraded through the gate after successful campaigns, the last time being in 1945 when victorious Red Army troops took Berlin. The upper part of the gate, together with its chariot and Goddess of Peace, were destroyed during the war, but in 1957 the original molds were discovered in West Berlin and a new quadriga was cast in copper and presented as a gift to the people of East Berlin—a remarkable, rare instance of cold war–era East-West cooperation.

A short distance west, walking along Strasse des 17 Juni, you ⓫ will reach the **Soviet Victory Memorial,** until 1990 a Russian enclave in the West. Built directly after the end of World War II, before power plays between opposing sides had been set in motion, it was located in the western rather than the eastern sector. Through an East-West arrangement it has been allowed to remain there, although no longer guarded by Soviet troops, and now serves as a major attraction. The semicircular monument, which shows a bronze statue of a soldier, rests on a marble plinth taken from Hitler's former Berlin headquarters, flanked by what are said to be the first two tanks to have fought their way into Berlin in 1945.

Continuing on foot, turn south from the memorial and cross the tip of the Tiergarten to **Potsdamerplatz,** a somewhat dull-looking expanse that was once among the busiest squares in prewar Berlin. Potsdamerplatz is the point where the British, American, and Russian sectors met and is often referred to as the three-sector corner. The Wall cut through the center of the square. Not far from the square, on part of the wasteland on the other side of the dividing border, is a little knoll marking the remains of Hitler's reinforced concrete bunker where he spent his last days. The entire area has reawakened since buses and taxis were allowed to pass through the Brandenburg Gate. Cornerstones for the British and American embassies have already been established. In a lighter vein, circuses often lease sections of the area and set up tents on Potsdamerplatz.

In nearby Kemperplatz, west of Potsdamerplatz, lies the **Kulturforum** (Cultural Forum), a large square where you'll find a series of museums and galleries. Their contents will be shifting as state collections that were split in the war and stuck on opposite sides of the Wall are finally reunited. At press time, two new buildings were scheduled to join the complex. One of them planned to open in 1993, housing the **Kupferstichkabinett** (Drawings and Prints Collection) and the **Kunstbibliothek** (Art Library). The exhibitions at the Kupferstichkabinett include European woodcuts, engravings, and illustrated books from the 15th century to the present. Also on display are several pen-and-ink drawings by Dürer, 150 drawings by Rembrandt, and a photographic archive. The Kunstbibliothek contains art posters, a costume library, ornamental engravings, and a commercial art collection. *Admission free. Open Tues.–Fri. 9–5, weekends 10–5.*

The other, slated for completion in 1996, will display paintings dating from the late Middle Ages to 1800, many of them now at the Gemäldegalerie at Dahlem (*see* Outlying Sights and Attractions, *below*) and at the Bodemuseum on Museumsinsel (*see* Tour 4, *below*). Contact the Berlin Tourist Office for word on inevitable closings.

The roof that resembles a great wave belongs to the **Philharmonie** (Philharmonic Hall). Built in 1963, it is home to the renowned Berlin Philharmonic Orchestra. The functional design of the concert hall allows an audience of 2,000 to sit on all sides of the orchestra. The brilliant acoustics more than make up for ticketholders who face the backs of the orchestra. The main hall reopened in the spring of 1992 after an ambitious renovation. *Philharmonie ticket office: Matthäikirchstr. 1. Open weekdays 3:30–6 and weekends 11–2.*

The Philharmonie added the **Musikinstrumenten-Museum** (Musical Instruments Museum) to its attractions in 1984. It is well worth a visit for its fascinating collection of keyboard, string, wind, and percussion instruments. *Tiergartenstr. 1, tel. 030/ 254–810. Admission: DM 4. Free on Sun. and holidays. Open Tues.–Fri. 9–5, weekends and holidays 10–5. Guided tours on Saturdays at 11 with a noon presentation of the Wurlitzer organ.*

Opposite the Philharmonie is the **Kunstgewerbemuseum** (Museum of Decorative Arts). Inside this three-story building you'll find a display of the development of the arts and crafts in Europe from the Middle Ages to the present day. Among its treasures is the Welfenschatz (Guelph Treasure), a collection of 16th-century gold and silver plate from Nürnberg. The most impressive single piece is a reliquary in the form of a domed Byzantine church. Made in Köln in 1175, it is believed to have held the head of St. Gregory when it was brought back from Constantinople in 1773. Other displays of particular interest are the ceramics and porcelains. *Matthäikirchstr. 10, tel. 030/ 266-2911. Admission: DM 4 adults, DM 2 children. Free on Sun. and holidays. Open Tues.–Fri. 9–5, weekends and holidays 10–5.*

Leave the museum and walk south past the mid-19th-century church of St. Matthaeus to the **Neue Nationalgalerie** (New National Gallery), a modern glass-and-steel building designed by Mies van der Rohe and built in the mid-1960s.

The gallery's collection consists of paintings, sculptures, and drawings from the 19th and 20th centuries, with an accent on works by such Impressionists as Manet, Monet, Renoir, and Pissarro. Other schools represented are German Romantics, Realists, Expressionists, Surrealists, and the Bauhaus. The gallery also has a growing collection of contemporary art from Europe and America. *Potsdamerstr. 50, tel. 030/266-2666. Admission: DM 4 adults, DM 2 children. Free on Sun. and holidays. Open Tues.–Fri. 9–5, weekends and holidays 10–5.*

A Tageskarte (Day Card) covers 1-day admission to all museums at Kulturforum. Cost: DM 8. The card is available at each museum.

The last stop on the tour of the Cultural Forum is the **Staatsbibliothek** (National Library), opposite the Neue Nationalgalerie. This modern building, housing one of the largest libraries in Europe, with 4 million volumes, was designed by Hans Scharoun, the architect of the Philharmonie. *Potsdamerstr. 33, tel. 030/2661. Admission free. Open Mon.– Fri. 9–9, Sat. 9–5.*

From here you can walk to KaDeWe department store on Tauentzienstrasse, or to the Zoologischer Garten station, where you can take a train to return to your hotel; otherwise, if there's still time, you can amble along Kurfürstendamm (*see* Tour 1, *above*).

Tour 3: From Checkpoint Charlie to Alexanderplatz

Begin this tour of East Berlin on the corner of Kochstrasse and Friedrichstrasse (near the U-bahn Kochstrasse station). This site was once the most famous of the Berlin Wall crossing points, **"Checkpoint Charlie,"** as well as the setting of many memorable spy novels and films.

The physical checkpoint, a wooden pavilion, was hoisted away by crane in an emotional ceremony shortly after the Wall crumbled, but the red-and-white barrier and the threatening gray watchtower are still there, kept as a reminder of this particular chapter of Berlin's history. The watchtower is being taken over by the nearby **Haus am Checkpoint Charlie,** a museum tracing the history of the Wall and vividly describing the most ingenious of the successful escapes. Here you'll find a miniature submarine that brought one East German unscathed through the river frontier, and a coffinlike assembly of two hollowed-out surfboards in which a West German smuggled his girlfriend west. Keeping up with the times, the museum also has some spectacularly decorated pieces of the Wall on display. *Haus am Checkpoint Charlie, Friedrichstr. 44, tel. 030/2511031. Admission: DM 7.50 adults, DM 4 children. Open daily 9 AM–10 PM.*

A drab, gray section of the Wall still stands as a memorial just beyond the Checkpoint Charlie barrier. On the corner, at the barrier itself, is the famous **Cafe Adler,** (Friedrichstr. 206, tel. 030/251–8965), once a lonely outpost of Western hospitality in the shadow of the Wall but now just part of the general city scene.

Heading north on Friedrichstrasse, you can observe the burgeoning commercial development of eastern Berlin in microcosm. An attempt is being made to return this wide shopping boulevard to something approaching the flair it had in its prewar days. Large, fashionable stores will soon be lining the street again. An American Express office, the designer Escada, the jewelers Christ, and Mercedes-Benz have already established residence on Friedrichstrasse. Galeries Lafayette, the French department store, is scheduled to open its Berlin branch here at the end of 1994. Also in the vicinity of the main boulevard are the offices of n-tv, Germany's answer to CNN.

Turn right from Friedrichstrasse onto Johannes-Dieckmann-Strasse and straight ahead are two prominent cupolas beckoning you into one of the finest squares in all Europe, the **⑮ Gendarmenmarkt.** The cupolas belong to two monumental churches, the 18th-century **Deutscher Dom** (German Cathedral) and the **Französischer Dom** (French Cathedral), flanking in perfect harmony the beautiful neoclassical **Schauspielhaus,** one of the greatest works of the Berlin architect Karl Friedrich Schinkel and now home to the Berlin Symphony Orchestra. (Don't confuse the Deutscher Dom with the massive Berliner Dom, the city's own cathedral, which sits squarely beside the Spree River a short walk away.) The Deutscher Dom is an earlier cathedral with an impressive bronze cupola, but it is by no means as important. It was built by Berlin's Lutherans in 1701–08, and although it commands no great place in Berlin history, the broad steps you see before the church once displayed the coffins of revolutionaries who died in the uprisings of March 1848. At press time, it was scheduled to reopen sometime during 1994.

Immediately north of the Deutscher Dom is the Schauspielhaus, which opened again to the public as recently as 1984 after laborious reconstruction. *Schauspielhaus* means "theater," but now only concerts are performed here (*see* The Arts, *below*), possibly explaining the rather concerned look on the face of Friedrich von Schiller, who stands in statue form in the middle of the square. Completing the harmonious trio of classically proportioned buildings is the Französischer Dom, built at the same time as its near twin, the Deutscher Dom, for Huguenot settlers who found refuge in Berlin. The nostalgic Huguenots built it as a copy of their home church in Charenton, France; today it houses a Huguenot museum and a restaurant-in-the-round, 70 feet up under the dome. There are 254 steps to climb before you reach the restaurant (Französischer Hof), but there's a refreshing glass of wine or beer waiting at the top. *Hugenottenmuseum, Gendarmenmarkt. Admission: DM 2 adults, DM 1 children. Open Tues., Wed., Thurs., Sat. 12–5; Sun. 1–5.*

Time Out Save the Französischer Hof for a leisurely lunch or dinner before or after a concert. For a quick snack, try one of these nearby café/restaurants: the **Café Arkade** (Französischerstr. 25), on the northwest corner of the square, or the **Cafe zur Laube** (Otto Nuschkestr. 20), a local favorite that boasts its own *Konditorei* (pastry shop).

Leave the Gendarmenmarkt by Französischerstrasse and follow it east into Werderstrasse. The redbrick, neo-Gothic church on your left, the **Friedrichswerdersche Kirche,** was designed by Schinkel in 1824–30 in a style that combines vertical Gothic lines with a heavy solidity. You'll either hate the building's rather dirty red appearance and frivolous brass-ball-capped turrets or be fascinated by them; it was quite the rage at the time, and became a model for many churches in Prussia. The interior, no longer a church but a museum dedicated to the work of Schinkel and his contemporaries, is surprisingly light and airy, with a very delicate ribbed ceiling. *Schinkelmuseum, Friedrichswerdersche Kirche, Werderstr., tel. 030/208–1323. Admission: DM 1 adults, 50 pf children. Open Wed.–Sun. 10–6.*

Continue along Werderstrasse, crossing the Spree River over the Schleusen Bridge (there's a fine view from either side), and on the left you will see the enormous **Marx-Engels-Platz** (part of which has been renamed Lustgarten). On this windy, barren square once stood the Berliner Schloss (Berlin Palace), an Italian Baroque royal and imperial residence that grew from a 15th-century castle. The palace was bombed out during the war, and instead of attempting to rebuild it East Berlin's communist rulers blew up the remaining walls, cleared the ground, and erected the bombastic bronzed glass-and-concrete **Palast der Republik** (Palace of the Republic), which dominates the square today. The Palast was the seat of the Volkskammer, the East German Parliament, but it also gave space to several restaurants, a theater, a dance hall, and even a bowling alley. The locals call it the Palazzo Prozzo (a play on the German word *protzen,* meaning to show off in a gaudy way). Mercifully, the fine Baroque portal of the former palace was saved, carted off stone by stone across the square and inserted into the facade of the government building on your right, a particularly jarring juxtaposition.

Farther along this side of the Marx-Engels-Platz, at the top of Breitestrasse, are the former royal stables, the **Marstall,** a grand complex in imperial Prussian style. The Neue Marstall is now the city library, and the Alte Marstall hosts special loan exhibitions. On the corner of the Marstall you'll see one of the still-existent representations of Marx himself, a bronze relief showing the father of international socialism watching benignly over participants in the 1918–19 communist uprisings. Your attention is bound to be drawn by the starkly contrasting Renaissance facade of the house directly bordering the Marstall in Breitestrasse. This is the **Ribbeckhaus,** Berlin's only remaining Renaissance building. It was built for businessman Hans Georg von Ribbeck in 1624 and now serves as a government office.

From Breitestrasse walk back to Rathausstrasse, named after the former East Berlin city hall standing on the corner of Spandauerstrasse. It's called the **Rotes Rathaus**—the Red City Hall—not because of its communist associations but for its red-brick construction. Erected in 1861–70 on the site of Berlin's original, medieval town hall, in what was considered a suitably historical style—neo-Renaissance—the Rotes Rathaus looks oddly Venetian. A novel touch is the tiled frieze running along its facade, representing scenes from Berlin's history. If you're hungry, you can duck down into the cellar, where you'll have a choice of two restaurants (*see* Dining, *below*).

The ultimate destination of this tour is clearly visible from here: the 365-meter-high (1,198-foot-high) **Fernsehturm,** the television and radio tower that was once the futuristic symbol of East Berlin. The tallest structure in the entire city, it soars into the sky from the center of vast **Alexanderplatz** (nicknamed Alex), in prewar days a stylish piazza (named for the Russian czar Alexander I) but now a jumble of fast-food stands, nondescript 1950s high rises, Kaufhof department store, and the unattractive Hotel Stadt Berlin. Architecture buffs will want to note the two 1930s buildings opposite the railroad bridge, on the southwest side of Alexanderplatz, by Peter Behrens, an early modernist who employed the young Walter Gropius and Mies van der Rohe as junior partners in his firm. These Bauhausian structures, strikingly abstract in their day, are in a sad state of disrepair. To get away from it all, take a high-speed elevator to the tower's observation platform and soak up the best view of Berlin you can have short of buying a plane ticket. *Fernsehturm, Alexanderplatz. Elevator: DM 5 adults, DM 2.50 children. Open daily 9 AM–11 PM.*

It's no small irony that one of Berlin's oldest churches, the Gothic **Marienkirche,** stands on the edge of Alexanderplatz, almost in the shadow of the soaring television tower. The modest brick church shelters several treasures, including a 15th-century bronze baptismal font, a beautiful pulpit created in 1701 by Andreas Schluter, and the remarkable *Totentanz* fresco, a vivid, nightmarish representation of the "dance of death" theme, dating from 1450. *Open Mon.–Thurs. 10–noon and 1–4, Sat. noon–4. Guided tours of the church are conducted daily at 1 PM, and organ recitals regularly take place Saturdays at 4:30 PM.*

Time Out If it's chilly outside, you might want to warm up with a steaming hot bowl of soup at the **Suppenterrine** on Alexanderplatz. You'll rub shoulders at a communal zinc-topped bar with eastern Berliners sipping cabbage broth and local beer. It's not very classy, but it's cheap and cheerful. Alternatively, snack outdoors on a bulging *Dönnerkebab* sandwich, stuffed with succulent grilled lamb slices, onions, tomatoes, and cooked red cabbage. You'll find several food and beer stands near the Alexanderplatz S-bahn, where Rathausstrasse leads into the square.

Tour 4: On and around Unter den Linden, Museumsinsel

Unter den Linden is repeatedly described as eastern Berlin's Champs-Élysées, but that does justice to neither street. The mile-long thoroughfare that runs east from the Brandenburger

Tor into Karl-Lieb-Knecht-Strasse at Museumsinsel lacks the Paris boulevard's grand scale and sweep, but it's lined for much of the way with imperial buildings that the French could well envy. Wartime bombing left great gaps that in the 1950s were filled in by hurriedly thrown-up blocks of buildings, and virtually all the original lime trees—the *Linden*—were either destroyed by bombs or chopped down for fuel. The replacement trees aren't mature yet, but they're a pretty sight in summer. The ugly blocks of indifferent shops are still there, but that scene is changing, too, as western entrepreneurs move in. So Unter den Linden is on the way toward recapturing its prewar appearance and charm. Don't hurry your stroll along its length; in fact, if you have time and energy, take one side of the street at a time. You'll be slowed constantly anyway by the demands for your attention made by the historic buildings from Berlin's Prussian past that stand like sentinels on either side and imperiously seek your gaze.

None of them, however, date from the beginnings of Under den Linden, which was originally a bridle path, widened by the Prince-Elector Friedrich Wilhelm in 1647 to accommodate the hunting parties he and other members of the nobility led out into the woodland that is now the Tiergarten. Grand homes arose along its length, and in the 18th century Friedrich II built an opera house, a stately library, a cathedral, and a palace for the crown prince. They are there today, some rebuilt after wartime devastation and some serving different purposes (the crown prince's palace is Berlin's renowned Humboldt University), but all contributing to a harmonious historical entity that's unique in Germany.

The first large building you'll encounter as you head east along the boulevard from Pariser Platz, in front of the Brandenburger Tor, is a monumental diplomatic "palace," the **Soviet Embassy,** now reduced—like all former embassies to East Germany—to the role of a consular mission. Behind the forbidding railings is one of the few Lenin busts you'll find these days in Berlin. One block up on the same side is eastern Berlin's newest and most expensive hotel, the Grand (with a tempting shopping arcade). Behind it you'll see the gables of the **Komische Oper,** home of the eponymous company, whose productions are known for being innovative. The **Alte Palais,** the former palace of Emperor Wilhelm I, is next on the right, and flanking it in the middle of Unter den Linden is a striking bronze equestrian sculpture of **Friedrich II,** riding his favorite horse, Conde. The sculptor Rauch, who completed the work in 1851, decorated the plinth with reliefs of various German historical figures, mischievously positioning right under the horse's tail the heads of two outspoken critics of Friedrich II: Gotthold Lessing and Immanuel Kant. For years the sculpture was exiled to Potsdam, the ruler's favorite abode, but in 1980 the communist government apparently thought him sufficiently rehabilitated to reinstall him.

The lime-tree-framed square that recedes to the right, ❷❷ **Bebelplatz,** played a less happy role in German history: It was here, before the buildings that represented a high point in German culture, that Hitler's Nazi philistines burned the books of banned authors on May 11, 1933, an episode that has come to be known as the *Bücherverbrennung*. The square presents a much more cultivated face these days, flanked on one side by one of Berlin's main opera houses, the Deutsche Staatsoper, and on the other by the delicate Baroque-style Prinzessinnenpalais (Princesses' Palace), a copy of the original from 1733. In the background sits the elegantly curved facade of the former royal library, the Alte Bibliothek, dubbed the **"Kommode"** (chest of drawers) by irreverent Berliners because of its shape. A brass plate on the outside wall recalls that Lenin did some of his early research here in 1895.

The Deutsche Staatsoper, first designed by Georg von Knobelsdorff, the architect of Friedrich II's beloved Sanssouci Palace, in 1741–43 in a combination of Rococo and Classical styles, was one of the world's first opera houses. It burned down in 1843, and Karl Ferdinand Langhans, son of Carl Gotthard Langhans, rebuilt it in the neoclassical form you see today. It's a curiously charming building, monumental but modest beside the great structures that otherwise make up Unter den Linden. A visit to the Deutsche Staatsoper is a must even for the tone-deaf (*see* The Arts, *below*); tickets aren't difficult to get. *Unter den Linden 7. Box office tel. 030/200–4262. Open weekdays, noon–6.*

Time Out   No princess lives there anymore, but you can spoil yourself royally in the gilded splendor of the **Operncafe,** an elegant café/restaurant on the ground floor of the Prinzessinenpalais. The cake display case is a spectacle to rival anything at the nearby opera house. For more substantial fare, try the **Schinkel Klause,** a tavern named after the architect Schinkel and housed in the **Palais Unter den Linden** (once the Kronprinzenpalais), on Überwallstrasse, which runs down the side of the Operncafe. The palace is now a government guest house, but the Schinkel Klause is open to all.

㉓ Just behind the Deutsche Staatsoper is **St. Hedwig's Cathedral,** a substantial, circular building that's similar to the Pantheon in Rome. Note the tiny street called Hinter der Katholische Kirche; it means "Behind the Catholic Church." When the cathedral was erected in 1747 it was the first Catholic church built in resolutely Protestant Berlin since the Reformation in the 16th century. Although Knobbelsdorff was the official architect of the church, it's thought that Friedrich II contributed substantially to its design.

On the other side of Unter den Linden you'll see a surprisingly modest creation by architect Karl Friedrich Schinkel (his first ㉔ building, in fact), the **Neue Wache,** built in the style of a Roman temple in 1816–18 as a guardhouse and given a new use after World War II as a war memorial. An eternal flame burns in the center of the small, pillared hall, and before it lie the tombs of the "unknown warrior" and an "unknown resistance fighter." Until the unification of Germany, helmeted and jack-booted East German soldiers stood guard there, and the changing of the guard was a top tourist attraction. The sight is no more—it was one of the first rituals of the East German communists to be discarded.

Just west of the Neue Wache is the palace complex of the renowned **Humboldt University.** It was built in 1748–68 as a palace for Friedrich II's brother Prince Heinrich, and in 1810 the von Humboldt brothers, Wilhelm and Alexander, founded a university within its walls. The names of the famous men of letters and science who either studied or taught here comprise an

We can wire money to every major city in Europe almost as fast as you can say, "Zut alors! J'ai perdu mes valises".

How fast? We can send money in 10 minutes or less, to 13,500 locations in over 68 countries worldwide. That's faster than any other international money transfer service. And when you're *sans* luggage, every minute counts.

MoneyGram from American Express® is available throughout Europe. For more information please contact your local American Express Travel Service Office or call: 44-71-839-7541 in England; 33-1-47777000 in France; or 49-69-21050 in Germany. In the U.S. call 1-800-MONEYGRAM.

MoneyGram
INTERNATIONAL MONEY TRANSFERS.

519 M.P.H.

190 M.P.H.

75 M.P.H.

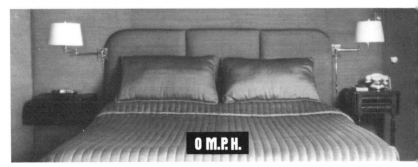

0 M.P.H.

WE LET YOU SEE EUROPE AT YOUR OWN PACE.

Regardless of your personal speed limits, Rail Europe offers everything to get you over, around and through anywhere you want in Europe. For more information, call your travel agent or 1-800-4-EURAIL.

OFFICIAL DISTRIBUTOR

Rail Europe

OF THE EURAIL PASS

illustrious list, including Marx, Engels, Hegel, Einstein, and Max Planck. Statues of Wilhelm and Alexander von Humboldt stand proudly before their university. On the other side of the Neue Wache, right at the end of Unter den Linden, is the former arsenal, the Zeughaus, 1695–1705. It was the first large building to grace the avenue. A masterpiece of early Baroque, it was used at the turn of the century as a hall of fame glorifying Prusso-German militarism. Today it's the **Deutsches Historisches Museum** (German History Museum), covering the period from 1789 to the present; its galleries on the GDR have been closed down. At press time, plans for the next exhibition were unsettled. *Unter den Linden 2, tel. 030/200–941. Admission: DM 4 adults, DM 2 children. Open Mon.–Thurs. 9–5, weekends 10–5.*

Heading east you'll come to the **Karl-Liebknecht-Brücke** (formerly the Marx-Engels-Brücke), a charming bridge designed by Schinkel and punctuated by classical statues. The bridge leads into a large island, the northwestern part of which is called **Museumsinsel** (Museum Island), on the site of one of Berlin's two original settlements, Cölln, dating from 1237. Today you'll find a complex of four remarkable museums here, which are described below. *Bodestr. 1–3, tel. 030/220–0381. Admission to each museum: DM 4. Free on Sun. and holidays. Open Mon.–Thurs. 9–5, weekends and holidays 10–5. A Tageskarte (Day Card) covers 1-day admission to all museums on Museum Island. Cost: DM8. The card is available at each museum.*

The **Altes Museum** (Old Museum; entrance Lustgarten) is an austere neoclassical building just north of Marx-Engels-Platz that features postwar East German art; its large etching and drawing collection, from the Old Masters to the present, is a treasure trove. The **Nationalgalerie** (National Gallery; entrance on Bodestrasse) houses an outstanding collection of 18th-, 19th-, and early 20th-century paintings and sculptures and often hosts special temporary exhibits. Works by Cézanne, Rodin, Degas, and one of Germany's most famous portrait artists, Max Liebermann, are part of the permanent exhibition.

Even if you aren't generally inclined toward the ancient world, make an exception for the **Pergamonmuseum** (entrance on Am Kupfergraben). It is not only the standout in this complex but one of Europe's greatest museums. The museum's name is derived from its principal and best-loved display, the Pergamon altar, a monumental Greek temple found in what's now Turkey and dating from 180 BC. Adorning it are finely carved figures of gods locked in battle against giants. As much as anything, perhaps, this vast structure illustrates the zeal of Germany's 19th-century archaeologists, who had it shipped piece by piece from a mountaintop to Berlin. Equally impressive is the Babylonian Processional Way in the Asia Minor department. As you walk through the museum, you cannot help wondering how they ever got away with dismantling and exporting these vast treasures.

Last in the complex is the **Bodemuseum** (entrance on Monbijoubrücke), with its superb Egyptian, Byzantine, and early Christian relics, sculpture collections, and coin gallery. The Sphinx of Hatshepsut, from around 1500 BC, is stunning, as are the Burial Cult Room and the Papyrus Collection. There is also a representative collection of Italian Renaissance paintings.

Museum Island will eventually house all the state archaeological collections. For example, the Egyptian holdings currently at Charlottenburg (*see* Tour 7, *below*) will be united with the Egyptian collection at the Bodemuseum, and the Far Eastern art at the Pergamonmuseum will move to Dahlem, which will concentrate on ethnological collections. The 19th-century **New Museum,** still in ruins from World War II bombings, will be rebuilt, and the Nationalgalerie will display only 19th-century paintings, including those now at the Neue Nationalgalerie at the Kulturforum (*see* Tour 2, *above*). The changes will be gradual and will take years to complete; visitors should contact the Berlin Tourist Office for the current status of these collections.

From the museum complex, follow the Spree Canal back to Unter den Linden and the enormous, impressive 19th-century **27** **Berlin Cathedral** (Berliner Dom). The small Märkisches Museum inside (entrance on Unter den Linden) records the postwar reconstruction of the building. If you climb the cathedral stairs, you can reach a balcony from which you can observe up close the vast nave and dome. The impact of the sight leaves many a visitor speechless. *Am Gendarmenmarkt. Balcony open 10–6. Museum admission free. Cathedral carillion plays automatically at noon, 3, and 7; live performances Tues. at 2, Sat. at 3.*

Continue west on Unter den Linden, turning right into Friedrichstrasse. The upper Friedrichstrasse is undergoing reconstruction. Among its landmarks are the tall **International Trade Center,** next to the Friedrichstrasse rail station, and, farther up, the **Friedrichstadtpalast,** featuring a nightclub, dancing, and occasional musical shows. Despite the rebuilding, the street still houses a number of small shops, bookstores, and neighborhood establishments. Just after crossing the Spree, turn left onto Schiffbauerdamm to see the **Berliner Ensemble** (*see* The Arts, *below*), founded by Bertolt Brecht, which continues to be a showcase for his works. Rejoin Friedrichstrasse and walk up beyond the bend, where the street turns into the Chausseestrasse (or take the U-6 to Oranienburger Tor) to find **28** the **Brecht-Haus** and a library for Brecht scholars. *Chausseestr. 125, tel. 030/282–3103. Admission: DM 2 adults, DM 1 children. Open Tues.–Fri. 9–3.*

Brecht is actually buried next door, along with his wife Helene Weigel and more than 100 other celebrated Berliners, in the **Dorotheenstädtischer Cemetery.** They include Hegel, Heinrich Mann, the neoclassical architects Schinkel and Schadow as well as the Berlin printer Litfass, the man who invented those stumpy cylindrical columns you'll find across Europe carrying advertisements and theater schedules.

Head back toward the center and turn left down Oranien-**29** burgerstrasse to the ruins of the massive city **synagogue,** which is in the process of being restored. It's an exotic amalgam of styles, the whole faintly Middle Eastern, built between 1894 and 1905. It was largely ruined on the night of November 11, 1938, the infamous Kristalnacht (crystal night), when Nazi looters and soldiers rampaged across Germany and Austria, burning synagogues and smashing the few Jewish shops and homes left in the country. It was further ruined during the bombing of the city toward the end of the war. From here, take the subway from Oranienburger Tor back to the center of the city.

Tour 5: Nikolaiviertel, Fischerinsel

The true heart of Berlin is a small patch of land, little more than 30 acres bordered on the east by the Spree River and with the city's oldest church, the Nikolaikirche, as its geographical and spiritual center. This is the **Nikolaiviertel,** the Nikolai quarter, a picturesque re-creation (or evocation) of old Berlin. It's just southwest of the Rotes Rathaus (*see* Tour 3, *above*)—cross Spandauerstrasse and you're there. By subway take U-2 from Alexanderplatz to Spittelmarkt and cross the Spree on Mühlendamm; the quarter is on the left. The area can be covered in an hour at the most, unless, of course, you linger in any of the more than 20 taverns, restaurants, and cafés that cram each of its four main alleys.

The **Nikolaikirche,** dedicated to a very important Berlin saint—Nicholas, patron of traders and fisherfolk—was built between 1230 and 1240 in solid, late-Romanesque style. Gothic refinements were added, and the twin towers weren't built until the 19th century. But wartime bombing destroyed all but the early foundation walls, rough-hewn stonework that forms the base of the rebuilt church you see today. The interior is almost entirely Gothic, but without the gloomy solemnity of so many churches of the period. Light streams through the high, arched windows, illuminating the gaily decorated interior and, incidentally, the exhibits about medieval Berlin in the side aisles and choir. *Admission: DM 1 adults, 50 pf children. Open Tues.–Fri. 9–5, weekends 9–6.*

In front of the church is an early representation in carved stone of the arms of Berlin, borne by a bear and enclosed by finely wrought iron. To one side you'll see the first of several replicas of historic old houses that crowd the area, the **Knoblauchhaus,** once the home of a wealthy silk merchant, Christian Knoblauch. The house now contains a museum tracing the family history (which is very much a history of Berlin) and a wine tavern, the Historische Weinstube. Head along Poststrasse in the direction of Mühlendamm and you'll find another interesting tavern on the corner. It's called Zur Rippe (The Rib), and if you look above the entrance you'll see why: There's a huge rib bone hanging there. The story goes that it's a giant's rib. At any rate, by all appearances it's certainly a real rib. Don't be tempted to stop for a drink there (the pub itself is disappointing, marred by a slot machine and laminated tables), but walk a few yards up Mühlendamm toward the Spree and then take your pick of a number of delightful restaurants and cafés spread out along the riverbank.

On the corner of Poststrasse and Mühlendamm is Berlin's finest Rococo house, the **Ephraimpalais.** Friedrich II had it built in 1761–66 for his court jeweler, Veitel Ephraim. Ephraim was Jewish, and in 1935 the Nazis tore down his beautiful house, ostensibly to make way for road improvements. But in 1987 the house, actually a small palace, was rebuilt using pieces of the original facade that were found in West Berlin. Today it houses an art gallery (open Tues.–Fri. 9–5, weekends 10–6) and an excellent restaurant.

Time Out If you haven't already stopped off at one of the cafés lining the Nikolaiviertel's riverbank, Spreeufer, round out your tour of the area by hunting out the **Zum Nussbaum** tavern, sitting snugly at the corner of Propststrasse and the alley called Am Nussbaum, right by the church. A replica, this was Berlin's oldest inn, and was serving its fine Berlin brew long before Friedrich II ascended the throne.

Head north to Rathausstrasse, then turn left. After crossing the Spree, walk left onto Breitestrasse. The immediate area possesses an array of fine old buildings, some rebuilt, some actually moved to this location from elsewhere in Berlin. Continue on Breitestrasse, and after crossing Mühlendamm, you'll be

③ in the **Fischerinsel** area, which retains some of its medieval character. It provides a refreshing change, too, from some of the heavy and uninspired postwar architecture.

Cross over the Gertraudenstrasse and wander up the south

③ bank of the canal to the redbrick **Märkisches Museum,** the museum of city history. It includes a special section on the city's theatrical past and a fascinating collection of mechanical musical instruments. These are demonstrated on Sun. 11–noon, Wed. 3–4. Next door to the museum live the (live) bears, Berlin's symbol. *Am Köllnischen Park 5. Admission: DM 3 adults, DM 1 children. Open Wed.–Sun. 10–6.*

Tour 6: Kreuzberg, Schöneberg

Once a separate village until it was absorbed by Berlin in the 19th century, **Kreuzberg** is the largest Turkish town outside Turkey, a colorful area that immigrant workers from Anatolia and Istanbul have made their own. Racial tensions sometimes surface, but for the most part there's a live-and-let-live atmosphere in the lively streets of this precinct south of Checkpoint Charlie and north of Tempelhof airfield, and nowhere else in Berlin will the visitor receive a warmer welcome. The food is good, authentic, and cheap, and the company noisy and friendly. Especially in east Kreuzberg, restaurants and pubs jostle for space with basement discotheques and back-room delicatessens. Maybe it's not the place to stay, but you haven't seen Berlin until you've walked a street or two in Kreuzberg. Take

③ the U-1 or U-8 line, alighting at **Kottbusser Tor.** The real heart of Kreuzberg life beats between Kottbusser Tor, Planufer, and Naunynstrasse. Walk east on Skalitzerstrasse, turn left into Mariannenstrasse, and you'll come to Muskauerstrasse, where you'll find one of Berlin's liveliest markets, the Eisenbahn-Markthalle. Visit it with a keen appetite and you won't leave disappointed or hungry. It's open daily from 7:30 AM.

③ The **Kreuzberg** is a hill—Berlin's highest—after which the district is named. Get there by taking the U-1 subway to Hallisches Tor and changing to the southbound U-6, toward Alt-Mariendorf. At the next stop, Mehringdamm, leave by the Kruezbergstrasse exit and you'll see the Kreuzberg on your left, crowned by an iron cross resembling a Gothic spire. Designed by Schinkel, the monument was erected in 1821 to commemorate the 1813–15 Wars of Liberation. The view from the top embraces the center of East Berlin to the north and Tempelhof airfield to the south. A vineyard on the sheltered southern slope of the Kreuzberg produces Germany's rarest wine, the Kreuzneroberger. It is produced in such small quantities that it is served only at official Berlin functions.

The district of **Schöneberg**—one of Berlin's oldest, and, like Kreuzberg, once a separate community—is bounded by Kreuzberg on the east, Wilmersdorf on the west, and the Tiergarten to the north. Schöneberg has a colorful market, the building of the former radio and television station RIAS, a pleasant park named after the dramatist, poet, and prose writer Heinrich von Kleist, a planetarium, and some good restaurants and watering holes, especially around Winterfeldtplatz. Nevertheless, this middle-class residential area is chiefly of interest for its famous city hall, the **Rathaus Schöneberg** (Schöneberg Town Hall). If you're walking from the Kreuzberg, leave the park by the western exit on Monumentenstrasse and continue until you reach the intersection with Potsdamerstrasse on the right. Turn left onto Hauptstrasse and continue south until you reach Dominicus-Strasse. Turn right here and take the first turning on your left, Elsas-Strasse. It will lead you straight to the building. Instead of walking, you can take the subway to Nollendorfplatz and change to the U-4 line for the Rathaus Schöneberg stop. Walk east along Volkspark, then turn left into Martin-Luther-Strasse. You'll see the city hall on the left.

Since the division of the two Berlins in 1948, the Rathaus Schöneberg has been home to the West Berlin Chamber of Deputies and their Senate. The Rathaus is of special interest to Americans, for it was here, on June 26, 1963, that John F. Kennedy made his memorable "Ich bin ein Berliner" speech just months before his assassination.

Completed in 1914, the Rathaus has a 237-foot-high tower from which a replica of the Liberty Bell is rung each day at noon. The bell was given by the American people as a symbol of their support for the West Berliners' struggle to preserve freedom. A document bears the signatures of 17 million Americans who pledged their solidarity with the people of West Berlin. *Rathaus Schöneberg Bell Tower. John-F.-Kennedy-Platz. Open Wed. and Sun. 10–4.*

Tour 7: Charlottenburg

Before it was swallowed up by Greater Berlin in 1920, **Charlottenburg** was the wealthiest municipality in all of Prussia. Wealth poured into the area because of its royal associations, which began with the patronage of Prussia's King Friedrich I in 1701. He established a royal country residence in Schloss Lützenburg and then renamed the palace Charlottenburg, after his wife Sophie Charlotte. The area around the palace, built in 1695, grew into a small town, graced by the homes of palace officials, and it acquired the name of the palace. Friedrich was its first lord mayor. **Schloss Charlottenburg** and its gardens became the showpiece of the former West Berlin, rivaled now by the newly accessible architectural treasures of the eastern part of the city but still an imperative stop in any visitor's itinerary.

As additional buildings were annexed to the original palace—and Berlin grew—this sumptuous palace became the city residence for the Prussian rulers. It has on occasion been referred to as Berlin's very own Versailles. Indeed, some claim that it was Napoléon, when he invaded Berlin in 1806, who first made the comparison to the Sun King's spectacular château near Paris. The comparison hardly seems appropriate. Charlottenburg is on a smaller, more intimate scale than Versailles. Its proportions are restrained; the formal gardens are not nearly as vast. Nor are you likely to encounter the kind of crowds that flock to Versailles. But you are sure to be suitably impressed.

A full day is not too much time to devote to Charlottenburg. In addition to the apartments of the Prussian nobility there are the landscaped gardens to be visited, and several excellent museums set within and just outside the grounds.

Friedrich II—Frederick the Great—was captivated by Charlottenburg, and he made a number of additions, such as the dome and several wings in the Rococo style. In time the complex evolved into the massive royal domain you see today.

The palace was severely damaged during World War II but has been painstakingly restored. Many of the original furnishings and works of art survived the war and are on display.

Behind heavy iron gates, the Court of Honor—the courtyard in front of the palace—is dominated by a fine Baroque statue, the *Reiterstandbild des Grossen Kurfürsten* (the Equestrian Statue of the Great Elector). A 156-foot-high domed tower capped by a gilded statue of Fortune rises above the main entrance to the palace.

Inside, in the main building, the suites of Friedrich I and his wife, Sophie Charlotte, are furnished in the prevailing style of the era. Paintings include royal portraits by Antoine Pesne, a noted court painter of the 18th century. On the first floor you can visit the Oak Gallery, the early 18th-century Palace Chapel, and the suites of Frederick Wilhelm II and Frederick Wilhelm III, furnished in the Biedermeier style.

Visits to the royal apartments are by guided tour only. Tours are in German but are worth taking even if you don't speak the language; they leave every hour on the hour from 9 to 4. Parks and gardens can be visited for free and offer a pleasant respite from sightseeing.

A gracious staircase leads up to the sumptuous State Dining Room and the 138-foot-long Golden Gallery. West of the staircase are the rooms of Frederick the Great, in which the king's extravagant collection of works by Watteau, Chardin, and Pesne are displayed. In one glass cupboard you'll see the coronation crown, stripped of its jewels by the king, who gave the most valuable gemstones to his wife. Also in the so-called New Wing is the **Galerie der Romantik,** the National Gallery's collection of masterpieces from such 19th-century German painters as Karl Friedrich Schinkel and Caspar David Friedrich, the leading member of the German Romantic school. *Schloss Charlottenburg. Luisenpl., tel. 030/320–911. Admission DM 4; with guided tour DM 8. Open Tues.–Fri. 9–5, weekends 10–5.*

The park surrounding the palace was first laid out in 1697. Destroyed during the war, it has since been restored to its original Baroque design. An avenue of cypress trees leads to the lake.

There are several buildings in the park that deserve particular attention, among which are the Belvedere, a teahouse overlooking the lake and Spree River that now houses a collection of Berlin porcelain, and the Schinkel Pavilion behind the palace near the river. The pavilion, modeled on a villa in Naples where the king stayed in 1822, was designed in 1824–25 by Schinkel on an appropriately intimate scale. It houses late-18th-century furniture and paintings by Caspar David Friedrich. Also of interest in the park is the mausoleum, also by Schinkel, which contains the tombs of King Frederick Wilhelm II and Queen Louise.

Just to the south of the palace are four small, distinguished museums. The first, across from the palace, is the **Ägyptisches Museum** (Egyptian Museum). The building, once the east guardhouse and residence of the king's bodyguard, is now home to the famous portrait bust of the exquisite Queen Nefertiti. The 3,300-year-old Egyptian queen is the centerpiece of a collection of works that span Egypt's history from 4,000 BC and include one of the best-preserved mummies outside Cairo. *Schloss Str. 70, tel. 030/320–911. Admission: DM 4 adults, DM 2 children. Open Mon.–Thurs. 9–5, weekends 10–5.*

Opposite the Ägyptisches Museum in the former west guardhouse is the **Antikenmuseum** (Antique Museum). The collection comprises ceramics and bronzes as well as everyday utensils from ancient Greece and Rome and a number of Greek vases from the 6th to the 4th century BC. Also on display is a collection of Scythian gold and silverware and jewelry found in the Mediterranean basin. *Schloss Str. 1, tel. 030/320–911. Admission: DM 4. Open Mon.–Thurs. 9–5, weekends 10–5.*

Next door to the Antikenmuseum is the delightful **Bröhan-Museum,** which, with its collection of Jugendstil and Art Deco decorative arts in period settings, provides for some a welcome break from the art of the ancients. The porcelain is particularly noteworthy. Special exhibitions are on display in an airy gallery two flights up. *Schloss Str. 1a, tel. 030/3214029. Admission: DM 4. Open Mon.–Thurs. 9–5, weekends 10–5.*

The final museum, the **Museum für Vor- und Frügeschichte** (Museum of Pre- and Proto-history), is located in the western extension of the palace opposite Klausener Platz. The museum depicts the stages of the evolution of man from 1,000,000 BC to the Bronze Age. *Spandauer Damm, tel. 030/320–911. Admission DM 4. Open Mon.–Thurs. 9–5, weekends 10–5.*

A Tageskarte (Day Card) for DM 8 covers a guided tour of Schloss Charlottenburg palace and 1-day admission to the museums. The card is available at each museum.

All the collections at Charlottenburg (except that at the Bröhan-Museum) will eventually be moving: the ancient art to Museumsinsel, the 19th-century paintings to the Kulturforum. The process will be gradual; contact the Berlin Tourist Office for the latest information on closings.

One of Charlottenburg's curiosities is a late-19th-century mansion on the upper part of Kurfürstendamm (No. 218), formerly the Chinese Embassy. The Chinese moved out in 1980, leaving behind a richly furnished house full of antique furniture, silk carpets, lamps, and exquisite ceramics. The house, with all its treasures, passed into private ownership and now includes a fine Chinese restaurant, perhaps the only one in Berlin with landmark status (*see* Dining, *below*), and a café and chocolate shop.

Outlying Sights and Attractions

Numbers in the margin correspond to points of interest on the Greater Berlin map.

Although the historic and cultural core of eastern Berlin is to be found along the central stretch of the Spree, amid the monumental architecture on and around Unter den Linden and in the picturesque alleys and corners of the Nikolai quarter, the center of everyday life is farther east, in the hilltop **Prenzlauer Berg** district. Here is where the typical eastern Berliner resides, in a tiny, poorly serviced apartment, or, if he is lucky or has good connections, a chic one. Here is where the average eastern Berlin worker has his favorite *Kneipe*, or neighborhood pub, and where the young and upwardly mobile flit from disco to basement dive. Factory worker and former communist executive rub shoulders on its drab streets or in its few well-restored boulevards.

To search for what makes this fascinating area tick, start from Alexanderplatz (bus No. 100 from Breitscheidplatz gets you there), walking along Karl-Liebknecht-Strasse, which becomes Prenzlauerallee. About halfway up the hill, turn left onto Wörtherstrasse, then left again onto Rykestrasse. Ahead

❶ of you is the **Prenzlauer Berg** itself, a hilltop crowned by a 150-year-old brick water tower. On the way there, at the end of Rykestrasse, you'll find a synagogue that escaped the worst of the Nazi terror, a 100-year-old brick structure with fine tile decoration and a courtyard that offers a haven of peace from the bustle of the Prenzlauer Berg street scene.

The "Berg" is actually a small park, with steps leading up to the water tower. At its base you'll find a plaque commemorating a group of anti-Nazi activists who were killed here in 1933 by Hitler's stormtroopers. Leave the park by the opposite side and head north along Kollwitzstrasse, to **Käthe-Kollwitz-Platz,** named after one of Berlin's best-loved figures, the artist Käthe Kollwitz, whose images of the proletarian world around her are filled with genuine pathos. She lived nearby (her home was destroyed in an air raid) and died a few weeks before war's end. In the center of the small Parisian-style park that forms the square you'll find an utterly charming sculpture by the artist, *The Mother*, bulky but graceful and throbbing with character. To see her work, visit the Käthe Kollwitz Museum in western Berlin.

Time Out If you're thirsty after climbing the Prenzlauer Berg, the ice-cream café on Käthe-Kollwitz-Platz serves not only *Eis* but a good cup of coffee and a locally brewed beer. In summer, you can sit in the small garden in front of the café.

At the corner of Käthe-Kollwitz-Platz and Wörtherstrasse begins one of eastern Berlin's most extraordinary streets, **Husemannstrasse,** which alone is a highlight of any visit to this part of the city. The stately houses on Husemannstrasse were built toward the end of the 19th century using, for the first time anywhere in Berlin, factory-produced stucco facades. During the postwar years of neglect and municipal penury, Husemannstrasse went the way of the rest of East Berlin. But in 1986 East Germany's communist rulers ordered it to be returned to its former glory, to the pastel-colored harmony you see today.

Greater Berlin

FRIEDRICHS-HAIN

Bersarin Str.
Dimitroff Str.
Warschauer Str.
Frankfurter Allee
Karl Marx Str.

Prenzlauer Berg (1)

Karl-... Prenzlauer Allee

Oranien Str.
Skalizer Str.
Urban Str.
Gneisenau Str.
Columbia Damm
Duden Str.

KREUZ-BERG

Sonnen Allee
Karl Marx Str.
Buschkrug Str.

NEUKÖLLN

Hermann Str.
Silberstein Str.
Grade Str.

Under Den Linden
Friedrich Str.

INNER BERLIN

TEMPEL-HOF

Germania Str.
Teile Str.
Arnulf Str.
Marien Dorfer Damm
Tempelhofer Damm

TIERGARTEN

Str. Des 17 Juni
Moabit Alt
Invaliden Str.
Beusel Str.
Bismark
March Str.

FORMER LOCATION OF BERLIN WALL

STADTRING GOERDELER

Leitzenburger Str.
Potsdamer Str.
Yorck Str.
Grunewald Str.
Damm
Sachsen-Damm
Haupt Str.
Rhein Str.
Steglitzer Damm
Grazer Damm

Bundes Allee
Weisbadener Str.

Kaiser Damm
Kant Str.
Kurfürstendamm
Spandauer Damm

Hohenzollern Damm

Clay Allee
Königin-Luise Str.

Dahlem Museum Complex (2)

U. D. Eichenschloss
Berliner Str.

Reichs Str.

CHARLOTTEN-BURG

Charlottenburger Str.
Heerstrasse
Ruhlebener Str.

Zitadelle (5)

Seegefelder Str.
Juliusturm
Nonnendamm
Brunsbüteler Damm
Heerstrasse
Magistrats W.
Weinmeisterhorn
Potsdammer Chaussee
Gatower Str.
Kladower Damm

WILMERS-DORF

Koenigs Allee
Teltsee Chaussee
Teufelsee
Heerstrasse

Grunewald (3)

Havelchaussee

Verbindungschaussee
AVUS
AVUS

Hutten Weg
Argentinische Allee
Fischerhütten Str.
Spanische Allee

ZEHLEN-DORF

Grosser Wannsee (4)

Havel

N

```
KEY
      Rail Lines
----  Subway Lines
0        500 yards
0        500 meters
```

But don't walk too far down Husemannstrasse—the money for its restoration ran out and only half the street was completed.

That completed half, however, is magnificent, a breath of fresh air after the uniform drabness of its surroundings, with elegant dark-green, wrought-iron balconies adding a whiff of Paris. A comparison with a film set isn't out of place, either, for if you peep into the backyards of Husemannstrasse you'll see the peeling parts that the painters and restorers didn't reach.

The street contains two offbeat museums: the **Friseurmuseum**, a hair-dressing museum claiming to be the only one of its kind in the world, and the **Museum Berliner Arbeiterleben um 1900** (Museum of Berlin Workers' Life Around 1900). In the Friseurmuseum you'll step into another, more leisurely era, when even the back-street bureaucrats of Berlin popped into the barber's shop for their morning shave. Here you'll find re-created Jugendstil barbershops, with instruments that once belonged to Kaiser Wilhelm's royal barber and a very early example of the safety razor that changed the shaving scene so radically. Lovingly mounted snippets from the hair of Iron Chancellor Bismarck and (so it's claimed) Goethe are among the museum's many curiosities. *Husemannstr. 8. Admission free. Open Mon.–Wed. 10–5. Guided tours: Mon., Tues. 10, 12, 1, and 5.*

The Museum Berliner Arbeiterleben um 1900 is two houses up, and gives a fascinating picture of Berlin working-class life around the turn of the century. *Husemannstr. 12. Admission: DM 2 adults, DM 1 children. Open Tues.–Thurs., Sat. 10–6, Fri. 10–3.*

Husemannstrasse is also full of small shops and boutiques of a quality seldom seen in eastern Berlin. Smokers should make for No. 4, a beautifully preserved tobacco shop whose dark-paneled interior is redolent with the aroma of fine cigars and rare tobaccos. On the other side of the street, at No. 11, the Raritäts Galerie is packed with small antiques and objets d'art. On the corner, a good Berlin beer is served at the Budike bar, and in the evenings, the Jugendstil-decorated Cafe-Stube attracts a stylish eastern Berlin crowd.

Return to Käthe-Kollwitz-Platz and follow Kollwitzstrasse down the hill to where it joins with Schönhauserallee, the district's main street. Return a short distance along Schönhauserallee and at No. 23 you'll find the Prenzlauer Berg's **Jewish Cemetery,** where the portraitist Max Liebermann and the opera composer Giacomo Meyerbeer are buried. Turn back toward the city center now, and on the way you'll pass one of Berlin's most charming memorials, a surprisingly humorous one in such drab surroundings. The sculptured group portrays Alois Senefelder, pioneer of lithography, sternly watching two urchins scribbling his name on the base of his statue. The pair have written his name in reverse, and one of them is holding a piece of chalk, a witty reference to Senefelder's discovery that figures and outlines written with chalk on a certain kind of slate absorbed color, creating a form of printing surface. At the bottom of Schönhauserallee you'll cross into Rosa-Luxemburg-Strasse, which leads back to Alexanderplatz.

Time Out Stop in at the **Theaterklause** (Rosa-Luxemburg-Strasse 39), opposite the famous eastern Berlin theater, the Volksbühne. It's a typical eastern Berlin dining room, with few flourishes, but the food is wholesome and cheap (the Steak Strindberg costs DM 10), and in the evenings you might find yourself sharing a table with one of the Volksbühne cast.

Eastern Berlin has its Museumsinsel; western Berlin's version is Dahlem, a complex of outstanding museums in the neighborhood of the same name (take the U-2 subway from Wittenbergplatz toward Krumme Lanke and get out at Dahlem-Dorf station). You'll emerge into a leafy district that seems more like a sleepy village. Walk south on Fabeckstrasse and enter the **2 Dahlem Museum Complex** to your right at either Arnimallee 23–27 or Lansstrasse 8.

The complex consists of seven museums, all but one of which is under a single gigantic roof. The greatest of these are the **Gemäldegalerie** (Picture Gallery), the **Museum fur Völkerkunde** (Ethnographic Museum), and the **Skulpturengalerie** (Sculpture Gallery). By 1997 the displays at Dahlem will be devoted exclusively to ethnographic art, with the Gemäldegalerie and Skulpturengalerie collections moving to the Kulturform (*see* Tour 2, *above*) and the Islamic collection shifting to Museumsinsel (*see* Tour 4, *above*). The changes will be gradual, with individual galleries closing. Contact the Berlin Tourist Office for the latest status of each museum.

Begin your tour with the **Gemäldegalerie.** One of Germany's finest picture galleries, it houses a broad selection of European paintings from the 13th to the 18th century. Rembrandt devotees will be particularly pleased to find the world's second-largest Rembrandt collection located on the second floor.

Several rooms on the first floor are reserved for paintings by German masters, among them, Dürer, Cranach, and Holbein. An adjoining gallery houses the works of the Italian masters— Botticelli, Titian, Giotto, Filippo Lippi, and Raphael—and another gallery on the first floor is devoted to paintings by Dutch masters of the 15th and 16th centuries: van Eyck, Bosch, Brueghel, van Dyck, and van der Weyden.

Flemish and Dutch paintings from the 17th century are displayed on the floor above. In the Rembrandt section, where there are 21 paintings by the master, you can see "The Man with the Golden Helmet," a painting formerly attributed to Rembrandt that has since proved by radioactive testing to have been the work of another artist of the same era. *Arnimallee 23– 27, tel. 030/83011. Admission: DM 4 adults, DM 2 children. Open Tues.–Fri. 9–5, weekends 10–5.*

The **Museum für Völkerkunde** (Ethnographic Museum) is internationally famous for its arts and artifacts from Africa, Asia, the South Seas, and ancient America. American visitors homesick for a taste of their own history should look out for the North American Indian wigwams and the feather cape that once belonged to Hawaii's 18th-century King Kamehameha I. Also of interest is the display of native huts from New Guinea and New Zealand. *Entrance: Lansstr. 8, tel. 030/83011. Admission free. Open Tues.–Fri. 9–5, weekends 10–5.*

The **Skulpturengalerie** (Sculpture Gallery) houses Byzantine and European sculpture from the 3rd to the 18th century. Included in its collection is Donatello's *Madonna and Child,* sculpted in 1422. *Entrance: Arnimallee 23–27. Admission free. Open Tues.–Fri. 9–5, weekends 10–5.*

Beyond the tour of monuments, museums, and other aspects relating to the Wall and the divided city, no visit to Berlin would be complete without seeing the vast world of lakes and greenery along its western extremities. In no other city has such an expanse of uninterrupted natural surroundings been preserved within city limits.

Along the city's fringes are some 60 lakes, connected by rivers, streams, and canals, in a verdant setting of meadows, woods, and forests. Excursion steamers ply the water wonderland of the Wannsee and Havel. (*See* Guided Tours, *above*, for details.) You can tramp for hours through the green belt of the Grunewald. On weekends in spring and fall and daily in summer the Berliners are out in force, swimming, sailing their boats, tramping through the woods, riding horseback. To the north, close to the line of the old barbed-wire political boundary, there are still a few working farms. Time and progress seem to have passed right by the rustic village of Lubars.

❸ Grunewald is the playground of the western half of the city, an expanse of woodland and lakes in which you could spend a week's holiday without doubling your tracks. A weekend is all most Berliners can manage, however, and on fine-weather Saturdays and Sundays in both winter and summer the area is invaded by walkers, joggers, cyclists, sunbathers, and **❹** swimmers. The area's largest lake, the **Grosser Wannsee**—actually an arm of the Havel River—has Berlin's biggest bathing beach, a sandy shore as wide and long as many along the Mediterranean. There are several smaller lakes tucked away in remote corners of the Grunewald. Amazingly, most of them are within yards of bustling Berlin streets and highways. The entire area is bisected by Germany's first motor-racing track, the Avus, which is now the main highway between downtown Berlin and Potsdam. The 9-km (5.5-mile) stretch was opened in 1921, and in 1937 racing star Bernd Rosemeyer established a world record of 276.3 kph (166 mph) on it. The highway is still used as a racing track for twice-yearly meets; some cynics say it has never lost its racetrack status with motoring Berliners. So if you drive to Grunewald and the Wannsee, beware. Otherwise, travel there on the S-1 or S-3 S-bahn lines.

The Wannsee and the Havel River are crisscrossed by excursion boats, and you'll find one landing pier on the bridge near the Grunewald S-bahn station. The bridge marks the boundary between the Grosser Wannsee and the much smaller **Kleiner Wannsee**, a narrow stretch of water lined by luxurious villas. On the northern bank you can visit the grave of the German playwright, poet, and prose writer Heinrich von Kleist, at the spot where he killed himself in November 1811 in a suicide pact with his lover, Henriette Vogel.

About a mile through the woods (follow the signs) lies the lovely **Pfaueninsel** (Peacock Island), idyllically set in a wide arm of the Havel. The island gets its name from the peacocks that the Prussian king Friedrich Wilhelm II released there after taking over the property in 1793, and there are still scores of them living wild in the undergrowth. Before the king fell under the spell of the island, the Berlin alchemist Johann Künkel von Löwenstein had tried to make gold in a secret workshop there, and although all his efforts failed, he did manage to produce a beautiful ruby-colored glass. Examples of his invention can be seen in the extravagant folly of a castle King Friedrich Wilhelm II built on the southern tip of the island for his mistress, Countess Lichtenau. She never lived there, however, for shortly after the castle was completed the king died. The castle itself has long outlived both, a gleaming white replica of what its original owner described as a "ruined Roman country mansion," sitting uncomfortably in the lush green vegetation like something from a Hollywood film set. *Admission: DM 3 adults, DM 1.50 children. Open Apr.–Sept., daily 9–5; Oct., daily 9–4.*

Time Out In the woods on the mainland opposite the castle (there's a frequent, cheap ferry service to and from the Pfaueninsel) is an entrancing country restaurant, a historic survivor from an earlier, leisured age: the **Blockhaus Nikolskoe,** built in Russian dacha style in 1819 by King Friedrich Wilhelm III for his daughter Charlotte and her husband, Czar Nicholas, and subsequently used by the czar's coachmen and ostlers. It's an ideal spot for lunch or afternoon tea, with a lovely view of the water. The wine list, by the way, is excellent.

Other points of interest on the banks of the Havel and the Wannsee include the Kaiser-Wilhelm memorial tower, better known as the **Grunewaldturm,** built in redbrick Märkish style in 1897–98 in memory of Kaiser Wilhelm I. You can enjoy a fine view of the area from the observation platform 450 feet up, beneath the tower's turret.

Of all Berlin's many bridges, none grabs the imagination as completely as the **Glienicker Brücke** over the Havel River between Wannsee and the Jungfernsee. Until November 1989, the fortified border between East and West Berlin ran across the center of the bridge, which became the established point for exchanging espionage agents. Many a Western spy came in from the cold across the Glienicker Brücke. Today the historic cast-iron bridge is a main traffic route between downtown Berlin and Potsdam. Above the bridge rises one of Berlin's most beautiful parks, the **Volkspark Klein-Glienicke,** with its elegant little palace, the **Schloss Klein-Glienicke** (Konigstr., tel. 030/805–3041; not open to the public). The palace was built on the orders of the Prussian Prince Carl, who asked the famous Schinkel and other Berlin architects and builders to create for him a Berlin version of the kind of country house he had admired on a tour of Italy. Schinkel's influence is everywhere to be found in the palace's harmonious mixture of Neoclassical and Romantic styles.

Schinkel went on to exercise his fantasy in the park itself, building pavilions at two vantage points and calling them Kleine Neugierde and Grosse Neugierde—Little Curiosity and Big Curiosity. Although the industrialization of nearby Potsdam has marred the vista somewhat, one can still enjoy a magnificent panorama of the Havel, Wannsee, and beyond.

Time Out King Friedrich Wilhelm IV married a Bavarian princess in 1823 and built a country house for her in the style of her homeland on the edge of the park, beside a tranquil pool called the Moorlake. Later it became a hunting lodge favored by the Hohenzollern rulers, and today it's a charming restaurant, the **Wirtshaus Moorlake.** In summer you can dine and drink outside in a pretty garden beside the lake. In winter the oak-beamed interior encloses you in a warm welcome (*see* Dining, *below*).

North of this area is **Spandau,** best known, of course, for the prison that held, among other convicted Nazi war criminals, Rudolf Hess. Hitler's deputy remained there until his death, which occurred under mysterious circumstances. Hess was Spandau's last prisoner, and the jail has been torn down (it was located at Wilhelmstrasse 23), although the story of Hess still hangs over this otherwise quite bourgeois district of Berlin. Residents wince when they hear Spandau described as a district of Berlin, and you'll hear locals talk about "going up to the city" whenever they set off for a shopping trip downtown. When the foundation stone of the Spandau city hall was laid in 1911, a plea was made to the Kaiser to "protect us from Great Berlin," and although Berlin's rapid growth engulfed Spandau in 1920, there's still a strong spirit of municipal independence in its attractive streets.

❺ Symbolic of Spandau's aggressive local patriotism is its unusual castle, the sturdy **Zitadelle** (reached by the U-7 line to the Zitadelle station), built by the city's princely rulers in 1560–94 in the Gothic style. You can set back the clock to those early times in the vaulted restaurant within the Zitadelle's massive tower, the Juliusturm, an earlier structure from the 12th century, where "medieval" banquets are served nightly (*see* Historische Gastätte auf der Zitadelle in Dining, *below*). The tower once held the Imperial War Treasure, from 1874–1919: some 120 million gold marks, most of which was paid to France after Germany's defeat in World War I.

Spandau stands at the confluence of Berlin's two rivers, the Spree and the Havel, and it's a center for Berlin water-sports enthusiasts. There are very pleasant walks along the riverbanks, and Spandau's old town center, Altstadt, beckons with boutiques, small shops, restaurants, and cafés.

Berlin for Free

Street entertainers are a fixture in every German city scene, of course, but the best seem to congregate in Berlin. They liven up **Breitscheidplatz,** parts of the **Ku'damm,** and **Tauenzienstrasse.** It's free entertainment, but a mark or two thrown into an upturned hat or open violin case is always appreciated.

Classical music fans can enjoy free **organ recitals** at most Berlin churches; check the calendar of events outside every church entrance or phone 030/319–00180 for concert schedules. Organ recitals are given most Saturdays at 4:30 at eastern Berlin's Marienkirche, on the edge of Alexanderplatz. Berlin's radio and television stations RIAS (tel. 030/85030) and SFB (tel. 030/30–310) sometimes issue free tickets to **concert rehearsals** throughout the city.

What to See and Do with Children

Top of the list of children's attractions in Berlin is, of course, the **Zoologischer Garten,** one of the world's best zoos. (*See* Tour 1, *above*.) The reunification of Berlin means the city now has two zoos. Eastern Berlin's **Tierpark Berlin,** at Am Tierpark 125 (U-5 to Tierpark station) is much smaller than the more famous zoo in the west but, as the Germans say, *"Klein aber fein"* (small but fine). *Tel. 030/515–310. Admission: DM 5 adults, DM 2 children. Open Mon.–Sat. 9 AM–dusk.*

All Berlin parks have **playgrounds** and **adventure areas;** the best in western Berlin are in the Freizeitpark Tegel, Volkspark Rehberge, Volkspark Hasenheide, and, in eastern Berlin, Treptower Park.

On a wet day, try the **Museum für Verkehr und Technik** in Kreuzberg. The history of mechanized transport is traced in fascinating detail, and among the examples of power sources is a fully operational solar-energy installation. *Trebbinerstr. 9, tel. 030/254–840. Admission: DM 3.50 adults, DM 1.50 children. Open Tues.–Fri. 9–5:30, weekends 10–6. U-bahn: Gleisdreieck or Möckernbrücke.*

Another museum that can't fail to please youngsters is the **Hundemuseum** in eastern Berlin's Blankenburg, where dogs and everything canine are the exclusive theme. *Alt Blankenburg 33. Admission: DM 2 adults, DM 1 children. Open Tues., Thurs., Sat. 3–6, Sun. 11–5. S-bahn: Blankenburg.*

The **Panorama** cinema in the center of western Berlin shows a half-hour film about Berlin, with a 360-degree screen and six-channel sound. *Budapesterstrasse 38. Admission: DM 10 adults, DM 8 children. Show times every hour 11 AM–10 PM.*

Star-struck children can take their pick from two excellent planetariums. The **Planetarium am Insulaner** in Schöneberg has lectures only. *Münsterdamm 90, tel. 030/790–0930. Admission: DM 5 adults, DM 3 children. Lectures: 7 PM and 9 PM Tues. and Thurs.–Sat. at 9 PM, and Sun. at 3, 4, 6, and 9 PM. S-bahn: Priesterweg.*

In eastern Berlin, there's the **Zeiss-Grossplanetarium** in Ernst-Thälmann-Park. *Prenzlauerallee 80, tel. 030/422–840. Admission: DM 4 adults, DM 2 children. Open Wed.–Sun. 1–8 PM. S-bahn: Prenzlaurerallee.*

Berlin has the world's first teddy bear museum, the **Teddy-Museum,** at Kurfürstendamm-Karree, admittedly as much an attraction for adult antiques collectors as for children. *Kurfürstendamm 206. Open Wed.–Mon. 3–10.*

Children will love the collection of dollhouses and antique toys on display at the **Museum für Deutsche Volkskunde,** (tel. 030/25071), part of the Dahlem Museum Complex (Dahlem-Dorf U-bahn station). They might not want to be reminded of school, but the **Schulmuseum,** (Wallstrasse 32, tel. 030/275–5346) gives an eye-opening and often amusing insight into classroom life of earlier centuries.

Off the Beaten Track

While **trams** are still an essential part of the transport system in eastern Berlin, only one line still exists in the western part of the city. It runs between Nollendorfplatz and Potsdamerstrasse, and for DM 1 (at press time, the price of a single ticket) you can join the locals and ride a piece of history.

Western Berliners and tourists rarely venture to eastern Berlin's **Müggelsee**, the largest lake in that part of the city. It's not really off-the-beaten-track territory, particularly on weekends, but here you'll be able to observe the eastern Berliner at play.

Berlin's *Hinterhöfe*—the backyards of city apartment blocks— are where the real life of this amazing city is to be found. So say those in the know, including the cultural tour operators Kultur-Kontor (Savignyplatz 9–10, tel. 030/310–888), which organizes "Hinterhöfe" tours on various weekends for approximately DM 20.

Sightseeing Checklist

Museums **Brecht-Haus** (*see* Tour 4, Exploring, *above*). Bertold Brecht's former home is now a museum devoted to the life and work of the great playwright of the proletariat. *U-bahn: Oranien-burger Tor.*

Dahlem Museum Complex (*see* Outlying Sights, *above*). The complex consists of the Gemaldegalerie, Skulpturengalerie, Museum für Indische Kunst, Museum für Islamische Kunst, Museum für Ostasiatische Kunst, and Museum fur Völker-kunde. *U-bahn: Dahlem-Dorf.*

Deutsches Historisches Museum (*see* Tour 4, Exploring, *above*). This museum of German history has in the past emphasized revolutionary movements of the 19th and 20th centuries. All the galleries on the GDR have been closed down, but plans are brewing to replace them with a new exhibition, which will be written and displayed according to Western, democratic think-ing. This will not take place, however, until 1996. *U-bahn: Französischestr.*

Haus am Checkpoint Charlie, (*see* Tour 3, Exploring, *above*). This museum examines the history of the Berlin Wall and docu-ments the most daring escapes over (and under) it. *U-bahn: Kochstrasse.*

Kunstgewerbemuseum, (*see* Tour 2, Exploring, *above*). This museum surveys arts and crafts from medieval times to the present. *Bus Nos. 341, 129, 148, 284, 187. U-bahn: Potsdamer-platz.*

Märkisches Museum (*see* Tour 5, Exploring, *above*). Eastern Berlin's cultural-historical museum contains exhibits on the prehistory of the Berlin area, Berlin's history from 1307 to 1848, and the development of Berlin art, handicrafts, and thea-ter. *U-bahn: Märkisches Museum.*

Museum fur Naturkunde. Eastern Berlin's outstanding natural history museum is part of Humboldt University. *Invalidenstr. 43, tel. 030/289–72540. Admission: DM 3 adults, 1.50 children. Open Tues.–Sun. 9:30–5. U-bahn: Oranienburger Tor.*

Museumsinsel (*see* Tour 4, Exploring, *above*). Eastern Berlin's major museum complex, on a Spree River island, consists of the Altes Museum, Bodemuseum, Nationalgalerie, and Pergamon-museum. *U-bahn: Friedrichstr.*

Musikinstrumenten-Museum (*see* Tour 2, Exploring, *above*). This historical collection of musical instruments run by the State Institute for Musical Research includes an original Wurlitzer organ, which is demonstrated every Saturday at noon. *Bus Nos. 129, 142, 148, 248, 341.*

Neue Nationalgalerie (*see* Tour 2, Exploring, *above*). Art of the 19th and 20th centuries is on display. *Bus Nos. 341, 129, 148, 284.*

Schinkelmuseum (*see* Tour 3, Exploring, *above*). Housed in the Friedrichswerdersche Kirche by Schinkel, the museum is devoted to the work of the neoclassical architect. *U-bahn: Spittelmarkt.*

Schloss Charlottenburg Museums (*see* Tour 7, Exploring, *above*). These consist of the Ägyptisches Museum (Egyptian Museum), Antikenmuseum und Schatzkammer (Antique Museum), Galerie der Romantik der Nationalgalerie (Romantic Gallery), and Museum für Vor- und Frühgeschichte (Museum of Pre- and Proto-history). *U-bahn: Sophie-Charlotte-Platz.*

Historic Buildings and Homes

Alte und Neue Marstall (*see* Tour 3, Exploring, *above*). The former royal stables now house eastern Berlin's art academy (and special exhibitions) and a state library, respectively. *U-bahn: Stadtmitte.*

Altes Palais (*see* Tour 4, Exploring, *above*). The palace, built in neoclassical style in 1834–37, is now part of Humboldt University. *U-bahn: Französischestr.*

Deutsche Staatsbibliothek. The former royal library is now part of Humboldt University (*see* Tour 4, Exploring, *above*). *U-bahn: Französischestr.*

Deutsche Staatsoper (*see* Tour 4, Exploring, *above*). The home of the premier opera company of eastern Berlin, it is one of the finest creations of the royal architect Georg Wenzeslaus von Knobelsdorff, built in 1741–43. *U-bahn: Französischestr.*

Hamburger Bahnhof. Berlin's oldest railway station, built in 1845–47, is now a railway and transport museum. *Invalidenstrasse 51. Admission free. Tues.–Sun. 9–5. U-bahn: Hamburgerstr.*

Humboldt University (*see* Tour 4, Exploring, *above*). Eastern Berlin's university was originally a palace built for the brother of Frederick the Great and converted to its present use by the Humboldt brothers in 1809. *S-bahn: Unter den Linden.*

Jagdschloss Grunewald. This former hunting lodge (really a large country house) deep in the Grunewald woods is a survivor from the Renaissance and now contains a small but select collection of German and Flemish paintings from the 15th to the 19th century and an exhibition of hunting weapons. *Am Grunewald See, Zehlendorf, tel. 030/813–3597. Admission: DM 2 adults, DM 1 children. Open Tues.–Fri. 10–2, weekends 11–4. S-bahn: Zehlendorf.*

Kongresshalle (*see* Tour 2, Exploring, *above*). America's contribution to the 1957 International Building exhibition, Interbau, is often called "The Oyster" because of its bizarre form. *U-bahn: Bellevue.*

Martin-Gropius-Bau. The former arts and crafts museum was designed in 1822 by Martin Gropius, an uncle of Bauhaus pioneer Walter Gropius. The historic building now contains art galleries that show special art exhibitions. *Stresemannstr. 110, tel. 030/254–8600. Admission varies with exhibitions. Open Tues.–Sun. 10–8. U-bahn: Kochstr.*

Neue Wache (*see* Tour 4, Exploring, *above*). Built as a neoclassical sentry post by Schinkel, it is now a memorial to the victims of fascism and militarism. *S-bahn: Unter den Linden.*

Rathaus Schöneberg (*see* Tour 6, *above*). The city hall of the suburb of Schöneberg is the site of John F. Kennedy's famous "Ich bin ein Berliner" speech, and a copy of the Liberty Bell, a gift from the American people, hangs in the tower. *U-bahn: Rathaus Schöneberg.*

Reichstag (*see* Tour 2, Exploring, *above*). Berlin's century-old parliament building will eventually return to its former use as the home of the German Bundestag. *S-bahn: Unter den Linden.*

Ribbeckhaus (*see* Tour 3, Exploring, *above*). Berlin's only Renaissance house is now the home of city offices. *U-bahn: Französischestr.*

Rotes Rathaus (*see* Tour 3, Exploring, *above*). Eastern Berlin's city hall is called red not because of the communists who once met there but for the bricks with which it was built. *U-bahn: Stadtmitte.*

Schauspielhaus (*see* Tour 3, Exploring, *above*). Schinkel's greatest work in Berlin, the theater now serves as a concert hall. *U-bahn: Französischestr.*

Schloss Bellevue (*see* Tour 2, *above*). The Berlin residence of the German president, the palace is surrounded by grounds that contain the English Gardens, a favorite park among Berliners. *S-bahn: Bellevue.*

Schloss Britz. This 18th-century Prussian nobleman's home in the Neukölln district was converted to its present form in the late 19th century and is maintained as a museum of the *Gründerzeit* (German Empire) style. Its park is also a living example of Gründerzeit garden design. *Alt-Britz 73, tel. 030/606–6051. Admission (guided tour only): DM 2 adults, DM 1 children. Open Wed. 2–6. U-bahn: Parchimer Allee.*

Schloss Charlottenburg (*see* Tour 7, Exploring, *above*). Berlin's only remaining Hohenzollern palace was built for Queen Sophie Charlotte in 1695 and subsequently expanded by Friedrich II, among others. *U-bahn: Sophie-Charlotte-Platz.*

Schloss Friedrichsfelde. One of East Berlin's few surviving Baroque mansions, it was built in 1695 and extended in neoclassical style in the early 18th century. Chamber music concerts are regularly held here. *Am Tierpark 125, tel. 030/510–0111. Admission by guided tour only: Tues.–Sun. 11, 1, 3. U-bahn and S-bahn: Friedrichsfelde.*

Schloss Niederschönhausen. This beautiful small palace, built in 1664 as a country residence for the Countess von Dohna, was extended in 1704 and for more than 50 years was the home of Friedrich II's despised wife, Elisabeth Christine. Only the park is open to visitors. *Ossietzkystr., Pankow. S-bahn: Pankow.*

Schloss Pfaueninsel (*see* Outlying Sights, *above*), a romantic castle on an island in the Havel built by King Friedrich Wilhelm II for his mistress. *S-bahn: Grunewald.*

Zitadelle Spandau (*see* Outlying Sights, *above*) is Spandau's stout fort, which houses a museum and restaurant. *U-bahn: Zitadelle.*

Architecture   **Brandenburger Tor** (*see* Tour 2, Exploring, *above*). This is probably Berlin's most famous monument and symbol, a triumphal arch built by Carl Langhans in 1788–91. *S-bahn: Unter den Linden.*

Radio and Television Towers. Here's one respect where western Berlin lags far behind the east: its radio and television tower, the Funkturm (Messedamm/Masuremallee), only 500 feet high. It's a dwarf compared with eastern Berlin's Fernsehturm on Alexanderplatz, which is more than double the height. All that said, the western tower is older, having been built in 1924–26.

Churches and   **Berliner Dom** (*see* Tour 4, Exploring, *above*). Berlin's cathe-
Temples   dral, built in 1893–1905 in Italian High Renaissance style, has a crypt that contains many Hohenzollern royal family tombs. *U-bahn: Friedrichstr.*

Deutscher Dom (*see* Tour 3, Exploring, *above*). Berlin's "German Cathedral," built in 1701–08, is a component of the harmonious Gendarmenmarkt. It is currently closed for restoration. *U-bahn: Französischerstr.*

Dorfkirche Buckow. Berlin has around 50 medieval village churches and this one, built in the mid-13th century, is one of the finest. You'll find it in the Buckow district. *Marienfelder-chaussee 66. U-bahn: Johannisthalerchaussee, then take Bus No. 172.*

Französischer Dom (*see* Tour 3, Exploring, *above*). Berlin's "French Cathedral," on the Gendarmenmarkt, contains a Huguenot museum and, in the tower, a good restaurant with a marvelous view of the square from a tiny terrace. *U-bahn: Französischerstr.*

Marienkirche (*see* Tour 3, Exploring, *above*). This north German Gothic church built on Romanesque remains is famous for its Gothic *Dance of Death* fresco. *U-bahn: Französischer-str.*

Nikolaikirche (*see* Tour 5, Exploring, *above*). Reputedly Berlin's oldest church, it's the center of the picturesque Nikolaiviertel. *U-bahn: Stadtmitte.*

St. Hedwig's Cathedral (*see* Tour 4, Exploring, *above*). The cathedral of the Berlin diocese, the church on Bebelplatz was designed in the 18th century along the lines of the Pantheon in Rome. Rebuilt after the war, it has a totally modern interior. Organ recitals are given every Wednesday at 3 PM. *U-bahn: Französischerstr.*

Sophienkirche. Named after Queen Sophie Luise, this 18th-century church is the only one in Berlin with a Baroque tower. *Grosse Hamburger Strasse. U-bahn: Hamburger Strasse.*

Statues and   **Friedrich II equestrian statue** (*see* Tour 4, Exploring, *above*).
Monuments   This fine sculpture of Prussia's greatest king can be found in the middle of Unter den Linden opposite Humboldt University. *S-bahn: Unter den Linden.*

Grunewaldturm (*see* Outlying Sights, *above*). This observation tower is deep in the Grunewald forest. *S-bahn: Grunewald.*

Kaiser-Wilhelm-Gedächtniskirche (*see* Tour 1, Exploring, *above*). The late-19th-century church dedicated to Germany's last emperor is now, in its ruined state, a war memorial. *U-bahn: Kurfürstendamm.*

Kreuzberg Monument (*see* Tour 6, Exploring, *above*). This Gothic monument of iron was designed by Schinkel to honor the Prussian soldiers who died fighting Napoléon. *U-bahn: Mehringdamm.*

Neptunbrunnen. Berlin isn't a city of fountains, but this graceful group of figures was one of the world's biggest when built in 1888–91. It faces the Rotes Rathaus. *U-bahn and S-bahn: Alexanderpl.*

Plötzensee Memorial. The buildings where more than 2,500 dissidents were executed by the Nazis are a chilling reminder of the city's dark past. *Hüttigpfad 13, tel. 030/344–3226. Admission free. Open daily 8–6. U-bahn: Putlitzstr.*

Siegessäule (*see* Tour 2, Exploring, *above*). Berlin's victory column was erected in 1873 in front of the Reichstag but moved to its present site by the Nazis. *S-bahn: Tiergarten.*

Parks and Gardens **Botanischer Garten.** This botanical garden in Dahlem is one of the world's leading botanical gardens, with the world's highest tropical house. Laid out in 1899–1910, the gardens and hot houses have more than 18,000 different plant species. *Königin-Luise-Strasse 6–8, tel. 030/830–060. Admission: DM 3 adults, DM 1.50 children. Open daily 9 AM–dusk. S-bahn: Botanischer Garten.*

Pfaueninsel (*see* Outlying Sights, *above*). An idyllic Havel River island bought by King Friedrich Wilhelm II in 1793. *S-bahn: Grunewald.*

Tiergarten (*see* Tour 2, Exploring, *above*). The name means "zoological garden," but Berlin's zoo takes up only a corner of this large, central park that contains or borders on some of the city's most famous landmarks. *U-bahn and S-bahn: Tiergarten.*

Volkspark Klein-Glienicke (*see* Outlying Sights, *above*). The park was laid out in 1824–60 on the banks of the Havel and contains pavilions and a palace by Schinkel. *S-bahn: Wannsee.*

Zoos **Tierpark Berlin.** Eastern Berlin's zoo is much smaller than western Berlin's Zoologischer Garten, but the setting, within the grounds of the Schloss Friedrichsfelde, couldn't be better. *Am Tierpark 125, tel. 030/512–3143. Admission: DM 5 adults, DM 2 children. Open Mon.–Sat. 9 AM–dusk. U-bahn: Tierpark.*

Zoologischer Garten (*see* Tour 1, Exploring, *above*). Berlin's oldest and largest zoo is in the center of western Berlin. *U-bahn and S-bahn: Zoologischer Garten.*

Other Places of Interest **Berlin Wall** (*see* Tour 3, Exploring, *above*). A bit of the Wall has been kept for posterity on Mühlenstrasse, between the Jannowitz and Überbaum bridges. Artists from all over the world have been busy painting on the 1.3-km (.8-mi)-long remnant, dubbed the East Side Gallery, contributing to a work on the theme of peace and human rights. *S-bahn: Friedrichshain.*

Breitscheidplatz (*see* Tour 1, Exploring, *above*). Western Berlin's true center, this square bordered by Europa Center and the Kaiser-Wilhelm-Gedächtniskirche is where the city hums 24 hours a day. *U-bahn: Kurfürstendamm.*

Glienecker Brücke (*see* Outlying Sights, *above*). The cast-iron bridge on the former southwest border between East and West Berlin is where spies were traditionally exchanged. *S-bahn: Wannsee, then bus No. 116.*

Husemannstrasse (*see* Outlying Sights, *above*). This is one of eastern Berlin's showpiece streets, but its restoration is only facade-deep. *U-bahn and S-bahn: Alexanderpl.*

Olympiastadion. Site of the 1936 Olympic Games and the accompanying Nazi pageantry, it is still used for sports and musical events. Even by today's standards, it is immense. *Charlottenburg, tel. 030/304–0676. Admission (for visiting only): DM 1 adults, 50 pf children. Open daily 7 AM–dusk. U-bahn: Olympia-Stadion (Ost).*

Shopping

Berlin is still a divided city when it comes to shopping, with the western part of the city still far ahead in the size, scope, and quality of its stores and the merchandise they offer. However, this situation is changing rapidly. Clothes are *the* thing to buy in western Berlin, which claims to be Germany's leading fashion center. Prices are generally lower than in cities like Munich and Hamburg. Berlin's recent history, from the fall of the Wall to the reunification celebrations, is emblazoned on virtually every T-shirt you'll find in the shops around Breitscheidplatz. Nobody wants to leave Berlin without a piece of the Wall, and you'll have no difficulty finding prepacked, painted pieces of it, complete with guarantees of authenticity. But the guarantees are worth no more than the paper they're printed on, for how do you test the authenticity of a piece of concrete? So if you buy what's claimed to be a piece of the Wall, swallow your skepticism.

Stores usually open at 9 AM and close at 6 PM (1 or 1:30 PM on Saturday), although some smaller shops open earlier and close for lunch. On Thursday the larger stores stay open until 8:30 PM or later, and on the first Saturday of every month most shops stay open until 4 PM.

Shopping Districts Western Berlin has one of Germany's most famous shopping streets, the Kurfürstendamm, universally known as the **Ku'damm,** but the best buys are to be found in side streets leading off this glittering boulevard, especially between **Breitscheidplatz** and **Olivaerplatz.** The multistory **Europa Center** on Breitscheidplatz has more than 100 boutiques, stores, cafés, and restaurants, but this is no place to bargain-hunt. Less expensive options can be found on two streets leading into the square, **Budapesterstrasse** and **Tauenzienstrasse.** At the end of Tauenzienstrasse (about three minutes' walk from Breitscheidplatz) is Berlin's biggest department store, the **Kaufhaus des Westens** (popularly known as the **KaDeWe**), which boasts that it stocks everything possible on its six floors.

For trendier and more elegant clothing, try the boutiques lining the Kurfürstendamm, from Meinekstrasse to Olivaerplatz. Here you'll find designer boutiques from Sonia Rykel, Yves St.

Laurent, and Cartier, as well as fine porcelain stores and the best of the German automobile showrooms.

For budget shopping and the kind of wares you won't find at home, try **Kantstrasse, Wilmersdorferstrasse,** or **Karl-Marx-Strasse** in Neukölln, **Schloss Strasse** in Steglitz, **Turmstrasse** in Moabit, **Berlinerstrasse,** and the **Tegel-Center** in Reinickendorf. More adventurous souls might venture out to **Spandau** and explore the Altstadt.

In eastern Berlin, **Unter den Linden** and **Friedrichstrasse** are being restored to the premier position they once held among the glittering shopping boulevards of Berlin, but in 1992 they still had some way to go before being able to compete with the Ku'damm. Alexanderplatz now includes branches of the German department stores Herties and Kaufhof. Some of eastern Berlin's luxury hotels—the Palast and the Grand, for example—have Western-style shopping malls.

Department Stores Berlin has Europe's largest department store, the Kaufhaus des Westens, or **KaDeWe,** a grand-scale emporium in modern guise at Wittenbergplatz. Be sure to visit the sixth floor, which is entirely devoted to food and drink; only Harrods in London can boast anything comparable. The Ku'damm has several department stores, the largest of which is **Wertheim.** Although it's not as attractive as KaDeWe, it nonetheless offers a large selection of fine merchandise. Department stores in eastern Berlin, such as **Kaufhof** (formerly Centrum), on the north side of Alexanderplatz, have been upgraded to match western standards. You can still find good buys in such eastern German specialties as wooden toys and ceramics.

Gift Ideas Fine **porcelain** is still produced at the former Royal Prussian Porcelain Factory, now called **Staatliche Porzellan Manufactur,** or KPM. This delicate, handmade, hand-painted china is sold at KPM's store at Kurfürstendamm 26A (tel. 030/881–1802), but it may be more fun to visit the factory salesroom at Wegelystrasse 1. It also sells seconds at reduced prices. If you long to have the Egyptian Museum's Queen Nefertiti on your mantelpiece at home, try the **Gipsformerei der Staatlichen Museen Preussicher Kulturbesitz** (Sophie-Charlotte-Str. 17, tel. 030/321–7011, open weekdays 9–4). It sells plaster casts of this and other treasures from the city's museums. Take home a regiment of **tin figures,** painted or to paint yourself, from the **Berliner Zinnfigurenkabinett** (Knesebeckstr. 88, tel. 030/310802).

Street Markets Every Berlin district has its market (usually twice a week), but the best are both to be found in **Schöneberg:** in front of the Schöneberg city hall (Tuesday and Friday 8–1) and at Winterfeldtplatz (Wednesday and Saturday 8–1). You'll find everything here, from fresh fruit and vegetables to new and secondhand clothing. The **Türkenmarkt** (Turkish market) on Neukölln's Maybachufer (Tuesday and Friday noon–6:30) is the nearest thing to an Oriental bazaar this side of the German border, and it's become a top tourist attraction. The **Ackerhalle** on the corner of Invalidenstrasse and Ackerstrasse in Berlin's Mitte district is the city's only surviving 19th-century covered market; take your camera.

Antiques and Apart from the Strasse des 17 Juni market (*see* Crafts, *below*),
Flea Markets other leading sources of antiques and secondhand goods can be found in **Kreuzberg** (the Krempelmarkt, on the corner of Reichpietschufer and Linkstrasse, Saturday and Sunday 8–3:30),

Wilmersdorf (Fehrbellinerplatz, Sunday 7–4), and **Schöneberg** (the Flohmarkt in a part of the disused Nollendorfplatz U-bahn station, daily except Tuesday 11–7. The stalls are located in 16 old subway cars, and on Sunday mornings the Nolles Salonorchester livens things up still further with jazz and swing). In eastern Berlin there's the **Trödelmarkt** at Arkonaplatz (near the Rosenthaler Platz subway station, Saturday 9–4).

Crafts On Saturday and Sunday from 10 to 5, the colorful and lively antiques and handicrafts fair on a stretch of Strasse des 17 Juni (east of Ernst-Reuter-Platz) swings into action. Much of what's on offer is kitsch, although some fine workmanship and imaginative artistry can be found among the stalls. Farther along is a secondhand and antiques section. Homemade curries and chili are offered at the food stands that dot the area, and in winter mulled wine is ladled out to chilled shoppers.

Food In addition to neighborhood markets and the food floor at KaDeWe, Berlin's other major food markets are the **Arminius-Markthalle** (Arminiusstrasse 2) and the **Eisenbahn-Markthalle** (Eisenbahnstrasse 43–44). They're both open Monday–Friday 8–6 and Saturday 8–1. They're great sources for a quick, inexpensive lunch.

Specialty Stores
Antiques Not far from Wittenbergplatz is **Keithstrasse,** a street given over to antiques stores. There are also several small antiques stores in the converted subway cars of the **Nollendorfplatz Flohmarkt.** Eisenacherstrasse, Fuggerstrasse, Kalckreuthstrasse, Motzstrasse, and Nollendorfstrasse—all close to Nollendorfplatz—have many antiques stores of varying quality. Another good street for antiques is **Suarezstrasse,** between Kantstrasse and Bismarckstrasse. The venerable auction house **Christie's** recently opened an outpost at Fasanenstrasse 72 (tel. 030/882–7778), just off the Ku'damm. The antique glass and jewelry at **Lee** (Kurfürstendamm 32, tel. 030/881–7333) are exceptional.

In eastern Berlin, antiques are sold in the **Metropol** and **Palast hotels,** in the **Nikolai quarter,** and in the restored **Husemannstrasse.** Some private stores along the stretch of **Friedrichstrasse** north of the Spree Bridge offer old books and prints. **Southeby's** auction house has set up shop at the Palais am Festungsgraben (Unter den Linden, tel. 030/200–4119).

Books **Düwal** (Schlüterstr. 17, Charlottenburg), and **Koch** (Kurfürstendamm 216), both offer a very wide range of antique books, old maps, and prints.

International Press The leading hotels stock American and British newpapers. Other outlets include **KaDeWe** and the souvenir shops at Joachimstrasse 1 (next to the Bahnhof Zoo) and Kurfürstendamm 206–209.

Jewelry Fine handcrafted jewelry can be found at **Wurzbarcher** (Ku'damm 36, tel. 030/883–3892). Eastern Berlin's **Galerie "re"** (Friedrichstr. 2, tel. 030/2086870) offers good values.

Men's Clothing **Mientus** (Wilmersdorferstr. 73), a large, exclusive men's store, caters to expensive tastes, as does **Brand** (Ku'damm 184). They offer conventional/businesswear as well as sporty and modern looks, and carry many top designer labels; Brand, however, serves more conservative tastes. For men's shoes, try **Budapester Schuhe** (Ku'damm 199). **Norbert's** (Bleibtreustrasse 24, between the Ku'damm and Leitzenburgerstr.) also stocks the leading designer labels. Slightly less expensive and exclusive but still up there is **Erdmann** (in the Europa Center facing Tauenzienstr). At the other end of the scale, nothing in the **Kleidermarkt** (Bergmannstr. 102) is more expensive than DM 40 (there are women's fashions, too).

Women's Clothing   Berlin fashion designers claim to lead the field in Germany. Whether that's true or not, Berlin's fashion boutiques are second to none. Among the best are **News of Fashion** (Kurfürstendamm 56–57) and **Rival** (Nürnbergerstr. 14). For German designer wear, try **Zenker** (Ku'damm 45). It's not cheap, but the styling is classic. If you're looking for international labels, drop by **E. Braun & Co.** (Ku'damm 43) or **Kramberg** (Ku'damm 56), and then go next door to **Granny's Step,** where you'll find evening wear styled along the lines of bygone times. For modern, Berlin-designed chic, check out **Filato** (Nürenbergstr. 24A). If you're feeling daring, browse through the extraordinary lingerie store **Nouvelle** (Bleibtreustr. 24). Elegant '20s intimate wear made of fine, old-fashioned materials is its specialty. For German folk-inspired outfits, try **Pupi's Loden** (Schlüterstr. 54 and Ansbacherstr. 30a).

Sports and Fitness

Bicycling   There are bike paths throughout the downtown area and the rest of the city. *See* Getting Around, *above,* for details of renting bikes.

Golf   Berlin's leading club is the **Golf- und Landclub Wannsee** (Stölpchenweg, Wannsee, tel. 030/805–5075).

Jogging   The **Tiergarten** is the best place for jogging in the downtown area. Run its length and back and you'll cover 5 miles. Joggers can also take advantage of the grounds of **Charlottenburg** castle, 2 miles around. For longer runs, anything up to 20 miles, make for **Grunewald.**

Riding   Horses are rented out by the **Reitschule Onkel Toms Hütte** (Onkel-Tom-Str. 172, tel. 030/813–2081). Children's ponies are stabled at **Ponyhof Lange** (Buckower Chaussee 82, Marienfelde, tel. 030/721–6008), **Ponyhof Wittenau** (Wittenauerstr. 80, tel. 030/402–8535), **Reitzentrum Gropivsstadt** (Kölner Damm 1, Rudow, tel. 030/604–6044), near the U-bahn line 7 (direction Rudow, Lipschitzallee exit); and **Preussenhof** (Staakener Str. 64, Spandau, tel. 030/331–7965).

Sailing and Windsurfing   Boats and boards of all kinds are rented by **Jürgen Schöne** (tel. 030/381–5037) and **Scharfe Lanke** (tel. 030/361–5066).

Swimming   The **Wannsee** and **Plötzensee** both have beaches; they get crowded during summer weekends, however. There are pools throughout the city, so there's bound to be at least one near where you're staying. For full listings, ask at the tourist office. The most impressive pool is the **Olympia-Schwimmstadion** at Olympischer Platz (U-bahn: Olympiastadion). The **Blub Padeparadis** lido (Buschkrugallee 64, tel. 030/606–6060) has indoor and outdoor pools, hot tubs, and a solarium (U-bahn: Grenzallee).

Tennis and Squash   There are tennis courts and squash centers throughout the city; ask your hotel to direct you to the nearest. **Tennis & Squash City** (Brandenburgischestr. 31, Wilmersdorf, tel. 030/879–097) has seven tennis courts and 11 squash courts. You can even step off the Ku'damm and onto a tennis court, at **"Tennisplätze am Ku'damm"** (Cicerostr. 55A, tel. 030/891–6630).

Dining

Dining in Berlin can mean sophisticated nouvelle specialties in upscale restaurants with linen tablecloths and hand-painted porcelain plates, or hearty local specialties in atmospheric and inexpensive inns: The range is as vast as the city. Specialties include *Eisbein mit Sauerkraut*, knuckle of pork with pickled cabbage; *Rouladen*, rolled stuffed beef; *Spanferkel*, suckling pig; *Berliner Sülze*, potted meat in aspic; *Schlachteplatte*, mixed grill; *Hackepeter*, ground beef; and *Kartoffelpuffer*, fried potato cakes. *Bockwurst* is a chubby frankfurter that's served in a variety of ways and sold in restaurants and at sausage stands all over the city. *Schlesisches Himmerlreich* is roast goose or pork served with potato dumplings in rich gravy. *Königsberger Klopse* consists of meatballs with a herring and capers sauce—it tastes much better than it sounds.

Eastern Germany's former ties to the Eastern Bloc persist in restaurants featuring the national cuisine of those other one-time socialist states, although such exotica as Japanese, Chinese, Indonesian, and French food are slowly appearing. Wines and spirits imported from other countries can be quite good; try Hungarian, Yugoslav, and Bulgarian wines (the whites are lighter), and Polish and Russian vodkas. But like everything else, their prices are no longer cheap.

Highly recommended restaurants are indicated by a star ★.

Category	Cost*
Very Expensive	over DM 100
Expensive	DM 75–DM 100
Moderate	DM 50–DM 75
Inexpensive	under DM 50

**per person for 3-course meal, excluding drinks*

Western Berlin

Very Expensive
★

Bamberger Reiter. One of the city's leading restaurants, this is presided over by Tirolean chef Franz Raneburger. He relies on fresh market produce for his *Neue Deutsche Küche* (German nouvelle cuisine), so the menu changes daily. Fresh flowers set off this attractive oak-beamed restaurant, which features an enclosed garden for dining during summer months. *Regensburgerstr. 7, tel. 030/218–4282. Reservations essential. Jacket and tie required. DC, V. Closed lunch, Sun., Mon., and Aug. 1–20.*

Frühsammer's Restaurant an der Rehwiese. Here you can watch chef Peter Frühsammer at work in his open kitchen. His choice of daily menu is never remiss; the salmon is always a treat. The restaurant is in the annex of a turn-of-the-century villa in the Zehlendorf district (U-bahn to Krumme Lanke and then bus No. 53 to Rehweise). *Matterhornstr. 101, tel. 030/803–8023. Reservations essential. Jacket and tie required. MC, V.*

Berlin Dining

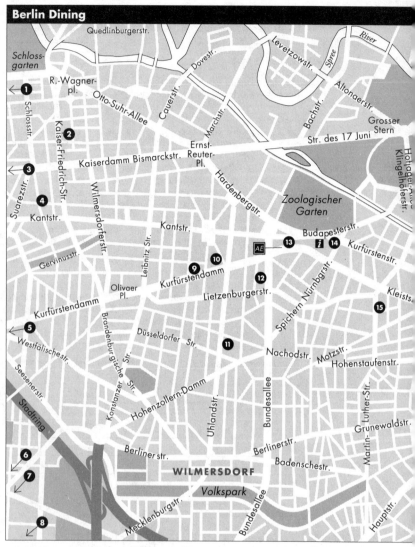

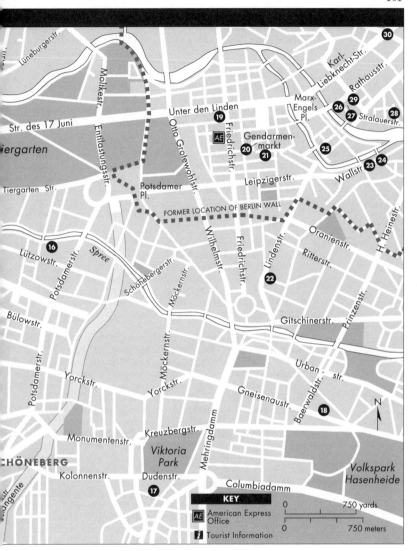

KEY

AE American Express Office

🛈 Tourist Information

0 — 750 yards

0 — 750 meters

Closed lunch, Sun., and 3 weeks during the school summer holidays.

Grand Slam. Overlooking a lake and nestled among the trees on the property of the exclusive Rot-Weiss tennis club in Grunewald, this restaurant is German fine dining at its best, with excellent service and no pretentiousness. Four-course lunch menus and six-course dinner menus are available for DM 149. Try the salmon and caviar appetizer and the marinated duck breast with a tinge of quince. *Gottfried von Cramm-weg 47–55, tel. 030/825–3810. Reservations essential. Jacket and tie recommended. AE, DC, MC, V. Closed Sun. and Mon.*

Expensive **Alt-Luxembourg.** There are only nine tables at this popular restaurant in the Charlottenburg district, with attentive service enhancing the intimate setting. Chef Kurt Wannebacher produces a divine lobster lasagna. *Windscheidstr. 14, tel. 030/323–8730. Reservations essential. Jacket and tie required. DC, V. Closed Sun., Mon., 3 weeks in Jan., and 3 weeks during June and July.*

Moderate **Alt-Nürnberg.** Step into the tavernlike interior and you could be in Füssen or Garmisch in Bavaria; the waitresses even wear dirndls. The Bavarian colors of blue and white are everywhere, and that region's culinary delights, such as *Schweinshaxe* (knuckle of pork), dominate the menu. If you prefer to eat Prussian style, order calves' liver. *Berliner Art Europa-Center, tel. 030/261–4397. Reservations advised. Dress: informal. AE, DC, MC, V.*

Hecker's Deele. Antique church pews complement the oak-beamed interior of this restaurant that specializes in Westphalian dishes. The *Westfälische Schlachtplatte* (a selection of meats) will set you up for a whole day's sightseeing—the Ku'damm is right outside. *Grolmannstr. 35, tel. 030/88901. Reservations advised. Dress: informal. AE, DC, MC, V.*

Ho Lin Wah. Until 1980 this was the Chinese Embassy in Berlin, and much of the restaurant's decor was retained after the Chinese moved out. China's loss was Berlin's gain: This is one of the city's best Chinese restaurants, family-run and with first-class (mostly Cantonese) cuisine and attentive service. *Kurfürstendamm 218, tel. 030/882–3271. Reservations advised. Dress: informal. AE, DC, MC, V.*

Mundart Restaurant. Five chefs work the kitchen of this popular restaurant in the Kreuzberg district. You can't go wrong with the fish soup or any of the daily specials. *Muskauerstr. 33–34, tel. 030/612–2061. Dress: informal. Reservations advised. No credit cards. Closed lunch, Mon., and Tues.*

November. This restaurant specializes in German and Continental nouvelle cuisine at its best. It's located near the National Gallery, overlooking the Schöneberger Ufer and quietly tucked away among art galleries, offices, and exclusive apartments. Because this is a relatively small place, divided into two sections, ask for a table in the room away from the hustle of the bar. The marble walls and striking lighting effects may remind you of a sleek New York City restaurant. The imaginative creations include such specialties as fresh pasta with spinach topped with quail eggs. Meat dishes are recommended, particularly game entrées during the winter. *Schöneberger Ufer 65, tel. 030/261–3882. Reservations advised. Jacket and tie advised. AE, DC, MC, V. Closed Mon.*

★ **Ponte Vecchio.** Delicious Tuscan-style Italian food is served here in a handsome, light-wood dining room. Ask the friendly waiters for their recommendations—the food is excellent and simply presented. Try the delicate *Vitello tonnato*, veal with a tuna sauce. *Spielhagenstr. 3, tel. 030/342–1999. Reservations essential. Jacket and tie required. DC. Closed lunch (except Sun.), Tues., and 4 weeks in summer.*

Wibb's. Gabi, Martin and Christian Wibbke (the "Wibb" family) run this smart corner restaurant with friendly efficiency and exemplary kitchen skills. Competition in Uhlandstrasse is keen, with restaurants dueling for pavement space, but Wibb's stands out. Fresh-cut flowers on the tables and well-chosen prints on the walls give a splash of color to the slightly formal surroundings. The menu is relatively small but packed with good things, particularly the imaginative fish dishes. *Uhlandstr. 142, tel. 030/861–5310. Reservations advised. Dress: informal. AE, MC, V.*

Wirtshaus Moorlake. You need a car to reach this enchanting lakeside country-style restaurant, deep in the Grunewald, but the excursion is well worth it. Built in 1840 as a royal hunting lodge, it became an established stagecoach stop on the Berlin-Potsdam run. Now it's a popular destination for weekending Berliners, so go on a weekday; reserve a table upstairs under the exposed beams. Despite the Bavarian character of the surroundings, the menu is mostly Berlin fare. Try the *Königsberger Klopse. An der Moorlake, tel. 030/805–5809. Reservations advised. Dress: informal. AE, DC, MC, V. Closed Tues. and winter evenings.*

Zitadellen-Schänke. Here you'll dine like a medieval noble, served a multicourse menu by Prussian wenches and serenaded by a minstrel group. In winter, a roaring fire helps light and warm the vaulted restaurant, which is part of Spandau's historic Zitadelle. Its medieval banquets are popular, so be sure to reserve your spot at one of the heavy antique oak tables. *Am Juliusturm, Spandau, tel. 030/334–2106. Reservations advised. Dress: informal. AE, DC, MC, V.*

Inexpensive **Alt-Berliner Wiessbierstube.** A visit to the Berlin Museum must include a stop at the museum's pub-style restaurant. There's a buffet packed with Berlin specialties, and you can take in live jazz here on Saturday and Sunday mornings. *Berlin Museum, Lindenstr. 14, tel. 030/251–0121. No reservations. Dress: informal. No credit cards. Closed Mon.*

Blockhaus Nikolskoe. Prussian King Wilhelm III built this Russian-style wooden lodge for his daughter Charlotte, wife of Russian Czar Nicholas I. Located south of the city on Glienecker Park, it offers open-air riverside dining in the summer. Game dishes are prominently featured. *Nikolskoer Weg, tel. 030/805–2914. Reservations advised. Dress: informal. AE, DC, MC, V.*

Eierschale. Berlin is famous for its breakfast cafés, and this is one of the best—and the best located, on the corner of central Rankestrasse and the Ku'damm. It serves breakfast at all hours, but really gets going in the evenings, when jazz groups perform in a neighboring room. The lunch and supper menus feature filling Berlin fare, but if Mexican-style spareribs are on offer, they're especially to be recommended. Sunday morning is *Frühschoppen* time, when live jazz accompanies the buffet brunch; great fun and an opportunity to witness the highlight of a Berliner's weekend. *Rankestrasse 1, tel. 030/882–5305. Reservations advised. Dress: informal. MC.*

★ **Hardtke.** This is about the most authentic old Berlin restaurant in the city; it's popular with tourists. The decor is simple, with paneled walls and wood floor. The food is similarly traditional and hearty. It's a great place to try *Eisbein*. Wash it down with a large stein of beer. *Meinekestr. 27, tel. 030/881-9827. Reservations advised. Dress: informal. No credit cards.*

Karagiosi. A short walk from the Charlottenburg palace, this simply furnished, friendly Greek restaurant is just the place to round out a day's sightseeing. The decor is minimal, but the food is so authentic you could be in Athens, and if you're in luck there'll be live music the night you call. *Klausenerpl. 4, tel. 030/798-2379. No reservations. Dress: informal. V.*

Thürnagel. At this vegetarian restaurant in the Kreuzberg district, it's not only healthy to eat but fun. The seitan in sherry sauce or the tempeh curry are good enough to convert a seasoned carnivore. *Gneisenaustr. 57, tel. 030/691-4800. Reservations advised. No credit cards. Dinner only.*

Eastern Berlin

Prices in eastern Berlin have risen rapidly to approximately the same level as in the western part of the city. Our categories, therefore, correspond with those in the western Berlin dining section.

Expensive **Borchardt.** This is one of the most fashionable meeting places to
★ spring up in eastern Berlin since the Berlin Wall fell. The high ceiling, columns, red plush benches, and Art Nouveau mosaic (discovered during renovations) help create the impression of a 1920s café. The restaurant serves entrées with a French accent and is well known for its luscious seafood platter (DM 48). For meat lovers, the baby lamb with a medley of vegetables is recommended. Desserts include whiskey parfait with honey sauce and strawberry parfait with rhubarb foam. Sunday brunches are particularly popular, so plan ahead. *Französischestr. 47, tel. 030/229-3144. Reservations advised. Dress: informal but neat. AE.*

Ermeler-Haus. The Rococo grandeur of this wine restaurant located in a series of upstairs rooms reflects the elegance of the restored patrician home—which dates from the mid-16th century—in which it's housed. The atmosphere is subdued and formal, the wines are imported, and the service and German cuisine are excellent. There's dancing every Saturday evening. *Märkisches Ufer 10-12, tel. 030/279-4028. Reservations advised. Jacket and tie required. AE, DC, MC, V.*

Französischer Hof. Not for the infirm or those who are afraid of heights, this restaurant is tucked away below the cupola of the Französicher Dom, the church that sits in classical splendor on one side of the beautiful Gendarmenmarkt. The restaurant, which runs a circular course around the base of the cupola, is approached by a long, winding staircase—fine for working up an appetite but certainly not recommended for the fainthearted. The reward at the top of the stairs is a table in one of Berlin's most original and attractive restaurants. The menu is as short as the stairway is long, but there's an impressive wine list. *Französischer Dom, Gendarmenmarkt, tel. 030/229-3969. Reservations strongly advised (the frustration of being turned away after that climb could spoil anyone's day). No credit cards.*

Ratskeller. This is actually two restaurants in one, composed of a wine and a beer cellar, each highly popular and each with great atmosphere (entrances at opposite corners of the building). Menus are somewhat limited but include good solid Berlin fare. The brick-walled beer cellar is guaranteed to be packed during main dining hours, at which time reservations sometimes get ignored; Berliners simply line up to get in. The wine cellar is less crowded, in part because it is slightly more expensive. Among the menu selections are Hungarian goulash soup, chicken, and steaks. *Rathausstr. 15–18 (in the basement of the Rotes Rathaus, or Red Town Hall), tel. 030/212–4464 and 030/242–3819. Reservations advised. Dress: informal. No credit cards.*

★ **Schwalbennest.** On the edge of the Nikolai quarter, overlooking the Marx-Engels-Forum, this is a fairly new establishment, yet it is already known for its outstanding food and service. The choice is wide for main dishes and wines. The grilled selections are excellent, but note that the flambéed dishes cost extra, although no additional price is indicated on the menu. *Am Marstall (upstairs), Rathausstr. at Marx-Engels-Forum, tel. 030/242–6919. Reservations essential. Dress: informal at lunch, jacket and tie required at dinner. No credit cards.*

Zur Goldenen Gans. Regional specialties are featured here, particularly game and venison dishes prepared Thüringer Forest style. *Friedrichstr. 158–164, in the Grand Hotel, tel. 030/20920. Reservations advised. Dress: informal. AE, DC, MC, V.*

Moderate **Zille.** For authentic Berlin specialties you'll probably do no bet-
★ ter; the atmosphere is also thoroughly relaxing. *Alexanderpl., in the Hotel Stadt Berlin, tel. 030/2389–4245. Reservations advised. Dress: informal. AE, DC, MC, V.*

Inexpensive **Alt-Cöllner Schankstuben.** Four tiny restaurants are contained
★ within this charming, historic Berlin house. The section to the side of the canal on the Kleine Gertraudenstrasse, where there are tables set outside, serves as a café. The menu is relatively limited, but quality, like the service, is good. *Friederichsgracht 50, tel. 030/242–5972. No reservations. Dress: informal. No credit cards.*

★ **Raabe Diele.** The location of this restaurant is the basement of the 16th-century Ermeler-Haus (*see above*). It was largely rebuilt in 1969, meaning that the pine-paneled cellar is new—with canned music—and offers considerably less elegance and atmosphere than the handsome rooms upstairs. On the other hand, the prices are far lower and the menu consists of good Berlin-style cuisine. The service down here is just as attentive as it is upstairs. *Märkisches Ufer 10–12, in Ermeler-Haus, tel. 030/279–4036. Dress: informal. Reservations advised, particularly at night. AE, DC, MC, V.*

★ **Zur Letzen Instanz.** Unquestionably Berlin's oldest restaurant, established in 1525, this place is imbued with an Old-World charm rarely found in the modern city these days. The choice of food is, as usual, limited, but it is prepared in the genuine Berlin tradition and is truly hearty—you'll find beer in the cooking as well as in your mug. *Waisenstr. 14–16 (U-bahn Klosterstr.), tel. 030/242–5528. Reservations essential. Dress: informal. No credit cards.*

Zur Rippe. This famous eating place near Alexanderplatz serves wholesome food in an intimate setting with oak paneling and ceramic tiles. Specialties include the Märkische cheese platter and herring casserole. *Poststr. 17, tel. 030/217–3235. Reservations not necessary. No credit cards.*

Lodging

Berlin lost all of its grand old luxury hotels in the bombing during World War II; though some were rebuilt, many of the best hotels today are modern. Though they lack little in service and comfort, you may find some short on atmosphere. For first-class or luxury accommodations, eastern Berlin is easily as good as western, for the East German government, eager for hard currency, built several elegant hotels—the Grand, Palast, Dom (now called Hilton International), and Metropol—which are up to the very best international standards and place in the very top price category. If you're seeking something more moderate, the better choice may be western Berlin, where there are large numbers of good-value pensions and small hotels, many of them in older buildings with some character. In eastern Berlin, however, the hostels run by the Evangelical church offer outstanding value for your money.

There are no longer any restrictions on who can stay where in the former East Berlin, as there were in the past. In western Berlin, business conventions year-round and the influx of summer tourists mean that you should make reservations well in advance. If you arrive without reservations, consult the board at Tegel Airport that shows hotels with vacancies, or go to the tourist office at the airport. The main tourist office in the Europa Center can also help with reservations (*see* Important Addresses and Numbers, *above*).

Highly recommended hotels are indicated by a star ★.

Category	Cost*
Very Expensive	over DM 250
Expensive	DM 180–DM 250
Moderate	DM 120–DM 180
Inexpensive	under DM 120

for 2 people in double room, including tax and service

Western Berlin

Very Expensive
★
Bristol Hotel Kempinski. Destroyed in the war, rebuilt in 1952, and renovated in 1980, the "Kempi" is a renowned Berlin classic. Located on the Ku'damm in the heart of the city, it has the best shopping at its doorstep plus some fine boutiques of its own within. Rooms and suites are luxuriously decorated, English style, and with all amenities. *Ku'damm 27, tel. 030/884–340. 334 rooms with bath. Facilities: 3 restaurants, indoor pool, sauna, solarium, masseur, hairdresser, limousine service. AE, DC, MC, V.*

Grand Hotel Esplanade. Opened in 1988, the Grand Hotel Esplanade exudes luxury. Uncompromisingly modern architecture, chicly styled rooms, and works of art by some of Berlin's most acclaimed artists are its outstanding visual aspects. Then there are the superb facilities and impeccable service. The enormous grand suite comes complete with sauna, whirlpool, and a grand piano for DM 1,200 per night. *Lützowufer 15, tel. 030/261–011, fax 030/265–1171. 369 rooms, 33 suites. Facilities: 2 restaurants, pub, poolside bar, pool, sauna, whirlpool,*

American Express offers Travelers Cheques built for two.

American Express® Cheques *for Two*. The first Travelers Cheques that allow either of you to use them because both of you have signed them. And only one of you needs to be present to purchase them.

Cheques *for Two* are accepted anywhere regular American Express Travelers Cheques are, which is just about everywhere. So stop by your bank, AAA* or any American Express Travel Service Office and ask for Cheques *for Two*.

steam bath, solarium, masseur, hairdresser, boutique, medical station, library. AE, DC, MC, V.

Hotel Berlin. The hotel that bears Berlin's name is actually part of a prominent Scandinavian group, hence the birch-tree bright and light look, modern but furnished in enduring, understated good taste. The location is handy for both the Ku'damm and Unter den Linden. *Lützowplatz 17, tel. 030/ 26050, fax 030/2605–2716. 490 rooms and 21 suites with bath. Facilities: sauna, solarium, beauty center, boutiques, restaurant, beer tavern, piano bar. AE, DC, MC, V.*

★ **Inter-Continental Berlin.** The top-billed "Diplomaten Suite" is in a class of its own: It's as large as a suburban house and is furnished in exotic Oriental style. Other rooms and suites may not be so opulently furnished but still show individuality and taste. The lobby is worth a visit even if you're not staying here. It's one-fourth the size of a football field and lavishly decorated; stop by for afternoon tea and pastries. *Budapesterstr. 2, tel. 030/26020, fax 030/2602–80760..600 rooms with bath. Facilities: 3 restaurants, indoor pool, sauna, boutiques, Pan Am check-in service. AE, DC, MC, V.*

Steigenberger Berlin. The Steigenberger group's exemplary Berlin hotel is centrally situated, only a few steps from the Ku'damm but remarkably quiet. Small touches that lift the hotel above the usual run of chain establishments include a nightly weather forecast dropped on your bedside table to help you plan for the next day. *Los-Angeles-Platz 1, tel. 030/210–8117. 389 rooms and 11 suites, all with bath. Facilities: pool and poolside bar, sauna, solarium, massage room, 2 restaurants, cocktail bar, café, tavern. AE, DC, MC, V.*

Expensive **Hotel Hamburg.** The Ring group's Berlin establishment offers all the expected comfort and facilities in a quiet location handy for both parts of Berlin. If you book well in advance, you can take advantage of a two-night package for little more than the price of one night's stay, with a city tour, a welcome drink, complimentary breakfast, a dinner, and opera or theater tickets all thrown in. *Landgrafenstr. 4, tel. 030/269–161. 240 rooms with bath. Facilities: restaurant, bar. AE, DC, MC, V.*

★ **Landhaus Schlachtensee.** Opened in 1987, this former villa (built in 1905) is now a cozy bed-and-breakfast hotel. The Landhaus Schlachtensee offers personal and efficient service, well-equipped rooms, and a quiet location in the Zehlendorf district. The nearby Schlachtensee and Krumme Lanke lakes beckon you to swim, boat, or walk along their shores. *Bogotastr. 9, tel. 030/816–0060, fax 030/8160–0664. 19 rooms with bath. Facilities: breakfast buffet. AE, DC, MC, V.*

Schweizerhof Berlin. Recent refurbishing has not altered the rustic look of this centrally located hotel; the extras, such as room video players and minibars, are up-to-the-minute. Ask for a room in the west wing, where rooms are larger. Standards are high throughout. The indoor pool is the largest hotel pool in Berlin. *Budapesterstr. 21–31, tel. 030/26960. 430 rooms with bath. Facilities: sauna, solarium, pool, fitness room, hairdresser, beauty salon. AE, DC, MC, V.*

★ **Seehof.** This handsome lakeside hotel is close to the Berlin fairgrounds and within easy reach of downtown. Most rooms overlook Lietzensee Lake; ask for a balcony room on the second floor. The large indoor pool overlooks the lake, too, and has access to a bar. Dine in the Au Lac restaurant, with its frescoed ceilings and Gobelin tapestries; it specializes in French cuisine

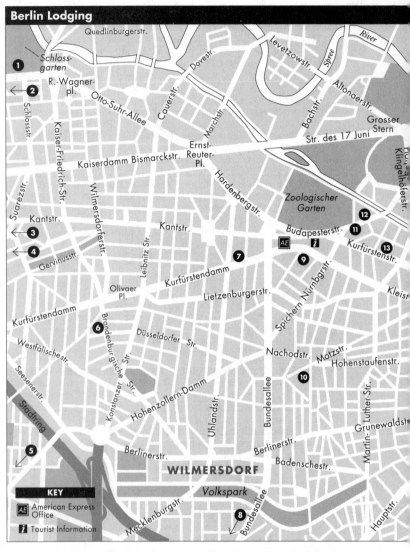

Berlin Lodging

Quedlinburgerstr.

River

Spree

Schloss-
garten ❶

Levetzowstr.

Altonaerstr.

Bachstr.

R.-Wagner-
pl. ❷

Dovestr.

Otto-Suhr-Allee

Cauerstr.

Marchstr.

Grosser
Stern

Str. des 17 Juni

Schlossstr.

Kaiser-Friedrich-Str.

Kaiserdamm Bismarckstr.

Ernst-
Reuter-
Pl.

Hardenbergstr.

Klingelhöferstr.

Suarezstr.

Wilmersdorferstr.

Kantstr. ❸

Zoologischer
Garten

❶❷ 12

Gervinusstr. ❹

Kantstr.

Budapesterstr.

11

Leibniz Str.

❼

AE 🛈

Kurfürstenstr. 13

Kurfürstendamm

❾

Spichern Nürnbgrstr.

Kleis

Olivaer
Pl.

Lietzenburgerstr.

Kurfürstendamm

Brandenburgische Str.

Düsseldorfer Str.

Nachodstr.

Motzstr.

Hohenstaufenstr.

Westfälischestr.

Konstanzer Str.

10

Seesenerstr.

Stadtring

Hohenzollern-Damm

Uhlandstr.

Bundesallee

Martin-Luther-Str.

Grunewaldstr.

❺

Berlinerstr.

Berlinerstr.

Badenschestr.

WILMERSDORF

Hauptstr.

Volkspark

Mecklenburgstr.

❽

Bundesallee

KEY

AE **American Express
Office**

🛈 **Tourist Information**

Atrium Hotel, **10**
Berolina, **24**
Bristol Hotel
Kempinski, **7**
Casino Hotel, **2**
Charlottenhof, **29**
Econtel, **1**
Forum Hotel
Berlin, **23**
Grand Hotel, **25**

Grand Hotel
Esplanade, **15**
Herbst, **4**
Hilton
International, **27**
Hospiz
Augustrasse, **20**
Hospiz am Bahnhof
Friedrichstrasse, **19**
Hotel Berlin, **14**
Hotel Hamburg, **13**
Hotel Krone, **28**
Hotel Müggelsee, **17**

Inter-Continental
Berlin, **12**
Landhaus
Schlachtensee, **5**
Metropol, **18**
Newa, **21**
Radisson Plaza, **22**
Ravenna, **8**
Riehmers
Hofgarten, **16**
Savigny, **6**

Schweizerhof
Berlin, **11**
Seehof, **3**
Steigenberger
Berlin, **9**
Unter den Linden, **26**

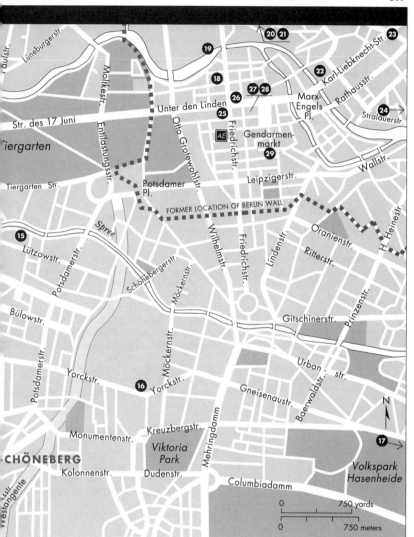

and serves a fine six-course gourmet menu. *Lietzensee-Ufer 11, tel. 030/320–020, fax 030/3200–2251. 77 rooms with bath. Facilities: restaurant, terrace with outdoor bar, indoor pool, sauna, solarium. AE, DC, MC, V.*

Moderate **Casino Hotel.** What was once a barracks has been skillfully con-
★ verted into an appealing hotel with large, comfortable rooms, all tastefully furnished and well equipped—the Prussian soldiers never had it so good! You'll detect the Bavarian owner's influence in the south German cuisine at the restaurant. The Casino is in the Charlottenburg district. *Königen-Elisabeth-Str. 47a, tel. 030/303–090. 24 rooms with bath. Facilities: restaurant, beer garden. AE, DC, MC, V.*

Riehmers Hofgarten. A few minutes' walk from the Kreuzberg hill in the heart of the colorful Kreuzberg district and close to Tempelhof airport, the Riehmers Hofgarten is a small hotel housed in a late-19th-century building. The high-ceilinged rooms are comfortable, with crisp linens and firm beds. *Yorckstr. 83, tel. 030/781–011. 21 rooms with bath. AE, DC, MC, V.*

Inexpensive **Atrium Hotel.** This little privately run hotel is located within reasonable reach of downtown. The modest rooms are comfortably furnished and clean, the staff efficient and helpful. The only drawback is that there's no restaurant. *Motzstr. 87, tel. 030/218–4057. 22 rooms with bath. MC.*

Econtel. This family-oriented hotel is within walking distance of the Charlottenburg palace. Rooms have a homey feel and are spotlessly clean. *Sommeringstr. 24, tel. 030/346–810. 205 rooms with bath. Facilities: snack bar. MC.*

Herbst. This plain and simple bed-and-breakfast pension is in the Spandau district, where Hitler's mysterious deputy Rudolph Hess spent more than 40 years in jail. There are good connections to downtown by S-bahn. *Moritzstr. 21, tel. 030/333–4032. 22 rooms with bath. AE, DC.*

★ **Ravenna.** A small, friendly hotel in the Steglitz district, Ravenna is near the Botanical Garden and Dahlem museums. All the rooms are well equipped. Suite 111B is a bargain: It includes a large living room and kitchen for only DM 200. *Grunewaldstr. 8–9, tel. 030/792–8031. 45 rooms with bath. AE, DC, MC, V.*

Savigny. A hotel in central Berlin doesn't come any cheaper: A double room costs just DM 110, and that includes breakfast. The rooms are sparsely furnished, and there are no private bathrooms. But the service is friendly, and you're just 500 yards from the Ku'damm. *Brandenbürgischestr. 21, tel. 030/881–3001. 50 rooms, none with bath. Facilities: bar. No credit cards.*

Eastern Berlin

Very Expensive **Grand Hotel.** Eastern Berlin's most expensive hotel lives up to its name; opened in 1987, this hotel is grand in every sense of the word. From the moment you step into the air-conditioned atrium lobby, you'll wonder how this example of capitalism at its most elegant ever fitted into a socialist society. From there on in, all is couched in luxury, and really, you could be in any modern, commodious hotel in the world. *Friedrichstr. 158–164, corner Behrenstr., tel. 030/23270, fax 030/2327–3362. 315 rooms and 35 suites, all with bath. Facilities: 4 restaurants, winter garden, Bierstube (beer room), bars, concert café, casi-*

no, pool, sauna, squash courts, shopping arcade, hairdresser, theater ticket office, car and yacht rental. AE, DC, MC, V.

Hilton International. Berlin's newest hotel opened in 1991 as the Dom Hotel, and was soon taken over by Hilton. It overlooks the historic Gendarmenmarkt, with the German and French cathedrals and the neoclassical Schauspielhaus. Near Checkpoint Charlie, the location is central to the whole city. All the right touches are here, from heated bathtubs to special rooms for handicapped travelers, nonsmokers, and businesswomen. *Mohrenstr. 30, tel. 030/3820, fax 030/2382–4269. 366 rooms. Facilities: 3 restaurants, cafeteria, pub, wine cellar, bar, discotheque, indoor pool, sauna, solarium, fitness room, bowling, garage. AE, DC, MC, V.*

★ **Metropol.** This is the choice of businesspeople, not just for its excellent location across from the Friedrichstrasse train station and the International Trade Center; the service is outstanding. The best rooms are on the front side, facing north. All rooms are well equipped (but note that only public areas are air-conditioned); the hotel's antiques gallery is small but interesting, and the nightclub is an unusually good one, while the restaurants are only fair (except in price!); the exception is the hotel grill-restaurant off the lobby, which is about the best in eastern Berlin. *Friedrichstr. 150–153, tel. 030/203–070, fax 030/2030–7209. 300 rooms with bath. Facilities: 3 restaurants, nightclub, bars, garage, pool, sauna, fitness room, solarium, antiques gallery, shopping mall, car, horse-drawn carriage, and yacht rental available. AE, DC, MC, V.*

★ **Radisson Plaza.** This is a favorite with tour groups because of its proximity to eastern Berlin's Museum Island—and because it's another of the city's mega facility hotels. The best rooms overlook the Spree River; those on the Alexanderplatz side can be noisy. The shopping mall includes a travel agency, an antiques gallery, and eastern Berlin's central ticket agency. The restaurants are recommended. *Karl-Liebknecht-Str. 5, tel. 030/2382–7590. 583 rooms with bath. Facilities: 6 restaurants, 4 bars, garage, Bierstube, nightclub, pool, sauna, fitness room, solarium, bowling, travel office, theater ticket office, antiques gallery, shopping mall, car and yacht rental. AE, DC, MC, V.*

Expensive **Berolina.** If being a little way from the city's main tourist attractions is no deterrent, this is a pleasant place located near Alexanderplatz. Its rooftop-garden restaurant (Restaurant Krö-gel, on the 11th floor) will give you a fine view out over Berlin. *Karl-Marx-Allee 31, tel. 030/212–3302, fax 030/212–3409. 344 rooms with bath. Facilities: 3 restaurants, rooftop garden, souvenir shop, café, bar, sauna, garage. AE, DC, MC, V.*

Forum Hotel Berlin. With its 40 stories, the Forum Hotel Berlin at the top end of Alexanderplatz competes with the nearby Fernsehturm for the title of premier downtown landmark. The rooftop dining room features good food and service and stunning views (reservations are essential). As the city's largest hotel, it is understandably a bit impersonal. The bar on the 37th floor claims to be the highest in Europe and is open until 5 AM. *Alexanderpl., tel. 030/23890. 997 rooms with bath or shower. Facilities: 4 restaurants (including rooftop dining room), 3 bars, garage, shopping, beer garden, Bierstube, sauna. AE, DC, MC, V.*

Hotel Müggelsee. Berlin's biggest and some say most beautiful lake is just beyond your balcony in this establishment, which was once a favorite among East Germany's communist leaders. The hotel even has its own yacht for the use of its guests. *Am Grossen Müggelsee, tel. 030/658–820, fax 030/6588–2263. 166 rooms with bath. Facilities: boutiques, tennis court, 2 restaurants, bar, nightclub. AE, DC, MC, V.*

★ **Unter den Linden.** The international quality of the gigantic, newer hotels may be missing here, but the location couldn't be better. The restaurant is known for the best food on Unter den Linden. *Unter den Linden 14, corner Friedrichstr., tel. 030/ 220–031. 307 rooms with bath or shower. Facilities: restaurant. AE, DC, MC, V.*

Moderate **Charlottenhof.** This popular hotel-pension, ideally located on the beautiful Gendarmenmarkt, was taken over by a large western group in 1991. Happily, room prices have stayed moderate and the homey, friendly nature of the original establishment has remained unscathed. With this, the Charlottenhof has moved into the ranks of eastern Berlin's most recommendable hotels. *Charlottenstr. 52, tel. 030/392–8426. 86 rooms with bath. Facilities: restaurant, bar. AE, DC, MC, V.*

Hotel Krone. Opened in 1991, the Krone is part of the Hilton Hotel complex, sharing Hilton's excellent location on the beautiful Gendarmenmarkt, but not its high prices. The facilities offered by the Krone are correspondingly fewer, but rooms are comfortable and adequately furnished. There's no restaurant, but most of eastern Berlin's better eating haunts are within a 10-minute walk. *Gendarmenmarkt, tel. 030/2382–4212, fax 030/2382–4269. 148 rooms with bath. Facilities: restaurant, bar. AE, DC, MC, V.*

Newa. This older hotel, popular because of its affordability, is just a 10-minute streetcar ride away from the downtown area. Rooms in the back are quieter. At press time, the hotel was undergoing major renovations; call ahead to check on its status. *Invalidenstr. 115, tel. 030/5173. 57 rooms, most with bath. No credit cards.*

Inexpensive **Hospiz am Bahnhof Friedrichstrasse.** This Evangelical church-
★ run hostel, both because of price and a convenient location, gets booked up months in advance. It is enormously popular with families, so the public areas are not always particularly restful. The restaurant is cheap and usually busy. Not all rooms have their own bathrooms. *Albrechstr. 8, tel. 030/284–030. 110 rooms, most with bath. Facilities: restaurant. MC, V.*

Hospiz Augustrasse. Comfortable rooms and a friendly staff make this very low-priced hotel—also run by the Evangelical church—appealing. It is roughly a 10-minute streetcar ride into downtown Berlin. Breakfast is the only meal served here. *Augustr. 82, tel. 030/282–5321. 70 rooms, some with bath. No credit cards.*

The Arts and Nightlife

The Arts

Today's Berlin has a tough task living up to the reputation it gained from the film *Cabaret*, but if nightlife is a little toned down since the '30s, the arts still flourish. In addition to the many hotels that book seats, there are several ticket agencies, including **Theaterkasse Sasse** (Ku'damm 24, tel. 030/882–7360),

Theater-kasse Centrum (Mienekestr. 25, tel. 030/882–7611), and **Wildbad-Kiosk,** (Rankestr. 1, tel. 030/881–4507). Most of the big stores (KaDeWe, Hertie, Wertheim, and Karstadt, for example) also have ticket agencies, while in eastern Berlin tickets can be obtained from the tourist office in Alexanderplatz, and at ticket offices in the Palast and Grand hotels. Detailed information about what's going on in Berlin can be found in *Berlin Programm,* a monthly guide to Berlin arts (DM 2.80), and the magazines *Tip* and *Zitty,* which appear every two weeks and provide full arts listings.

Theater Theater in Berlin is outstanding, but performances are usually in German. The exceptions are operettas and the (nonliterary) cabarets. Of the city's more than 50 theaters, the most renowned for both its modern and classical productions is the **Schaubühne am Lehniner Platz** (Ku'damm 153, tel. 030/890–023). Also important are the **Schlosspark-Theater** (Schlossstr. 48, tel. 030/793–1515) the **Renaissance-Theater** (Hardenbergstr. 6, tel. 030/312–4202); and the **Freie Volksbühne** (Schaperstr. 24, tel. 030/881–3742). For *Boulevard* plays (fashionable social comedies), there is the **Komödie** (Kurfürstendamm 206, tel. 030/882–7893), and at the same address the **Theater am Kurfürstendamm** (tel. 030/882–3789), and the **Hansa Theater** (Alt Moabit 48, tel. 030/391–4460). Among the smaller, more experimental theaters is the **Tribune** (Otto-Suhr-Allee 18–20, tel. 030/341–2600), a youthful enterprise.

Eastern Berlin's leading theaters include: the **Berliner Ensemble** (Bertolt–Brecht–Pl., tel. 030/282–3160), dedicated to Brecht and works of other international playwrights; **Deutches Theater** (Schumannstr. 13–14, tel. 030/287–1225), for outstanding classical and contemporary German drama; **Friedrichstadtpalais** (Friedrichstr. 107, tel. 030/283–6474), a glossy showcase for variety revues and historic old Berlin theater pieces; **Kammerspiele** (Schumannstr. 13–14, tel. 030/287–1226), a studio theater attached to the Deutsches Theater; **Maxim-Gorki-Theater** (Am Festungsgraben, tel. 030/208–2783), featuring plays by local authors and some contemporary humor; and **Volksbühne** (Rosa-Luxemburg-Pl., tel. 030/282–8978), featuring classical and contemporary drama.

Berlin's savage and debunking idiom is particularly suited to social and political satire, a long tradition in cabaret theaters here. The **Stachelschweine** (Europa-Center, tel. 030/261–4795) and **Die Wühlmäuse** (1/30 Nümbergerstr. 33, tel. 030/213–7047) carry on that tradition with biting wit and style; eastern Berlin's equivalent is **Distel** (Friedrichstr. 100, tel. 030/200–4704). For children's theater, try **Klecks** (Schinkestr. 8/9, tel. 030/693–7731). **Puppentheater** (Greifswalderstr. 81–84, tel. 030/426–1343), eastern Berlin's puppet theater, is nominally for children but can be good entertainment for adults as well.

Concerts Berlin is the home of one of the world's leading orchestras, the **Berliner Philharmonisches Orchester** (Berlin Philharmonic— *see* Philharmonic, *below*) in addition to a number of other major symphony orchestras and orchestral ensembles. The **Berlin Festival Weeks,** held annually from August to October, combine a wide range of concerts, operas, ballet, theater, and art exhibitions. For information and reservations, write **Festspiele GmbH** (Kartenbüro, Budapesterstr. 50, 1000 Berlin 30).

Concert halls in Berlin include:

Grosser Sendesaal des SFB (Haus des Rundfunks, Masurenallee 8–14, tel. 030/303–11123). Part of the Sender Freies Berlin, one of Berlin's broadcasting stations, the Grosser Sendesaal is the home of the Radio Symphonic Orchestra.

Konzertsaal der Hochschule der Künste (Hardenbergstr. 33, tel. 030/318–52374). The concert hall of the Academy of Fine Arts is Berlin's second biggest—also known as the "symphony garage."

Philharmonie (Matthaikircherstr. 1, tel. 030/254–880 or 030/261–4383). The Berlin Philharmonic is based here. Tickets have to be reserved and purchased at the box office; telephone bookings are not accepted.

Schauspielhaus (Gendarmenmarkt, tel. 030/2090–2122). This beautifully restored hall is a prime venue for concerts in eastern Berlin.

Waldbühne (Am Glockenturm, close to the Olympic Stadium). Modeled along the lines of an ancient Roman theater, this open-air site accommodates nearly 20,000 people. Tickets are available through ticket agencies.

Opera, Ballet, and Musicals
The **Deutsche Oper Berlin** (Bismarckstr. 35, tel. 030/341–0249) is one of Germany's leading opera houses and presents outstanding productions year-round. The ballet also performs here. Tickets for both are expensive and sell out quickly. But tickets are often returned on the night of the performance; reduced prices are also available for students. At the **Neuköllner Oper** (Karl-Marx-Str. 131–133, tel. 030/687–6061) you'll find showy, fun performances of long-forgotten operas and humorous musical productions. The skillfully restored **Theater des Westens** (Kantstr. 12, tel. 030/319–03193) is the ideal setting for comic operas and musicals like *West Side Story*, *A Chorus Line*, and *Cabaret*. Experimental ballet and modern dance are presented at the **Tanzfabrik** in Kreuzberg (Möckernstr. 66, tel. 030/786–5861).

Eastern Berlin's main sites for opera, operettas, and dance are the **Deutsche Staatsoper** (Unter den Linden 7, tel. 030/200–4762), the **Komische Oper** (Behrenstr. 55–57, tel. 030/229–2555), and the **Metropol Theater** (Friedrichstr. 101, tel. 030/203–640).

Film
Berlin has around 90 movie theaters, showing about 100 movies a day. International and German movies are shown in the big theaters around the Ku'damm; the "Off-Ku-damm" theaters show less commercial movies. For (undubbed) movies in English, go to the **Odeon** (Hauptstr. 116, tel. 030/781–5667), **Kurbel** (Gniesebrechtstr. 4, tel. 030/883–5325), or the **Arsenal** (Welserstr. 25, tel. 030/218–6848). Films from eastern Germany's state archives are shown Tuesday and Friday at 5:30 and 8 at **Filmtheater Babylon** (Rosa-Luxemburg-Str. 30, tel. 030/282–8978).

In February, Berlin hosts the **Internationale Filmfestspiele**, an internationally famous film festival, conferring "Golden Bear" awards on the best films, directors, and actors. The organizers, under pressure from an increasingly popular film festival that takes place in Munich every June, are considering moving the two-week event to summer. Call tel. 030/254–890 for information.

Nightlife

Berlin's nightlife has always been notorious. There are scads of places in western Berlin to seek your nighttime entertainment, and the quality ranges widely from tacky to spectacular. Eastern Berlin's nightlife has not been on a par with that of the western sector, although that is changing. Dinner-dancing is generally offered at the international-style hotels; some also have nightclubs.

All Berlin tour operators offer **Night Club Tours** (around DM 100, including entrance fees to up to three shows, free drinks, and, in some cases, supper). Most places in western Berlin stay open late; some have all-night liquor licenses.

Clubs **Chez Nous** (Marburgerstr. 14, tel. 030/213–1810) lives up to Berlin's reputation as the drag-show center of Germany. Empire-style plush is the backdrop for two nightly shows (reservations recommended).

You'll find three more conventional stage shows at **Dollywood** (Kurfürstenstr. 114, tel. 030/218–8950) each night, plus a disco. **La Vie en Rose** (Europa-Centre, tel. 030/323–6006) is a revue theater with spectacular light shows that also showcases international stars (book ahead). If the strip show at the **New Eden** (Ku'damm 71, tel. 030/323–5849) doesn't grab you, maybe the dance music will (two bands nightly). The **New York Bar** (Olivaer Pl. 16, tel. 030/883–6258) is a mellow drinking haven compared with its rowdier neighbors. Despite Mississippi-inspired decor, the **Riverboat** (Hohenzollerndamm 177, tel. 030/878–476) has great Berlin atmosphere. You have a choice at **Zeleste** (Marburgerstr. 2, tel. 030/211–6445): Sit back and listen to jazz or dance the night away in its disco.

Jazz Clubs Berlin's lively music scene is dominated by jazz and rock. For jazz enthusiasts, *the* events of the year are the summer's **Jazz in the Garden** festival and the international autumn **Jazz Fest Berlin**. For information, call the **Berlin Tourist Information Center** (Europa-Center, tel. 030/262–6031). Traditionally, the best **live jazz** can be found at:

Eierschale (Podbielskiallee 50, tel. 030/832–7097). A variety of jazz groups appear here at the "Egg Shell," daily from 8:30 PM, admission free.
Flöz (Nassauischestr. 36A, tel. 030/861–1000). The sizzling jazz at this club is sometimes incorporated into theater presentations.
Kunstlerhaus Bethanien (Mariannenpl. 2, tel. 030/614–8010). Jazz and 'Free Music' concerts are held at this big venue.
Quartier Latin (Potsdamerstr. 96, tel. 030/262–9016). The Quartier Latin is one of the leaders in Berlin's jazz scene. Jazz and rock are both presented.

Discos **Dschungel** (Nürnbergerstr. 53, tel. 030/218–5776). A funky disco, "Jungle," is a current "in" spot. Dance until you drop, or at least until 4 AM. Closed Tuesday.
Hafenbar (Chauseestr. 20). This is a popular eastern Berlin disco decorated in '50s style. Closed Wednesdays.
Metropol (Nollendorfpl. 5, tel. 030/216–2787). Berlin's largest disco, which stages occasional concerts, is a hot spot for the younger tourist. The black dance floor upstairs is the scene for a magnificent light and laser show. The DM 10 cover includes your first drink.

Kneipen Berlin has roughly 5,000 bars and pubs; this includes the dives, too. All come under the heading of *Kneipen*—the place round the corner where you stop in for a beer, a snack, a conversation, and sometimes, to dance.

Bogen 597 (Savignypl., S-bahn passage). Sound effects are provided by the S-bahn—you'll hear and feel the trains passing on the tracks overhead. This is a cozy place that serves a fine selection of wines in addition to the inevitable beer.

Ku'dorf (Joachimstaler-Str. 15). The Ku'dorf makes it easy to go from one Kneipe to another—there are 18 located under one roof here, underground, just off the Ku'damm. Open Monday–Saturday from 8 PM.

Leydicke (Mansteinstr. 4). This historic spot is a must for out-of-towners. The proprietors operate their own distillery and have a superb selection of wines and liqueurs; definitely the right atmosphere in which to enjoy a few glasses.

Sperlingsgasse (Lietzenburgerstr. 82–84). Look for the replica of the Brandenburg Gate on the sidewalk. It'll point you in the direction of the 13 different Kneipen here. All open at 7 PM.

Wilhelm Hoeck (Wilmersdorferstr. 149). Berlin's oldest Kneipe is also its most beautiful. Its superb interior dates from 1892 and is all original. Frequented by a colorful cross section of the public, this is a place that's definitely worth a visit.

Wirthaus Wuppke (Schlüterstr. 21). Come here if you're seeking a mellower, quieter atmosphere. It gets as crowded as the others, but it's not so hectic. The food is good and inexpensive.

Yorckschlösschen (Yorckstr. 15). In the summer you can sit in the garden and enjoy a beer and a snack or a hearty meal. If you're lucky, there may be live music.

Zur Nolle (Nollendorfpl.). You can sit in an old subway car in this converted (aboveground) subway station and enjoy live Dixieland music. Berlin specialties are served from the buffet. Check it out on a Sunday morning as you stroll around the local flea market.

Zwiebelfisch (Savignypl. 7). Literally translated as the "onion fish," this Kneipe has become the meeting place of literary bohemians of all ages. It has a good atmosphere for getting to know people. The beer is good, the menu small.

Casinos Western Berlin's leading casino is in the Europa Center. It has 10 roulette and three blackjack tables, and is open 3 AM–3 PM. Eastern Berlin's poshest casino is at the Grand Hotel.

4 Excursions from Berlin

Including Potsdam and Magdeburg

Potsdam

Important Addresses and Numbers

Tourist
Information The tourist office is **Potsdam-Information** (Friedrich-Ebert-Strasse 5, Potsdam 1561; tel. 0331/21100, 0331/329217, and 0331/329220). It's open weekdays 9–8, weekends 9–6. Rooms in private homes (but not hotel rooms) can be reserved through Potsdam-Information, either at a special counter open until 6 or by telephoning 0331/23385 or 0331/21100, fax 0331/23012.

Emergencies **Police:** tel. 0331/110. **Ambulance:** tel. 0331/410 or 0331/412–581. **Medical emergencies:** Poliklinik, Turkstrasse, tel. 0331/410. **Doctor and dentist:** 0331/410. **Late-night pharmacies:** Zentralapotheke, Heinrich-Rau-Allee 40, tel. 0331/24069. When this pharmacy is closed, a sign is posted on its door identifying the nearest late-night pharmacy.

Getting There

Potsdam is virtually a suburb of Berlin, some 20 kilometers (12 miles) southwest of the city center and a half-hour journey by car, train, or bus. City traffic is heavy, however, and a train journey is recommended, even though there are no direct trains. Perhaps the most effortless way to visit Potsdam and its attractions is to book a tour with one of the big Berlin operators (*see* Guided Tours, *below*).

By Car From Berlin center (Strasse des 17 Juni), take the Potsdamerstrasse south until it becomes Route 1 and then follow the signs to Potsdam.

By Train Take the S-bahn, either the S-5 or the S-1 line, to Wannsee. Change there for the short rail trip (the trains leave only hourly) to Potsdam West (for Schloss Sanssouci and Schloss Charlottenhof), and Wildpark (for Neues Palais) stations. You also can take bus No. 113 from Wannsee to the Bassanplatz bus station. From there you can take bus No. 695 to Sanssouci park, or you can walk down Brandenburgerstrasse to Platz der Nationen and on to the Green Gate, the main entrance to Sanssouci Park.

By Bus There is regular bus service from the bus station at the Funkturm, Messedamm 8 (reached by U-1 to Kaiserdamm).

By Boat Boats leave hourly 10–6 from Wannsee landing.

Guided Tours from Berlin

Severin & Kühn (BVB, Kurfürstendamm 216, tel. 030/883–1015) offers a whole-day tour for DM 89 (including lunch). **Berliner Bären Stadtrundfahrt** (BBS, Rankestr. 35, tel. 030/213–4077) conducts an afternoon tour that includes tea in its DM 65 price. Berolina and Bus-Verkehr-Berlin also offer tours of Potsdam from Berlin.

Exploring Potsdam

Germany's most famous king, Friedrich II—Frederick the Great—spent more time at his summer residence in Potsdam than at the official court in Berlin, and it's no wonder. Freder-

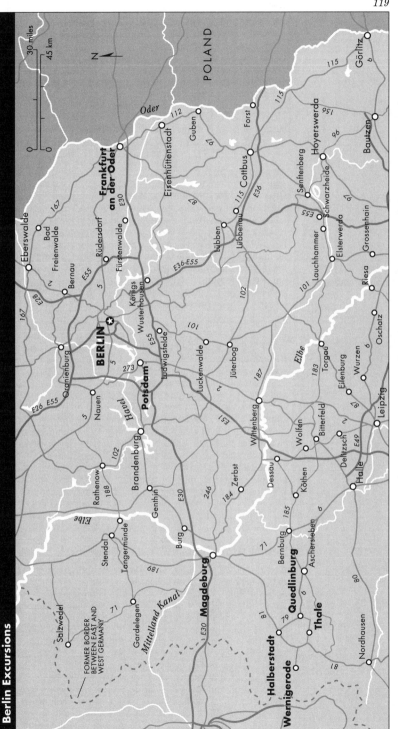

Berlin Excursions

30 miles
45 km

N

POLAND

POLAND

Oder

Görlitz

115

Frankfurt
an der Oder

Eisenhüttenstadt

Guben

Forst

115

Hoyerswerda

951

Bautzen

Eberswalde

Bad
Freienwalde

167

Rüdersdorf

Fürstenwalde

E30

Cottbus

115

E36

Senftenberg

Schwarzheide

96

Grossenhain

Bernau

E55

Königs
Wusterhausen

E36-E55

Lübben

Lübbenau

E55

Lauchhammer

Elsterwerda

Riesa

Oschatz

167

E28

BERLIN

E55

Ludwigsfelde

101

101

Jüterbog

187

Elbe

Torgau

183

Eilenburg

61

Wurzen

Leipzig

Oranienburg

Potsdam

5

273

Luckenwalde

2

Wittenberg

E51

Wolfen

Bitterfeld

7

Delitzsch

E49

Halle

E26 E55

Nauen

Havel

5

102

Brandenburg

E30

246

184 Zerbst

Dessau

Köthen

185

Rathenow

188

Genthin

Burg

71

Bernburg

Aschersleben

6

Stendal

Tangermünde

681

Magdeburg

E30

Quedlinburg

80

Salzwedel

Gardelegen

71

Mittelland Kanal

81

79

6

Thale

Nordhausen

Elbe

Halberstadt

Wernigerode

18

FORMER BORDER
BETWEEN EAST AND
WEST GERMANY

ick was an aesthetic ruler, and he clearly fell for the sheer beauty of a sleepy township lost among the hills, meadows, and lakes of this rural corner of mighty Prussia. Frederick's father, Friedrich Wilhelm I, had established the Prussian court at Potsdam, but the royal castle didn't match the demanding tastes of his son and heir, who built a summer palace of his own amid green lawns above the Havel River. He called it "Sanssouci," meaning "without a care" in the French language he cultivated in his own private circle and within the court. Designed by Georg Wenzeslaus von Knobelsdorff, Sanssouci became one of Germany's greatest tourist attractions (5 million visitors a year file through the palace and grounds).

As you walk through Potsdam's own **Brandenburger Tor** (a victory arch built 25 years after Sanssouci) and on past the Grünes Gitter, the main entrance, at Platz der Nationen, you will see the Hohenzollern palace complex, contained in a beautifully landscaped park. One of the most important European royal residences of its time, it is today largely re-created. Just weeks before the end of World War II, Potsdam was razed by British bombing, and the battle for Berlin finished it off. The East Germans did a magnificent restoration job. There is no charge to enter the grounds. It's recommended that you purchase the excellent map of the park sold at the Grünes Gitter; it's easy to get lost in this huge complex without it.

The vine-covered terraces on which **Sanssouci** stands are actually an artificial hill, rising in majestic steps from a side stream of the Havel. Executed according to Frederick's impeccable, French-influenced taste, the palace is extravagantly Rococo, with scarcely a patch of wall left unadorned. Strangely, Frederick occupied only five rooms; of these, his bedroom, study, and circular library (beautifully paneled with cedar wood) can be visited. Five rooms were kept for guests, one exclusively reserved for the French writer and philosopher Voltaire. Johann Sebastian Bach was also a welcome visitor; he and Frederick, a competent musician, performed together in the palace music chamber, considered one of Germany's finest Rococo interiors. To the west of the palace are the **Neue Kammern** (New Chambers), 1747, which housed guests of the king's family; originally it functioned as a greenhouse until it was remodeled in 1771–74. Just east of Sanssouci palace is the **Picture Gallery** (1755–63), which still displays Frederick's collection of 17th-century Italian, Flemish, and Dutch paintings, including Cavaggio's *Doubting Thomas*. Frederick opened the gallery to the public, creating the first museum of its kind in Germany.

At the end of the long, straight avenue that runs through Sanssouci Park you'll see a much larger and grander palace, the **Neues Palais** (New Palace). Frederick loosened the pursestrings in building this palace after the Seven Years' War (1756–63), and it is said that he wanted to demonstrate to his subjects that the state coffers hadn't been depleted too severely by the long conflict. Frederick rarely stayed here, however, preferring the relative coziness of Sanssouci. Still, the Neues Palais has much of interest, including an indoor grotto hall, a Jules Verne–like extravaganza of walls and columns set with shells, coral, and other aquatic decoration. There's a fascinating collection of musical instruments, which includes a 900-year-old portable organ; the Upper Gallery, which contains paintings by 17th-century Italian masters; and a recently restored bijou court theater in which performances are still given throughout the year by Potsdam's Hans Otto Theater.

After Frederick died in 1786 (he is buried on the terrace of Sanssouci Palace), the ambitious Sanssouci building program ground to a halt and the park fell into neglect. It was 50 years before another Prussian king, Frederick William III, restored Sanssouci's earlier glory. He engaged the great Berlin architect Karl Friedrich Schinkel to build a small palace for the crown prince. The result is the **Schloss Charlottenhof,** set in its own grounds in the southern part of Sanssouci Park. Schinkel gave it a classical, almost Roman appearance, and he let his imagination loose in the interior, too—decorating one of the rooms as a Roman tent, with its walls and ceiling draped in striped canvas.

Just north of the Schloss Charlottenhof, on the path back to Sanssouci, you'll find two other later additions to the park: Friedrich Wilhelm II's **Römische Bäder** (Roman Baths), 1836, and a **teahouse** built in 1757 in the Chinese style, which was all the rage at the time. Between the Neues Palais and the Sanssouci is the **Orangerie** (completed in 1860), which, with two massive towers (one of which is open, providing a splendid view) linked by a colonnade, evokes an Italian Renaissance palace. Today it houses 47 copies of paintings by Raphael. Elsewhere in the park, a delicious layercake **"mosque"** disguises pump works that operated the fountains in Sanssouci Park; the minaret concealed the chimney. The Italianate **Friedenskirche** (Peace Church, 1845–48) houses a 12th-century Byzantine mosaic taken from an island near Venice. The **Belvedere,** an 18th-century tower near the **Drachenhaus** (*see* Time Out, *below*), was scheduled to be restored by April 1994 and should provide stupendous vistas of the entire complex.

Time Out Halfway up the park's Drachenberg hill, above the Orangery, stands the curious **Drachenhaus** (Dragon House), modeled in 1770 after the Pagoda at London's Kew Gardens and named for the gargoyles ornamenting the roof corners. When built, it served as the residence of the palace vintner; it now houses a popular café.

Another corner of Potsdam—about five minutes by car from Sanssouci—is equally exotic. Resembling a rambling, half-timbered country manor house, the **Schloss Cecilienhof** was built for Crown Prince Wilhelm in 1913 in a newly laid out stretch of park bordering the Heiliger See, called the New Garden. It was here that the Allied leaders Truman, Atlee, and Stalin hammered out the fate of postwar Germany at the 1945 Potsdam Conference. You can see the round table where they held their meetings; in fact, you can stay the night under the roof where they gathered to make history, for the Cecilienhof is today a very comfortable hotel (*see* Lodging, *below*). Also in the New Garden is the substantial two-story **Marmorpalais** (Marble Palace), completed in 1792, using gray-white Silesian marble to ornament the red brickwork. Formerly housing a military museum, it is closed for restoration until 2000. *Information Center, Sanssouci: tel. 0331/22051. Open Apr.–Oct., daily 9–5. Schloss Sanssouci admission (guided tours only): DM 6 adults, DM 3 children. Open Apr.–mid-Oct., daily 9–5; mid-Oct.–Jan. 9–3; Feb. and Mar., daily 9–4; closed first and third Mon. of month. Neue Kammern admission (guided tours*

*only): DM 4 adults, DM 2 children. Open Sat.–Thurs. 9–5.
Picture Gallery admission: DM 2 adults, DM 1 children. Open
mid-May–mid-Oct., daily 9–5, closed fourth Wed. of month.
Neues Palais admission with tour: DM 6 adults, DM 3 children. Open Apr.–mid-Oct., daily 9–5; mid-Oct.–Mar., daily
9–3; closed second and fourth Mon. of month. Schloss
Charlottenhof admission (guided tours only): DM 4 adults,
DM 2 children. Open mid-May–mid-Oct., daily 9–5; closed
fourth Mon. of month. Römische Bäder admission free. Open
mid-May–mid-Oct., daily 9–5; closed third Mon. of month.
Chinese teahouse admission: DM 2. Open mid-May–mid-Oct.,
daily 9–5; closed one Mon. a month. Orangerie admission (additional charge for special exhibitions): DM 4 adults, DM 2
children. Open mid-May–mid-Oct., daily 9–5; closed fourth
Thurs. of month. Mosque admission: DM 3. Open mid-May–
mid-Oct., daily 9–5; closed fourth Mon. in month. Schloss
Cecilienhof admission (nonguests): DM 3 adults, DM 1.50
children. Open daily 9–5, closed second and fourth Mon. of
month.*

Don't leave Potsdam without looking over the town itself,
which still retains the imperial character lent to it by the many
years it served as royal residence and garrison quarters. The
central market square, the **Alter Markt,** sums it all up: the
stately, domed **Nikolaikirche** (1724), a square Baroque church
with classical columns; an **Egyptian obelisk** erected by Schloss
Sanssouci architect Georg von Knobelsdorff; and the officious
facade of the former city hall (1755), now the Haus Marchi-
witza, with a gilded figure of Atlas atop the tower. Wander
around some of the adjacent streets, particularly Wilhelm-
Külz-Strasse, to admire the handsome restored burghers'
houses.

Three blocks north of the Alter Markt is the **Holländisches
Viertel,** built by Friedrich Wilhelm I in 1732 to induce Dutch
artisans to settle in a city that needed migrant labor to support
its rapid growth. (Few Dutch came, and the gabled, hip-roofed
brick houses were used mostly to house staff.) The Dutch government has promised to finance some of the cost of repairing
the damage done by more than four decades of communist administration.

Dining

Am Stadttor. A five-minute walk from the Schloss Sanssouci
and located on Potsdam's main shopping street, the Stadttor is
the ideal spot for lunch. The menu isn't exactly imperial Prussian, but the dishes are filling and inexpensive. The soups are
particularly wholesome, and the Berlin-style liver is as good as
any you'll find in the city. The place is popular, so it's advisable
to book a table. *Brandenburgerstrasse 1–3, tel. 0331/21729.
Reservations advised. Dress: informal. No credit cards. Inexpensive.*

Lodging

Schloss Cecilienhof. This Tudor country-style mansion is
where Truman, Atlee, and Stalin drew up the 1945 Potsdam
Agreement. It's here that Truman received the news of the
first successful atom bomb test (July 16, 1945). Given the fateful events that took place here, the hotel rooms are somewhat

mundane, although comfortable and adequately equipped. The Schloss is set in its own parkland bordering the Jungfernsee and is a pleasant stroll from Sanssouci and the city center. *Neuer Garten, tel. 0331/231–4144, fax 0331/22498. 42 rooms with bath or shower. Facilities: sauna, masseur, restaurant. AE, D, MC, V. Moderate.*

Magdeburg

Magdeburg's great Gothic cathedral—Germany's oldest and, some say, the country's finest—is worth the trip from Berlin. Much of the city was rebuilt after the 1945 bombing in the dull utilitarian style favored by the communists, but there are nevertheless corners of the old town where Magdeburg's 1,200-year history still lingers. Apart from the cathedral, the monastery church of Unser Lieben Frauen contains much of interest. Both are a few strides from the Elbe River, where some fine walks open up through the wooded Kulturpark.

Important Addresses and Numbers

Tourist Information The tourist office is **Information-Magdeburg** (Alter Markt 9, Postfach 266, Magdeburg 3010; tel. 0391/31667). It's open weekdays 10–6, Saturday 8–11. The tourist office can make reservations for accommodations; call 0391/35362.

Emergencies **Police:** tel. 0391/4370. **Ambulance:** tel. 0391/115. **Doctors, dentists, and late-night pharmacies:** tel. 0391/51176. **Medical emergencies:** Poliklinik Mitte, Tränsberg 21–23m, tel. 0391/51176.

Getting There

By Car Magdeburg is located just off the E–8 motorway, the old transit road connecting Berlin and Hannover. It's 150 kilometers (90 miles) west of Berlin, a 90-minute drive as long as the motorway is clear. (In summer and on weekends, when the E–8 gets crowded, the two-hour train ride from Berlin might be preferable.) To get to the town center follow the signs for Magdeburg-Stadtmitte.

By Train Trains leave approximately every two hours from Bahnhof Zoo in Berlin; the trip takes about two hours.

By Bus Buses leave from the Funkturm bus station in Berlin.

Guided Tours

There are no guided tours of Magdeburg originating in Berlin. The Magdeburg tourist office (*see above*) offers daily two-hour bus tours of the town, leaving at 11 AM. Cost: DM 4.

Exploring Magdeburg

If you arrive in Magdeburg by train or bus, head east from the main railway station (the bus depot is beside it) for two blocks to the city center, the **Alter Markt,** which is dominated from the west side by the 17th-century **Rathaus** (City Hall), one of Magdeburg's few remaining Baroque buildings. In front of its arcaded facade is a 1966 bronze copy of Germany's oldest equestrian statue, the **Magdeburger Reiter,** completed by an unknown master in about 1240. The sandstone original is now in the nearby **Kulturhistorisches Museum,** where you can also see the simple invention with which the 17th-century scientist Otto von Güricke proved the extraordinary power created by a vacuum. The device consisted of just two iron cups; von Güricke sealed them together by pumping out the air—and then attached the hollow sphere to two teams of eight cart-horses, which were urged to pull the cups apart. The vacuum proved stronger. *Otto-von Güricke-Strasse 68–73. Admission: DM 1 adults, 50 pf. children. Open Tues.–Sun. 10–6.*

Head down Breiter Weg; to your left you'll see the mighty twin towers of Magdeburg's Gothic **Dom** (cathedral) of saints Maurice and Catherine rearing up above the rooftops. Opposite the post office on Breiter Weg turn left into Domplatz, and there is the soaring west front of the cathedral before you. The awesome structure was begun in 1209, making it the oldest Gothic church in Germany; it was completed in 1520. The founder of the Holy Roman Empire, Otto I, lies buried beneath the choir, his tomb overshadowed by graceful columns of Ravenna marble. Study the representations of famous Christian martyrs on the walls of the nave; you'll find them all standing determinedly on the heads of their persecutors (that's Nero under the heel of St. Paul). A more recent memorial is Expressionist artist Ernst Barlach's sculptured group warning of the horrors of war. It was removed by the Nazis in 1933, but it's back with all its original force. *Open Mon.–Sat. 10–noon and 2–4; Sun. 2–4. Guided tours: Mon.–Sat. 10 and 2, Sun 11:15 and 2.*

Just north of Domplatz and on the way back to the city center is Magdeburg's second great attraction, the Romanesque monastery church and cloisters of **Unser Lieben Frauen.** The church, built in the years 1064–1230, now serves as a concert hall and an art gallery. Gothic sculptures share space with modern East German works in sober surroundings that encourage meditation and reflection—there's also a café for more mundane requirements. *Regierungsstr. 4–6, tel. 0391/33741 (concert information). Open Tues.–Sun. 10–6.*

Dining

Herrenkrug. This charming restaurant set in English-style gardens on the grounds of Herrenkrug Park specializes in typical German cooking with a nouvelle cuisine accent. Try the delicious liver cooked with apple rather than the *Eisbein* (pigs' knuckles) and sauerkraut. A variety of fruit with ice cream is a good way to end the meal. *Herrenkrugstr. 194, tel. 0391/554118. Reservations advised. Dress: informal but neat. AE, DC, MC, V. Expensive.*

Zum Alten Dessauer. Locals favor this popular eating haunt, known in the area for its reliable German dishes. Here you can find juicy *Schnitzel* with sauerkraut and *Bratkartoffeln* (roast potatoes); for dessert, order *Rote Grütze* (red summer fruit), cooked and topped with vanilla sauce. *Breiteweg 250, tel. 0391/30150. Reservations not required. Dress: informal. No credit cards. Moderate.*

Lodging

Hotel International. Magdeburg's leading hotel is typically East German postwar modern, but it has all the necessary facilities and comforts and is centrally located. Rooms are function-

al and uninspired in their decoration; if you're looking for space
and above-average comfort, then reserve a suite apartment
(DM 300 or more). *Otto-von-Güricke-Strasse 2, tel. 0391/554–
140. 331 rooms and 9 suites with bath or shower. Facilities: sauna, garage, 3 restaurants, café, bar, nightclub. AE, DC, MC,
V. Expensive.*

Grüner Baum. This is one of the few hotels in eastern Germany
to have remained in private hands throughout the years of communist state control. At press time, there were plans to give it a
long-overdue renovation, so call beforehand to check on the
availability of rooms. The rooms are large, and it's to be hoped
they'll stay that way after refurbishing, which will give each
room a private bathroom. *Wilhelm-Pieck-Allee 40, tel. 0391/
30862. 40 rooms, none with bath (bathrooms are on each floor).
No credit cards. Inexpensive.*

Excursions from Magdeburg Magdeburg is an ideal center from which to explore the Elbe
River countryside between the Harz Mountains and the Bran-
denburg plains. The Reisebüro (tourist office), near the main
railway station (Wilhelm-Pieck-Allee 14), offers bus tours of
the region. Ships of the eastern German shipping line Weisse
Flotte (tel. 0391/3780) embark from Magdeburg on day trips
and longer cruises on the Elbe.

Luxury cruises from Magdeburg to Bad Schandau (south of
Dresden) and Vanov (near Prague, Czech Republic) are operated by the KD German Rhine Line, with ports of call that include Wittenberg, Meissen, and Dresden. For information,
contact the company in the United States (tel. 914/948–3600 or
415/392–8817) or in Köln (tel. 0221/20880).

Southwest of Magdeburg is a group of historic old towns easily
reached by train or car. From Magdeburg, Route 81 goes 53 kilometers (33 miles) to **Halberstadt,** the gateway to the Harz
Mountain area to the south. One of the key commercial and religious centers of the Middle Ages, about 85% of Halberstadt
was destroyed in April 1945. Rebuilding has left some remarkable contrasts: Half-timbered 17th-century houses stand
alongside stark modern blocks. Dominating the town, the twin-
towered cathedral is one of the most noteworthy examples of
German Gothic, completed in 1491 after 252 years of construction. Inside, note the tapestries and sculptures, the stained-
glass windows, and the numerous ancient burial tombs.

Time Out Just south of Halberstadt, the **Jagdschloss Spiegelberger,** a Baroque hunting lodge dating from 1782, now houses a pleasant
country restaurant. In the basement is the "great wine cask," a
huge wooden barrel constructed in 1594 and holding 132,760 liters (35,080 gallons) of wine.

Heading south on Route 81, look for the turnoff to the right
about 9 kilometers (5½ miles), marked for Wernigerode, which
is another 14 kilometers (9 miles) along. **Wernigerode** is a colorful small city of half-timbered houses from the Middle Ages,
watched over by the castle atop the nearby Agnesberg Hill.
The castle was last rebuilt in 1862–85, but parts date from the
1670s and even earlier. Today the Feudalism Museum occupies
37 of its rooms. *Tel. 03943/23303. Admission: DM 6. Open
Tues.–Sun. 9–5.*

The 1899 vintage **Harzquerbahn,** a fascinating narrow-gauge
railway line mostly using steam power, starts from Wernige-

rode on its three-hour, 60-kilometer (37½-mile) run through the northern Harz Mountain area to Nordhausen. *Tel. 03943/ 32085. Wernigerode-Nordhausen trip cost: DM 14.*

From Wernigerode, a scenic drive winds south about 10 kilometers (6 miles) to Elbingerode, then west about 15 kilometers (9 miles) to Blankenburg. Just south of the town, a road cuts east 8 kilometers (5 miles) to **Thale**, site of the renowned **Hexentanzplatz** (Witches' Dancing Place). This rock plateau, with an elevation of 454 meters (1,475 feet), can be reached year-round by a four-minute cable-car ride from the Hubertusbrücke in Bodetal. From the top there's a splendid view out over the neighboring countryside.

Fifteen kilometers (9 miles) beyond Thale is **Quedlinburg**, known for its picturesque half-timbered houses and detailed carved-wood ornamentation. Wander around the town to enjoy the medieval houses, taking special note of the two-story **Rathaus** (City Hall), completed in 1615, its ornate stone front entry dramatically punctuating the Renaissance facade. From 966 to 1802, the castle atop the **Schlossberg** hill was the official residence of the Abbess of Quedlinburg Abbey; adjacent is the 12th-century Romanesque St. Servatius abbey church. The castle today houses a museum of local history.

Return to Berlin via Route 6 to Bernburg and then Route 71/ E49 north to Magdeburg, where you can pick up the E30.

5 Saxony and Thuringia

Including Leipzig, Dresden, and Weimar

To those familiar with eastern Germany—the former German Democratic Republic—the name may still conjure up images of dour landscapes and grim industrial cities. This image cannot be changed overnight, even with the collapse of the communist government. It will take years before the polluted, dying forests in the south can rejuvenate, and the ancient soot-stained factories are replaced. The deteriorating public housing projects of the '50s and '60s cannot be razed any more than the acrid smell of brown coal smoke can be eliminated overnight. But the small towns of eastern Germany—in regions once known as Prussia, Saxony, Thuringia—will tell much more about an older Germany than the frenetic lifestyles of Frankfurt, Hamburg, Stuttgart, or Köln. The communist influence—hard-line as it was—here never penetrated as deeply as did the American impact on West Germany. East Germany clung to its German heritage, proudly preserving connections with such national heroes as Luther, Goethe, Schiller, Bach, Handel, Hungarian-born Liszt, and Wagner. And although bombing raids during World War II devastated most of its cities, the East Germans, over the years, carried out an extensive program of restoring and rebuilding the historic neighborhoods. Meissen porcelain, Frederick the Great's palace at Potsdam, the astounding collections of the Pergamon and Bode museums in Berlin, and those in the Zwinger in Dresden will now be incorporated in the total national heritage.

Traditional tourist sights aside, eastern Germany is also worth visiting precisely because it *is* in transition, poised at a remarkable moment in history. In the wake of ebullient newspaper headlines and photographs of wild parties amid the rubble of the Berlin Wall, it's all too easy to simplify what's going on in the former GDR as a quest for Western-style democracy. The initiative for unification came as much from the West as it did from the East, and former East Germans have not been altogether happy with the consequences. Though they enjoyed the highest standard of living of all the Eastern Bloc countries, a number of eastern Germans still see their western compatriots as the "haves," and themselves as the "have-nots."

These people, bound politically and economically to the Soviet Union for 45 years, are still uncomfortable with their newly acquired freedoms and responsibilities. For most of those years, despite being communism's "Western front," the GDR was isolated from Western ideas, and many now resent the less savory elements of Western society imposed on what was an orderly, if unexciting, way of life. Time has not stood still east of the former border, but it has taken much less of a toll than it has in the West; the rampant commercial overdevelopment that has blighted much of Germany's western landscape is virtually unknown in the eastern part of the country. As one former East Berliner noted following her first visit to the western sector of the city, "The lights are brighter, so you can see the trash more readily."

The main differences for travelers are the absence of a border, no need to change currencies, and—regrettably—higher prices. But the most important change is that visitors now have complete freedom to go wherever they want, to choose their own hotels, and to wander off the "transit corridors" and explore eastern Germany at will.

Essential Information

At press time, the former German Democratic Republic—the "new federal states," or "eastern Germany"—was still in a state of flux, particularly in those areas most likely to affect visitors. The transportation and communications systems of the two halves of a country so long divided have to be completely integrated, and that will take time. Former state-run hotels are passing into private ownership and hundreds of others are being built to accommodate the surge of tourists and business travelers who followed the fall of the Berlin Wall and the opening of the frontiers.

The upheaval reaches down to the smallest concerns of everyday life, with prices rising to match those in western Germany. Travelers who remember East Germany as a low-budget paradise will be disappointed to find an area nearly as expensive as western Germany, in which the cost of comfortable lodgings has gone through the roof. As this process of price adjustment is still under way, it is difficult to accurately predict costs. Museums and art galleries, for instance, were still converting their old admission charges into the new deutsche mark currency. Telephone exchanges in eastern Germany were also being expanded to accommodate the sudden surge in calls from the former West, and numbers were being altered at a frustrating rate. It's still a hopelessly difficult task to call eastern Germany from western Germany. One tip: If you are calling long-distance, ask the international operator to book an *Eilgespräch* (urgent call). It costs double, but the wait is less than halved.

We have given addresses, telephone numbers, and other logistical details based on the best available information, but remember that changes are taking place at a furious pace in everything from postal codes to street and even city names. We strongly recommend that you contact the German National Tourist Office (*see* Chapter 1) or your travel agent for the most up-to-date information.

Important Addresses and Numbers

Tourist Information
See Important Addresses and Numbers in Chapter 3 for tourist offices in Berlin. For tourist information for individual cities, contact:

Chemnitz: Strasse der Nationen 3, tel. 0371/6620.
Dessau: Friedrich-Naumann-Str. 12, tel. 0340/822–138.
Dresden: Box 201, Pragerstr. 10/11, tel. 0351/495–5025.
Eisenach: Bahnhofstr. 3–5, tel. 03691/58428.
Erfurt: Bahnhofstr. 37, tel. 0361/26267.
Freiberg: Weingasse 9.
Gera: Dr.-Rudolf Breitscheid-Str. 1, tel. 0365/26432.
Halle: Salzgrafenstrasse 3, tel. 0345/502–528.
Leipzig: Sachsenplatz 1, tel. 0341/79590.
Meissen: Willy-Anker-Strasse 32, tel. 03521/4470.
Weimar: Box 647, Marktstr. 4, tel. 03643/762–342.

Embassies
With the reunification of Germany the embassies of the United States and the United Kingdom in eastern Berlin have been downgraded to the rank of consulates or missions. The **Canadian Embassy** in Bonn (Friedrich-Wilhelmstrasse 18, tel. 0228/231061) is responsible for eastern Germany. The **United States'**

office in eastern Berlin is at Neustädtische Kirchstr. 4–5, tel. 030/238–5174; the **United Kingdom**'s mission is at Unter den Linden 32–34, tel. 030/392–9607.

Travel Agencies **American Express:** Hotel Bellevue, Köpckestr., **Dresden,** 15, tel. 0351/56620; Europäisches Reisebüro, Katherinenstrasse, **Leipzig,** tel. 0341/79210.

Car Rental

Cars can be rented at all major hotels and at airports. Rental cars can be driven into neighboring countries, including Poland and Czechoslovakia. Rental charges correspond with those in western Germany. All the major international car rental firms are now represented throughout eastern Germany, but don't expect quite the same range of choice in models and reserve well in advance. All major Western credit cards are accepted.

Avis: Karl-Marx-Strasse 264, tel. 030/685–2093, and Schönefeld airport, tel. 030/678–72441, **Eastern Berlin;** Dresden airport, tel. 0351/589–4600, **Dresden;** Leipzig airport, tel. 0341/391–1132, **Leipzig.**

Hertz: Behrens-Str. 23 (opposite Grand Hotel), tel. 030/200–2012, and Herzbergstr, 40–43, tel. 030/559–6164, **Eastern Berlin;** Köpckestr. 15 (in Hotel Bellevue), tel. 0351/584–169, Tiergartenstr. 94, tel. 0351/232–8218, and Dresden airport, tel. 0351/584–169, **Dresden;** Platz der Republik 2 (in Hotel Astoria), tel. 0341/722–4701, and Leipzig airport, tel. 034204/3026 or 034204/4188, **Leipzig.**

InterRent-Europcar: Rosa-Luxemburg-Str. 2, tel. 030/246–3209, Siegfriedstr. 49–60, Lichtenberg, tel. 030/558–9825, and Schönefeld airport, tel. 030/687–8059, **Eastern Berlin;** Liebstadterstr. 5, tel. 0351/232–3399, and Dresden airport, tel. 03751/589–4590, **Dresden;** Johannisplatz 14, tel. 0341/718–9300, and Leipzig airport, 03741/224–1820, **Leipzig.**

Sixt-Budget: Friedrichstrasse 150–153, tel. 030/242–5201, and Schönefeld airport, tel. 030/678–2608, **Eastern Berlin;** An der Frauenkirche 5 (in Hotel Dresdner Hof), tel. 0351/484–1696, Pragerstr. (in Hotel Newa) tel. 0351/496–7112 and Dresden airport, tel. 0351/589–4570, **Dresden;** Gerberstr 15 (in Hotel Merkur), tel. 0341/799–1149, and Leipzig airport, tel. 0341/224–1868, **Leipzig.**

Arriving and Departing by Plane

Berlin's **Tegel** airport is only 6 kilometers (4 miles) from downtown; eastern Berlin's **Schönefeld** airport lies about 24 kilometers (15 miles) outside the downtown area. **Dresden Airport** (tel. 0351/589–141) lies about 10 kilometers (6 miles) north of the city. Leipzig's **Schkeuditz** airport is 12 kilometers (8 miles) northwest of the city.

Arriving and Departing by Car and Train

By Car Expressways connect Berlin with Dresden and Leipzig.

By Train International trains stop at Friedrichstrasse or Ostbahnhof stations in eastern Berlin; from there, there is direct service to Dresden, Leipzig, and most towns covered below. Meissen requires a bus connection from the rail line.

Getting Around

By Car Nearly 1,600 kilometers (1,000 miles) of autobahn and 11,300 kilometers (7,000 miles) of secondary roads crisscross eastern Germany. Traffic regulations are strictly enforced, from parking rules to speed limits (130 kph/82 mph on autobahns, 80 kph/50 mph on main roads, and 50 kph/30 mph in towns). The eastern German police have been known to levy fines for the slightest offense, and drinking and driving is particularly forbidden. If not otherwise indicated, cars coming from the right have the right-of-way. On heavily traveled north–south routes, you can avoid some of the trucking by keeping to the roads that run parallel to the autobahn if you don't feel pressed for time.

Gasoline is available at either **Minol** or **Intertank** filling stations, although increasingly now you'll also find the familiar signs of gasoline brands you know. Diesel fuel may not be available at all stations, and unleaded fuel is sold only on expressways and in main towns. On back roads, filling stations may be scarce, so be careful not to let fuel reserves get too low.

By Train East Germany has three types of trains—Express, the fastest, shown as "IEx" or "Ex" in timetables; fast, shown as "D"; and regular/local services indicated with an "E." The Euro-City and InterCity services of the German Federal Railways, the Bundesbahn, are being progressively incorporated into the east German system. The fast categories have varying supplementary fares; local trains do not. Most long- and medium-distance trains have both first- and second-class cars and many have either dining or buffet cars, although these may be joined to the train only from and to specific destinations. First- and second-class sleeping cars and couchettes are available. As rail travel is popular and space is limited, trains are usually full and reservations—make them either via the Reisebüro der DDR or at any major train station—are recommended.

Railway buffs are increasingly welcome, particularly around the narrow-gauge lines in the mountainous south.

By Boat **"White Fleets"** of inland boats, including paddle sidewheelers, ply the Elbe River with their starting point at Dresden, going downstream and on into Czechoslovakia.

The **KD German Rhine Line** is now operating two luxury cruises in both directions on the Elbe River from May to October: a five-day voyage from Bad Schandau (south of Dresden) to Magdeburg, and a seven-day journey from Bad Schandau to Hamburg. Ports of call include Dresden, Meissen, and Wittenberg. From April to October, cruises run between Bad Schandau and Vanov, Czechoslovakia, near Prague, and between Magdeburg and Vanov. The cruises, aboard new modern power vessels, are in great demand, so reservations should be made several months in advance. For details of the cruises, contact the company in the United States at 170 Hamilton Avenue, White Plains, New York 10601–1788, tel. 914/948–3600, and at 323 Geary Street, San Francisco, California 94102–1860, tel. 415/392–8817; in Germany contact Köln-Düsseldorfer Deutsche Rheinschiffahrt AG, Frankenwerft 15, 5000–Köln 1, tel. 0221/20880.

By Bus Long-distance bus services link Frankfurt with Dresden and Leipzig. Within Saxony and Thuringia, most areas are accessible by bus, but service is infrequent, and mainly serves to connect with rail lines. Check schedules carefully.

Guided Tours

Information on travel and tours to and around eastern Germany is available from most travel agents. Most Berlin tourist offices carry brochures about travel in eastern Germany. For information about guided tours around the region, contact **Berolina Berlin-Service** (Meinekestr. 3, 1000 Berlin 15, tel. 030/882–2091) or **DER Deutsches Reisebüro Gmbh** (Augsburger Str. 27, 1000 Berlin 30, tel. 030/21–99–8100).

Exploring Saxony and Thuringia

Highlights for First-Time Visitors

Buchenwald (*see* Tour 2)
Erfurt (*see* Tour 2)
Schiller and Goethe houses, Weimar (*see* Tour 2)
Thomaskirche and Nikolaikirche, Leipzig (*see* Tour 1)
Waltburg Castle, Eisenach (*see* Tour 2)
Zwinger Palace, Dresden (*see* Tour 2)

Tour 1: Dessau to Leipzig

Numbers in the margin correspond to points of interest on the Eastern Germany map.

The southern districts of Germany—Thuringia and Saxony—represent the old Germany of medieval times, and as you travel these regions, you'll see ample evidence of the grandeur of the past, although much has been rebuilt to replace war damage. Alas, you'll also see the ongoing (and just as devastating) damage of a modern industrial society: landscape scarred by coal pits around Leipzig, chemical pollution in the air around Bitterfeld and Wolfen north of Leipzig, and to the southeast thousands of acres of woodland destroyed by that pollution. South of Dresden, as the Elbe River leaves its broad valley, it passes through a region of dramatic narrow channels confined by stone mountains, almost like a miniature Grand Canyon. To the south, the *Erzgebirge,* or ore mountains, form a natural boundary with Czechoslovakia.

Leaving Berlin, go south on the E-51, marked for Leipzig. About 120 kilometers (75 miles) from Berlin, you'll pass **❶ Dessau,** a name known to every student of modern architecture. Here the architect Walter Gropius in 1925–26 set up his Bauhaus school of design, probably the most widespread influence on 20th-century architecture and decorative arts. Gropius's concept was to simplify design to allow mechanized construction; 316 villas in the Törten section of the city were built in the '20s using his ideas and methods. Stop to view the refurbished Bauhaus building; this was the fountainhead of ideas that has determined the appearance of cities such as New York and Chicago. Still used as an architecture school, the building can be

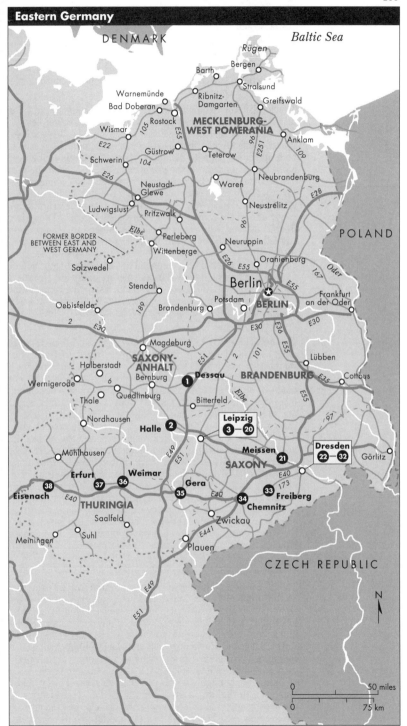

Eastern Germany

visited weekdays 10–5, and exhibits are also open weekends 10–12:30 and 2–5.

For a contrast to the no-nonsense Bauhaus architecture, look at Dessau's older buildings, including St. George's church, built in 1712 in Dutch Baroque style, or the 18th-century late-Baroque **Schloss Mosigkau,** 9 kilometers (5½ miles) southwest of Dessau, now a museum.

Try to visit the exquisite mid-18th-century country palace in late afternoon or early evening, when the setting sun lends a warm glow to the biscuit-colored facades of the three wings. Prince Leopold of Anhalt-Dessau commissioned the palace to be built for his favorite daughter, Anna Wilhelmine. She lived alone at the palace, for she never married, and when she died she left the property to an order of nuns. They immediately tore up the formal grounds to make an English-style park, and after a post–World War II attempt to restore the original Baroque appearance, money and enthusiasm ran out. The palace itself, however, was always well maintained, and the present custodians are so concerned about its preservation that you'll be asked to put on felt slippers on your tour of its rooms. Only about one-quarter of the rooms can be visited, but they include one of Germany's very few Baroque picture galleries. Its stucco ceiling is a marvel of Rococo decoration, a swirling composition of pastel-colored motifs. *Tel. 0340/831–139. Admission: DM 3 adults, DM 1 children. Open May–Oct., daily 9–6; Nov.–Apr., daily 10–2:30.*

The autobahn E51 branches left and right 40 kilometers (25 miles) south of Dessau: left to Leipzig, right to **Halle.** The temptation is to turn left and ignore Halle, particularly if you're in a hurry. The 1,000-year-old city, built on the salt trade, is one of eastern Germany's worst examples of communist urban planning, with a hastily built residential area whose name, Halle-Neustadt, has been shortened cynically by the locals to "Hanoi." But if you have the time, Halle is worth a visit, if only to view its fine central market place, the **Markt,** its northern side bristling with five distinctive, sharp-steepled towers. Four of them (two connected by a catwalk bridge) belong to the late-Gothic **Marienkirche** (St. Mary's Church), completed in 1529, where Martin Luther preached and George Friedrich Händel learned to play the organ. Händel was born in Halle in 1685, and you'll find several memorials to the great composer in and around the city. The house where he was born, the **Händelhaus,** is a few steps away from the Markt, at Grosse Nikolaistrasse 5–6. It's now a Händel museum. *Tel. 05201/ 24606. Admission: DM 2 adults, DM 1 children. Open Tues., Wed., and Fri.–Sun. 9:30–5:30; Thurs. 9:30–7.*

The fifth tower on the Markt is the celebrated Roter Turm (Red Tower), built between 1418 and 1506 as an expression of the city's power and wealth; it houses a bell carillon. The tower looks a bit incongruous against the backdrop of modern Halle, like an elaborate sandcastle stranded by the tide. Between the Roter Turm and Marienkirche is the **Marktschlösschen,** a late-Renaissance structure now serving as a gallery. On the northwest edge of the old town is a much more traditional expression of Halle's early might (which vanished with the Thirty Years' War), the **Moritzburg,** a castle built in the late-15th century by the archbishop of Magdeburg after he had claimed the city for his archdiocese. The castle is a typical late-Gothic fortress, with a sturdy round tower at each of its four corners and a dry moat. There's a cloisterlike peace in the central courtyard today, quite a contrast to the years when one army of occupation followed another with bloody regularity. In prewar years, the castle contained a leading gallery of German Expressionist paintings, which were ripped from the walls by the Nazis and condemned as "degenerate." Some of the works so disdained by the Nazis are back in place, together with some outstanding late-19th and early 20th-century art. You'll find Rodin's famous sculpture *The Kiss* here. *Staatliche Galerie Moritzburg, Friedemann-Bach-Platz 5, tel. 0345/37031. Admission: DM 2 adults, DM 1 children. Open Wed.–Sun. 10–1 and 2–6, Tues. 2–9.*

Some 200 yards southeast of the Moritzburg is Halle's cathedral, the **Dom,** an early Gothic church whose nave and side aisles are of equal height. The nearby former Episcopal residence, the 16th-century **Neue Residenz,** now houses a world-famous collection of fossils dug from brown coal deposits in the Geiseltal Valley near Halle. On the other side of the Saale River (cross the Schiefer bridge to get there) is another interesting museum, the **Halloren- und Salinemuseum,** which traces the history of the salt trade on which early Halle built its prosperity. It includes a full-scale replica of a salt mine, a chilling reminder of the price paid by the working man in centuries past for extracting one of life's necessities from the earth. *Mansfelderstr. 52, tel. 0345/25034. Admission: DM 2 adults, DM 1 children. Open Apr.–Sept., Tues.–Sun. 10–5; Oct.–Mar., Tues.–Sun. 10–4.*

From just outside Halle, take the autobahn 20 kilometers (12½ miles) to **Leipzig.** With a population of about 560,000, this is the second-largest city in eastern Germany (Berlin is the largest) and has long been a center of printing and bookselling. Astride major trade routes, it was an important market town in the Middle Ages, and it continues to be a trading center to this day, thanks to the trade fairs that twice a year (March and September) bring together buyers from the former East and West.

Those familiar with music and German literature will associate Leipzig with the great composer Johann Sebastian Bach (1685–1750), who was organist and choir director at the Thomaskirche (St. Thomas church); with the 19th-century composer Richard Wagner, who was born here in 1813; and with German Romantic poets Goethe and Schiller, both of whom lived and worked in the area.

In 1813 the Battle of the Nations was fought on the city's outskirts, in which Prussian, Austrian, Russian, and Swedish forces stood ground against Napoléon's troops. This battle (the *Völkerschlacht*) was instrumental in leading to the French general's defeat two years later at Waterloo, and thus helped to decide the national boundaries on the map of Europe for the remainder of the century.

Following the devastation of World War II, little is left of old Leipzig. Considerable restoration has been undertaken in the old city, however, and the impression is certainly that of a city with touches of Renaissance character, although some of the newer buildings (notably the university skyscraper tower) distort the perspective and proportions of the old city. Guided bus tours of Leipzig are conducted daily at 10 and 1:30 (from March to mid-October, there's also a tour at 4); tours leave from the information center downtown at Sachsenplatz 1 (tel. 0341/79590).

Numbers in the margin correspond to points of interest on the Leipzig map.

Railroad buffs may want to start their tour of Leipzig at the **Hauptbahnhof,** the main train station. With its 26 platforms, it is the largest in Europe. In 1991 it was expanded to accommodate the anticipated increase in traffic after reunification. But its fin-de-siècle grandness remains, particularly in the staircase that leads majestically up to the platforms. As you climb it, take a look at the great arched ceiling high above you; it's unique among German railway stations.

From the station, cross the broad expanse of the Platz der Republik, crowded with nascent capitalists selling everything from shaving soap to Czech Pilsner beer. Better shopping is to be found in the narrow streets opposite you. Behind them is a characterless square, Sachsenplatz, where you'll find Leipzig's main tourist office, Leipzig Information (open weekdays 9–7, Sat. 9:30–2). Continue south one block, along Katharinenstrasse, passing the "Fregehaus," No. 11, with its fine oriel and steep roof. In two minutes you'll enter Leipzig's showpiece plaza, the city's old market square, the huge **Markt.** One side is completely occupied by the recently restored Renaissance city hall, the **Altes Rathaus Stadtgeschichtliches Museum,** in which Leipzig's past is well documented. *Markt 1, tel. 0341/70921. Admission: DM 2 adults, 50 pf children. Open Tues.–Fri. 10–6, weekends 10–4.*

Starting from all sides of the Markt you'll find small streets that attest to Leipzig's rich trading past, and tucked in among them are glass-roofed arcades of surprising beauty and elegance. Invent a headache and step into the Apotheke at Hainstrasse 9, into surroundings that haven't changed for 100 years or more, redolent of powders and perfumes, home cures, and foreign spices. It's spectacularly Jugendstil, with finely etched and stained glass and rich mahogany. Or make for the antiquarian bookshops of the nearby Neumarkt Passage. Around the corner, on Grimmaischestrasse, is Leipzig's finest arcade, the **Mädlerpassage,** where the ghost of Goethe's Faust lurks in every marbled corner. Here you'll find the famous Auerbachs Keller restaurant, at No. 2, where Goethe set a scene in *Faust* (*see* Dining, *below*). A bronze group of characters from the play, sculpted in 1913, beckons you down the stone staircase to the cellar restaurant. A few yards away down the arcade is a delightful Jugendstil café called Mephisto, decorated in devilish reds and blacks.

Behind Grimmaischestrasse, on Nikolaistrasse, is a church that stands as a symbol of German reunification. It was here, before the undistinguished facade of the **Nikolaikirche,** that thousands of East Germans demanding reform gathered every Monday in the months before the communist regime finally collapsed under the weight of popular pressure. "Wir sind das Volk" ("We are the people") was their chant as they defied official attempts to silence their demands for freedom. In the white and pastel-colored interior of the church, much more impressive than the exterior would lead you to believe, is a soaring Gothic choir and a 16th-century nave, both cloaked in late-

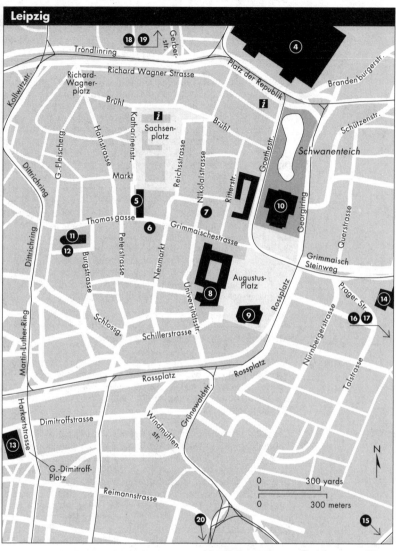

Leipzig

Altes Rathaus
Stadtgeschichtliches
Museum, **5**

Bosehaus, **12**

Botanischer
Garten, **15**

Exhibition
Pavilion, **16**

Gohliser
Schlösschen, **18**

Grassimuseum, **14**

Hauptbahnhof, **4**

Leipzig University
tower, **8**

Mädlerpassage, **6**

Museum der Bildenden
Künste, **13**

Neues Gewandhaus, **9**

Nikolaikirche, **7**

Opera House, **10**

Schiller's House, **19**

Schloss Dölitz, **20**

Thomaskirche, **11**

Völkerschlacht-
denkmal, **17**

18th-century surface decoration. A diamond-patterned ceiling is supported by classical pillars that end in green palm-tree-like flourishes, a curious combination of styles that meld successfully. Luther is said to have preached from the ornate 16th-century pulpit.

⑧ Towering over the Nikolaikirche and every other building in the center of the city is the 470-foot-high **Leipzig University tower,** dubbed the "Jagged Tooth" by some of the young wags who study there. They were largely responsible for changing the official name of the university, replacing the postwar title of Karl Marx University with its original one. In the shadow of the skyscraper, which houses administrative offices and lecture rooms, is the glass and concrete **Neues Gewandhaus,** the ⑨ modernistic home of the Gewandhaus Orchestra, one of Germany's greatest. (Its popular director, Kurt Masur, recently added to his duties the directorship of the New York Philharmonic Orchestra.) In the foyer you can see one of Europe's largest ceiling paintings, a staggering allegorical work devoted to the muse of music by Sighard Gilles, who employed 716 square meters to monumental effect. The statue of Beethoven that stands in the foyer won first prize for sculptor Max Klinger at the World Art Exhibition in Vienna in 1912. The acoustics of the Gewandhaus, by the way, are world renowned, enhancing the resonance of every tone by a full two seconds.

⑩ Opposite the Gewandhaus, on the north side of the Augustus-Platz, is the modern, boxy **Opera House,** the first postwar theater to be built in communist East Germany.

Time Out You'll find several cafés lining Grimmaischestrasse, leading out of the square, but why not buy an ice cream from one of the ubiquitous stands there. The eastern Germans are in love with *Eis* and consume it all year round. The Italian-style ice cream is quite authentic.

⑪ Continue west on Grimmaischestrasse to Thomasgasse and the **Thomaskirche,** the Gothic church where Bach was choirmaster for 27 years and where Martin Luther preached on Whit Sunday, 1539, signaling the arrival of Protestantism in Leipzig. Originally the center of a 13th-century monastery that was rebuilt in the 15th century, the tall church now stands by itself, but the names of adjacent streets recall the cloisters that once surrounded it. While in Leipzig Bach wrote five masses, two Passions, and the Magnificat, and composed most of his cantatas for the church's famous boys' choir, the Thomasknabenchor, which was founded during the 13th century; the church continues as the choir's home as well as a center of Bach tradition. During the Middle Ages, the choir was assembled to sing at every public function—from the installation of bishops to the execution of criminals. Its ranks thinned rapidly when the boys were engaged to sing while plague victims were carted to graves outside the city walls.

Bach's 12 children and the infant Richard Wagner were baptized in the church's early 17th-century font; Karl Marx and Friedrich Engels also stood before this same font, godfathers to Karl Liebknecht, who grew up to be a revolutionary, too!

The great music Bach wrote during his Leipzig years commanded little attention during his lifetime, and when he died he was given a simple grave, without a headstone, in the city's

Spend your
vacation
touring
castles.
Not train
stations.

acation Cars. Vacation Prices. Wherever your destination
Europe, there is sure to be one of more than 1,000 Budget locations nearby.
idget offers considerable values on a wide variety of quality cars, and if
u book before you leave the U.S., you'll save even more with a special
te package from the Budget World Travel Plan.℠ For information and
servations, contact your travel consultant or call Budget in the U.S. at
)0-472-3325. Or, while traveling abroad, call a Budget reservation center.

THE SMART MONEY IS ON BUDGET.®

e feature Ford and other fine cars.   *A system of corporate and licensee owned locations.*

Johannisfriedhof cemetery. It wasn't until 1894 that an effort was made to find where the great composer lay buried, and after a thorough, macabre search his coffin was removed to the cemetery church, the Johanniskirche. The church was destroyed by Allied bombs in December 1943, and Bach found his final resting place in the church he would have selected: the Thomaskirche. It's now a place of pilgrimage for music lovers from all over the world, and his gravestone below the high altar is never without a floral tribute. Fresh flowers also constantly decorate the statue of Bach that stands before the church. *Thomaskirchhof. Admission free. Open daily 9–6.*

⑫ The Bach family home, the **Bosehaus,** still stands, opposite the church, and is now a museum devoted to the life and work of the composer. (The exhibits are in German only; a guide to the museum in English can be purchased in the shop.) Of particular interest is the display of musical instruments dating from Bach's time. *Thomaskirchhof 16, tel. 0341/7866. Admission: DM 2 adults, DM 1 children. Open Tues. Thurs.–Sun. 9–5, Wed. 1 PM–9 PM.*

Time Out Tea time? On the corner of Thomaskirchhof, opposite the church, is the charming **Teehaus** café, offering more varieties of tea than you'd think it was possible to find in eastern Germany. Etched and beveled Jugendstil glass, brass, and dark wood paneling are the perfect complement to the delicate teas, which are served by an enthusiastic staff. *Open daily 10–6.*

From the Thomaskirche, follow Burgstrasse southward, past the 19th-century neo-Gothic monstrosity that now serves as Leipzig's city hall, and you'll come to the city's most outstanding museum, the **Museum der Bildenden Künste,** an art gallery ⑬ of international standard that is especially strong in early German and Dutch painting. The art collection occupies the ground floor of the former Reichsgericht, the court where the Nazis held a show trial against the Bulgarian communist Georgi Dimitroff on a trumped-up charge of masterminding a plot to burn down the Reichstag in 1933. *Georgi-Dimitroff-Platz 1, tel. 0341/2132626. Admission: DM 3 adults, DM 1.50 children. Open Tues. and Thurs.–Sun. 9–5, Wed. 1 PM–9:30 PM.*

Head up Rossplatz and turn right onto the short Grimmaisch ⑭ Steinweg to reach the **Grassimuseum** complex (Johannespl. 5– 11, tel. 0341/21420. Admission: DM 3 adults, DM 1.50 children). It includes the **Museum of Arts and Crafts** (open Tues.–Thurs. 10–6, Wed. 2–10, Fri. 10–1, weekends 10–5), the **Geographical Museum** (open Tues.–Fri. 9:30–5:30, Sat. 10–4, and Sun. 9–1), and the **Musical Instruments Museum** (enter from Täubchenweg 2; open Tues.–Fri. 9–5, Sat. 10–5, and Sun. 10–1).

⑮ The **Botanischer Garten** (Botanical Gardens) is a set of splendid open-air gardens and greenhouses. *Linnestr. 1, tel. 0341/ 282528. Admission: DM 2. Open weekdays 9–4, Sun. 10–4; greenhouses Sun. 10–12:30 and 2–4.*

Still farther out, via streetcar No. 15, 20, 21, or 25, is the ⑯ **Exhibition Pavilion** at Prager Strasse 210. Its main feature is a vast diorama portraying the Battle of the Nations of 1813 (open Tues.–Sun. 9–4). Slightly farther on Prager Strasse is the mas- ⑰ sive **Völkerschlachtdenkmal,** a memorial in the formal park; it, too, commemorates the battle (admission DM 2; open daily 10–5). Rising out of suburban Leipzig like some great Egyptian tomb, the somber, gray pile of granite and concrete is more than 300 feet high. Despite its ugliness, it's well worth a visit if only to wonder at the lengths—and heights—to which the Prussians went to celebrate their military victories, and to take in the view from a windy platform near the top (provided you can also climb the 500 steps to get there). The Prussians did make one concession to Napoléon in designing the monument: A stone marks the spot where he stood during the battle.

Outside of the center of Leipzig but reachable by public transportation (streetcar Nos. 20 and 24, then walk left up Poetenweg, or streetcar No. 6 to Menckestr.) is the delightfully
⑱ Rococo **Gohliser Schlösschen** (Gohliser House), the site of frequent concerts. *Menckestr. 23, tel. 0341/52979.*

⑲ Beyond that is **Schiller's House,** for a time the home of the German poet and dramatist Friedrich Schiller. *Menckestr. 42, tel. 0341/583187. Admission: DM 2 adults, DM 1 children. Open Tues., Wed., Fri., and Sat. 11–5.*

⑳ **Schloss Dölitz** (streetcar No. 22 or 24, walk up Helenstrasse) contains an exhibition of *Zinnfiguren,* historical tin soldiers. *Torhaus, Schloss Dölitz, Helenstr. 24, tel. 0341/323307. Admission: DM 2. Open Wed.–Sun. 10–5.*

Tour 2: Meissen and Dresden

Numbers in the margin correspond to points of interest on the Eastern Germany map.

㉑ Route 6 out of Leipzig will take you to **Meissen,** about 80 kilometers (50 miles) away. This romantic city on the Elbe River is known the world over for its porcelain, bearing the trademark crossed blue swords. The first European porcelain was made in this area in 1708, and in 1710 the royal porcelain manufacturer was established in Meissen, close to the local raw materials.

The story of how porcelain came to be produced in Meissen reads like a German fairy tale: Free-spending Prince August the Strong (ruled 1697–1704, 1710–33) urged alchemists at his court to search for the secret of making gold, which he badly needed to refill a Saxon state treasury depleted by his expensive building projects and extravagant lifestyle. The alchemists failed to produce gold, but one of them, Johann Friedrich Böttger, discovered a method for making something almost as precious: fine hard-paste porcelain. Prince August consigned Böttger and a team of craftsmen to a hilltop castle outside Dresden—Albrechtsburg in Meissen—and set them to work. August hoped to keep their recipe a state secret, but within a few years fine porcelain was being produced by Böttger's method in many parts of Europe.

The porcelain works outgrew their castle workshop in the mid-19th century, and today you'll find them in the town at the foot of the castle mount. There you can see demonstrations of pieces being prepared. In the same building, a museum displays Meissen porcelain, a collection that rivals that of the Porzellansammlung in Dresden. The 18th-century commemoration pieces and figurines are especially fine. Upstairs are the lesser known, 20th-century designs. Not surprisingly, there's a small gift shop on the premises. *Tel. 0351/484-0127. Open Sat.–Wed. 9–5.*

Meissen porcelain is to be found in one form or another all over town. A set of porcelain bells at the late-Gothic **Frauenkirche,** on the beautifully restored central market square, the Marktplatz, was the first of its kind anywhere when installed in 1929; they are rung six times a day. Opposite is the 500-year-old town hall, with three unusual dormers. The largest set of porcelain figures ever crafted can be found in another Meissen church, the **Nikolaikirche,** which also houses remains of early Gothic frescoes. Also of interest in the town center is the 1569 **Old Brewery,** graced by a Renaissance gable; **St. Francis,** now housing a city museum; and **St. Martins,** with its late-Gothic altar.

Time Out Snuggling up to the Frauenkirche is one of Meissen's oldest wine taverns, the **Weinschenke Vinzenz Richter** (Marktplatz 3). Meissen has some of Europe's northernmost and smallest vineyards, producing an excellent white wine. This is the place to try it. *Closed Mon. and Tues.*

It's a bit of a climb up Burgstrasse and Amtsstrasse to the **Albrechtsburg** castle, where the story of Meissen porcelain really began, but the effort is worthwhile. The 15th-century Albrechtsburg is Germany's first truly "residential" castle, a complete break with the earlier style of fortified bastion. It fell into disuse and neglect as nearby Dresden rose to local prominence, but it's still an imposing collection of late-Gothic and Renaissance buildings. In the central courtyard, a typical Gothic *Schutzhof* protected on three sides by high rough-stone walls, is an exterior spiral staircase, **the Wendelstein,** hewn from one massive stone block in 1525, a masterpiece of early masonry. Ceilings of the halls of the castle are richly decorated, although many date only from a restoration in 1870. Adjacent to the castle is a towered early Gothic cathedral, whose west entrance hall contains the graves of Saxon kings with covers designed by Cranach and Dürer that resemble giant etching plates. The sculptures of Otto I and his wife, Adelheid, are considered to be supreme examples of German medieval sculpture. *Tel. 03521/45290. Admission: DM 5. Guided tour: DM 7. Open daily 10–6.*

㉒ Another 20 kilometers (12 miles) southeast on Route 6 will take you to **Dresden.** Splendidly situated on a bend in the Elbe River, Dresden is a compact city easy to explore. In its Rococo yellows and greens, it is enormously appealing, and the effect is even more overwhelming when you compare what you see today—or what Canaletto paintings reflect of a Dresden centuries earlier—with the photographs of Dresden in 1945, after a British bombing raid almost destroyed it overnight. It was one of the architectural and cultural treasures of the civilized world, and the fact that, despite lack of funds and an often uncooperative communist bureacracy, the people of Dresden succeeded in rebuilding it is an enormous tribute to their skills and dedication.

Their efforts restored at least the riverside panorama to the appearance Canaletto would have recognized, but some of the other parts of the city center look halfway between construction and demolition. In the coming years the city will look more like a building site than ever as 20 new hotels are added to provide the accommodations it so desperately needs. Don't think of visiting Dresden without reserving a hotel room well in advance.

Dresden was the capital of Saxony as early as the 15th century, although most of its architectural masterpieces date from the 18th century, when the enlightened Saxon ruler August the Strong and his son, Frederick Augustus II, brought leading Italian and Bavarian architects and designers up from the south. The predominantly Italianate influence is evident today in gloriously overblown Rococo architecture. Streetcar tours leave from Postplatz Tuesday–Sunday at 9, 11, and 1:30; bus tours, leaving from Dr.-Külz-Ring, run on Tuesday, Wednesday, and Thursday, at 11 (call 0351/495–5025 for details).

Numbers in the margin correspond to points of interest on the Dresden map.

The best introduction to Dresden is to arrive by ship (*see* Essential Information, *above*), but for motorists or train passengers, the starting point of a Dresden tour will be the main railway station (which has adequate parking). To reach the old part of the city and its treasures you'll first have to cross a featureless expanse surrounded by postwar high rises, leading into the pedestrians-only Pragerstrasse (the tourist information office is at No. 8). Cross busy Dr.-Külz-Ring and you'll en-

㉓ ter a far different scene, the broad **Altmarkt,** whose colonnaded beauty has managed to survive the disfiguring efforts of city planners to turn it into a huge outdoor parking lot. The church on your right, the Kreuzkirche, is an interesting combination of Baroque and Jugendstil architecture and decoration. A church stood here in the 13th century, but the present structure dates from the late 18th century. (Its Renaissance tower, which can be seen in Canaletto's paintings of Dresden, collapsed in 1765.) The church is home to the famous Kreuzchor (choir of Kreuzkirche). The rebuilt Rathaus is on your left, as is the 18th-century yellow-stucco Landhaus, which contains the Museum für Geschichte der Stadt Dresden (City Historical Museum). The Rococo staircase in the entrance hall is particularly graceful. The museum is currently closed for construction. *Wilsdrufferstr. 2. Admission: DM 2 adults, DM 1 children. Open Mon.–Thurs. and Sat. 10–6.*

At the northern end of the Altmarkt cross Wilsdrufferstrasse (or pause for a window-shopping break on this broad boulevard) into the **Neumarkt** (New Market), which is, despite its name, the historic heart of old Dresden. The ruins on your right are all that remain of Germany's greatest Protestant church after the bombing raid of February 1945. These jagged, precariously tilting walls were once the mighty Baroque

㉔ **Frauenkirche,** so sturdily built that it withstood a three-day bombardment during the Seven Years' War only to fall victim to the flames that followed the World War II raid. Like the Gedächtniskirche in Berlin, the Frauenkirche has been kept in its ruined state as a war memorial, although plans were announced in 1991 to rebuild it as a European cultural center.

㉕ The large, imperial-style building looming behind the Frauenkirche is the famous **Albertinum,** Dresden's leading art museum. It is named after Saxony's King Albert, who between 1884 and 1887 converted a royal arsenal into a suitable setting for the treasures he and his forebears had collected. The upper sto-

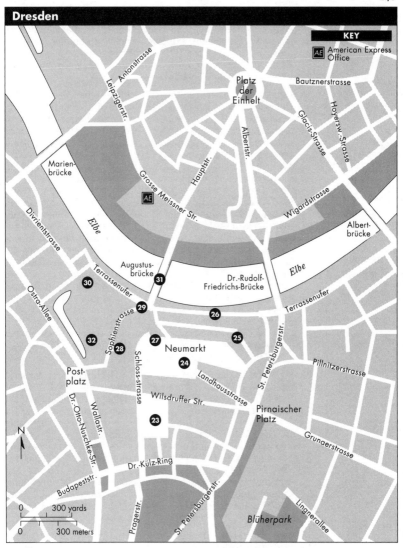

Dresden

KEY

Aᴇ American Express Office

Albertinum, **25**
Altmarkt, **23**
Augustusbrücke, **31**
Brühlsche
Terrasse, **26**
Frauenkirche, **24**
Johanneum, **27**

Katholische
Hofkirche, **29**
Residenzschloss, **28**
Semperoper, **30**
Zwinger, **32**

ry of the Albertinum, accessible from the Brühlsche Terrasse, houses the Gemäldegalerie Neue Meister (Gallery of Modern Masters). Permanent exhibits include outstanding work by German masters of the 19th and 20th centuries (Caspar David Friedrich's haunting *Das Kreuz im Gebirge* is here) and French Impressionists and Post-Impressionists.

Equally impressive is the Grünes Gewölbe (Green Vault). Named after a green room in the palace of August the Strong, this part of the Albertinum (entered from Georg-Treu-Platz) contains an exquisite collection of unique objets d'art fashioned from gold, silver, ivory, amber, and other precious and semi-precious materials. Among the crown jewels is the world's largest "green" diamond, 41 carats in weight, and a dazzling group of tiny gem-studded figures entitled *Hofstaat zu Delhi am Geburtstag des Grossmoguls Aureng-Zeb*. The name gives a false idea of the size of the work, dating from 1708, which represents a birthday gathering at the court of an Indian mogul; some parts of the tableau are so small that they can only be admired through a magnifying glass. Somewhat larger and less delicate is the drinking bowl of Ivan the Terrible, perhaps the most sensational of the treasures to be found in this extraordinary museum. Next door is the Skulpturensammlung (Sculpture Collection), which includes ancient Egyptian and classical works and examples by Giovanni da Bologna and Adriaen de Vries. *Am Neumarkt. Gemäldegalerie Neue Meister, tel. 0351/4955056. Admission: DM 5 adults, DM 2.50 children. Open Tues. and Thurs.–Sun. 9–5, Wed. 9–6. Grünes Gewölbe and Skulpturensammlung admission: DM 5 adults, DM 2.50 children. Open Fri.–Tues. 9–5, Wed. 9–6.*

㉖ If you leave the Albertinum by the **Brühlsche Terrasse** exit you'll find yourself on what was once known as the "Balcony of Europe," a terrace high above the Elbe, carved from a 16th-century stretch of the city fortifications; from the terrace a breathtaking vista of the Elbe and the Dresden skyline opens up. The southern exit of the Albertinum brings you back to the Neumarkt and to another former royal building that now serves

㉗ as a museum, the 16th-century **Johanneum,** once the regal stables. Instead of horses, the Johanneum now houses the Verkehrsmuseum, a collection of historical vehicles, including vintage automobiles and engines. *Neumarkt, tel. 0351/4953002. Admission: DM 4 adults, DM 2 children; half-price admission on Fri. Open Tues.–Sun. 10–5.*

Walk behind the Johanneum and into the former stable exercise yard, enclosed by elegant Renaissance arcades and used in the 16th century as an open-air festival ground. To spare the royalty on horseback the trouble of dismounting before ascending to the upper story to watch the jousting and jollities in the yard below, a ramp was built to accommodate both two- and four-legged guests. (From the top of the ramp you can look down on the ruined royal palace being reconstructed.) You'll find the scene today much as it was centuries ago, complete with jousting markings in the ground. More popular than even jousting in those days was *Ringelstechen*, a risky pursuit in which riders at full gallop had to catch small rings on their lances. Horses and riders often came to grief in the narrow confines of the stableyard.

On the outside wall of the Johanneum is a remarkable example of Meissen porcelain art: a painting on Meissen tiles of a royal

procession, 102 meters (336 feet) long. More than one hundred members of the royal Saxon house of Wettin, half of them on horseback, are represented on the giant jigsaw made up of 25,000 porcelain tiles, painted in 1904–07 after a design by Wilhelm Walther. Follow this unusual procession to the end and
28 you will come to the former royal palace, the **Residenzschloss,** where restoration work is under way behind the fine Renaissance facade. Although the work is expected to last well into the 1990s, some of the finished rooms are hosting historical exhibitions normally housed at the Zwinger (*see below*). The main gate of the palace, the Georgentor, has acquired its original appearance, complete with an enormous statue of the fully armed Saxon Count George, guarding the portal that carries his name. The palace housed August the Strong's Grünes Gewölbe before it was moved in its entirety to the Albertinum. *Sophienstr, tel. 0351/4953056. Admission: DM 5 adults, DM 2.50 children. Open Fri.–Tues. 9–5.*

Next to the Residenzschloss is the largest church in Saxony,
29 the **Katholische Hofkirche,** also known as the Cathedral of St. Trinitas. The son of August the Strong, Frederick Augustus II, (ruled 1733–63) brought architects and builders from Italy to construct a Catholic church in a city that had been the first large center of Lutheran Protestantism. They worked away by stealth, so the story goes, and Dresden's Protestant burgers were presented with a fait accompli when the church was finally consecrated in 1754. Seventy-eight historical and biblical figures decorate the Italian High Baroque facade; the chaste white interior's treasures include a beautiful stone pulpit by the royal sculptor Balthasar Permoser and a 250-year-old church organ said to be one of the finest ever to come from the mountain workshops of the famous Silbermann family. Peek behind the main altar into the two Rococo chapels, with charming illusionistic ceiling paintings and applied gold scroll decoration. In the cathedral's crypt are the tombs of 49 Saxon rulers and a precious vessel containing the heart of August the Strong.

Opposite the cathedral on the Theaterplatz is the restored
30 **Semperoper** (Semper Opera House), justifiably one of Germany's best known and most popular theaters. Richard Wagner's *Rienzi, Der Fliegende Holländer,* and *Tannhäuser,* and Richard Strauss's *Salome, Elektra,* and *Der Rosenkavalier* all premiered here. The masterful Dresden architect Gottfried Semper built the opera house in 1838–41, in Italian Renaissance style, and then saw his work razed in a fire caused by a careless candle lighter. Semper had to flee Dresden because of his participation in a democratic uprising, so his son Manfred rebuilt the theater according to his father's new designs, in the neo-Renaissance style you see today. Even Manfred Semper's version had to be rebuilt, after the devastating bombing raid of February 1945. On the 40th anniversary of that raid—February 13, 1985—the rebuilt Semperoper reopened with a performance of *Der Freischütz* by Carl Maria von Weber, another composer who did so much to make Dresden a leading center of German music and culture. The demand to experience the Semper Opera again in all its glory is enormous, and tickets are difficult to obtain in advance (*see* The Arts and Nightlife, *below*). If you're lucky enough to get in, however, an overwhelming experience awaits you. Even if you're no opera buff, the Semper's lavish interior, predominantly crimson,

white, and gold, can't fail to impress. Marble, velvet, and bro-
cade create an atmosphere of intimate luxury (it seats 1,323),
and the uninterrupted views and flawless acoustics are renowned.

Time Out On the riverbank side of the Theaterplatz you'll see the
pavilionlike **Italienisches Dörfchen,** constructed in 1911–13 on
the site of housing for the Italian workers who erected the
nearby Hofkirche. The café is a perfect spot for taking a break
over a glass of local beer or a pot of coffee.

③① The impressive bridge behind the cathedral, the **Augustusbrücke,** is a rebuilt version of a historic 17th-century bridge
blown up by the SS shortly before the end of World War II. Renamed for the Bulgarian communist accused by the Nazis of in-
stigating the Reichstag fire, Georgi Dimitroff, the restored
bridge, after the fall of communism, has regained its original
name honoring August the Strong.

Back on the Theaterplatz, in the center of the square directly in
front of the opera house, you'll see a proud equestrian statue of
King Johann, who ruled Saxony when Gottfried Semper was at
work. Don't be misled by Johann's confident pose in the sad-
dle—he was terrified of horses and never learned to ride.

The southwestern side of the square is taken up by another
Gottfried Semper creation, the **Sempergalerie,** part of the
③② largely 18th-century **Zwinger** palace complex (tel. 0351/484–
0120). Built by the great architect to house parts of the art collections of the Saxon royal house, it contains the world-re-
nowned Gemäldegalerie Alte Meister (Gallery of Old Masters).
The Zwinger complex also contains the Porzellansammlung
(Porcelain Collection), zoological museum, and Mathematisch-
Physikalischer Salon (displaying old scientific instruments).

Among the priceless paintings in the Sempergalerie collection
are examples by Dürer, Holbein, Jan van Eyck, Rembrandt,
Rubens, van Dyck, Hals, Vermeer, Raphael (*The Sistine Madonna*), Titian, Giorgione, Veronese, Velázquez, Murillo, Canaletto, and Watteau. On the wall of the entrance archway
you'll see an inscription in Russian, one of the few amusing reminders of World War II in Dresden. It reads, in rhyme: "Museum checked. No mines. Chanutin did the checking." Chanutin,
presumably, was the Russian soldier responsible for checking
one of Germany's greatest art galleries for anything more ex-
plosive than a Rubens nude. *Admission: DM 7. Open Tues.–
Sun. 10–6.*

The Sempergalerie forms one side of the fabulous Zwinger, the
pride of Dresden and perhaps one of the greatest examples of
Baroque architecture. There are two entrances to the Zwinger;
the Kronentor (Crown Gate), off of Ostra-Allee, is the one
through which August the Strong and his royal retinue once
paraded. August hired a small army of artists and artisans to
create a "pleasure ground" worthy of the Saxon court, building
it on a section of the original city fortifications (the "Zwinger").
They were placed under the general direction of the architect
Matthäus Daniel Pöppelmann, who was reluctantly called out
of retirement to design what came to be his greatest work,
started in 1707 and completed in 1728. Completely enclosing a
central courtyard, filled with lawns and pools, the complex
comprises six linked pavilions, one of which boasts a carillon of

Meissen, hence its name: Glockenspielpavillon. It's an extraordinary scene, a riot of garlands, nymphs, and other Baroque ornamentation and sculpture on the edge of an urban landscape etched in somber gray. The contrast would have been much greater if Semper had not closed in one side of the Zwinger, which was originally open to the riverbank. Stand in the center of this quiet oasis, where the city's roar is kept at bay by the palatial wings that form the outer framework of the Zwinger, and imagine the scene on summer evenings when August the Strong invited his favored guests to celebrate with him—the wedding, for instance, of his son, Prince Friedrich August, to Maria Joseph, archduchess of Austria. The ornate carriage-style lamps shone, the fountains splashed in the shallow pools, and wide staircases beckoned to galleried walks and the romantic Nymphenbad, a coyly hidden courtyard where nude female statues are protected in alcoves from a fountain that spits unexpectedly at unwary visitors.

The Porzellansammlung, stretching from the curved gallery adjoining the Glockenspielpavillon to the long gallery on the east side, is considered to be one of the best porcelain collections in the world. The focus, naturally, is on Dresden and Meissen china, but there are also outstanding examples of Japanese, Chinese, and Korean porcelain. *Porzellansammlung admission: DM 3 adults, DM 1.50 children. Open Sat.–Thurs. 9–5. Zoological Museum, Mathematisch-Physikalischer Salon admission: DM 3 adults, DM 1.50 children. Open Fri.–Wed. 9:30–5.*

Other less central curiosities in Dresden include the **Armee-museum** (Military Museum), which covers military history predating the German Democratic Republic (Olbrichtplatz, admission DM 1.50, open Tues.–Sun. 9–5); the **BuchMuseum** (Book Museum), which traces the history of books from the Middle Ages to the present (Marienallee 12, admission free, open Mon.–Fri. 9–4 (guided tour Sat. at 2 PM); and the **Deutsches Hygiene-Museum** (German Museum of Health), with historical displays of medical equipment and a unique glass anatomical figure (Lingnerpl. 1, admission DM 3 adults, DM 1.50 children. Open Tues.–Sat. 9–5).

Numbers in the margin correspond to points of interest on the Eastern Germany map.

From Dresden, you can either take the autobahn E40 or, if you have the time, the more scenic road via Freital to **Freiberg**. Once a prosperous silver-mining community, Freiberg is highlighted by two picturesque Gothic town squares, the Upper and Lower Markets. The late-Gothic cathedral, with its Golden Gate of 1230, has a richly decorated interior and a Silbermann organ dating from 1711.

Route 173 continues on via Oederan and Flöha to **Chemnitz** (on older maps, Karl-Marx-Stadt), about 65 kilometers (41 miles) down the E40 from Dresden. In recognition of the labor movement, East German officials renamed the city in 1953 to honor Karl Marx; in 1990 the population, now free to express a choice, overwhelmingly voted to revert to the original name. Badly damaged during World War II, Chemnitz has revived as a center of heavy industry, but it never had the architectural attractions of cities in the area. Stop to see the rebuilt 12th-century **Red Tower** in the center of the city; the **Altes Rathaus** (Old City

Hall), dating from 1496–98, now incorporating a variety of styles following many reconstructions; and the 250-million-year-old petrified tree trunks, unique in Europe, alongside the city museum. Look, too—assuming it's still there—at the massive stylized head of a meditative Karl Marx, sculpted by the Soviet artist Lew Kerbel, in front of the district council building in the new city center. Behind it is the motto, "Working Men of All Countries, Unite!"—in German, Russian, French, and English.

35 Take E40 out of Chemnitz to **Gera,** about 65 kilometers (41 miles) away. Once a princely residence and center of a thriving textile industry, the city has largely been rebuilt after the heavy damage sustained during World War II. Gera has often been compared with old Vienna, although today you have to search long and hard—and even then exercise some imagination—to discover any striking similarities between the German provincial town and the Hapsburg capital. After the combined destruction of a world war and more than four decades of communist mismanagement, some ornate albeit crumbling house facades, however, do betray Gera's rich past, although the palace in which prince-electors once held court was destroyed in the final weeks of the war and never rebuilt. The palace's 16th-century **Orangerie,** though, does still stand, in the former Küchengarten in the suburb of Untermhaus. An imposing semicircular Baroque pavilion, it now houses an art gallery and a separate collection of works by Gera's most famous son, the satirical Expressionist painter Otto Dix (1891–1969). The Dix gallery was renovated in 1991 for the centenary of the painter's birth. *Dimitroffallee 4. Admission free. Open Mon.–Thurs. 10–5, Sat.–Sun. 10–6.*

Don't leave Gera without lingering in the central town square, the Marktplatz, its Renaissance buildings restored with rare (for eastern Germany) care. The 16th-century city hall, the Rathaus, has a vividly decorated entrance. Note the weird angles of the lower-floor windows; they follow the incline of the staircase that winds up the interior of the building's picturesque 57-meter-high (185-foot-high) tower.

Time Out At the city hall's vaulted cellar restaurant, the **Ratskeller,** Gera's medieval past crowds in on you from all sides, with painted scenes on glass partitions and on the gnarled walls themselves. The restaurant is open daily from midmorning until midnight, so it's an ideal place for coffee, lunch, or dinner.

Close by is the Baroque **Regierungsgebäude** (government building), incorporating pieces from an earlier 16th-century building.

36 Take the E40 another 53 kilometers (33 miles) to **Weimar.** Sitting prettily on the Ilm River between the Ettersberg and Vogtland hills, Weimar has a place in German political and cultural history out of all proportion to its size (population: 63,000). It's not even a particularly old city by German standards, with a civic history starting as late as 1410. But by the early 19th century it had become one of Europe's most important cultural centers, where poets Goethe and Schiller were neighbors, Johann Sebastian Bach played the organ for his royal Saxon patrons, Carl Maria von Weber wrote some of his best music, and Liszt was director of music, presenting the first performance of *Lohengrin.* Walter Gropius founded his Staatliches Bauhaus here in 1919, and behind the classical pillars of the National Theater the German National Assembly in 1919–20 drew up the constitution of the Weimar Republic. After the collapse of the ill-fated Weimar government, Hitler chose the unsuspecting little city as the site for the first national congress of his new Nazi Party. On the outskirts of Weimar, the Nazis built—or forced prisoners to build it for them—the infamous Buchenwald concentration camp.

Weimar owes much of its greatness to a woman, the widowed Countess Anna Amalia, whose son Carl August ruled the duchy of Saxony-Weimar, and who went talent-hunting in the late-18th century for cultural figures to decorate the glittering court that her Saxon forebears had set up in the town. Goethe was among them, and he served the countess as a counselor, advising on financial matters and town design. Schiller followed, and the two became valued visitors to the countess's home. Their statues stand today before the **National Theater,** on Theaterplatz, two blocks west of the Markt, the central market square. The famous pair—Goethe with a patronizing hand on the shoulder of the younger Schiller—should be gleaming, having just been restored. The theater, sadly, isn't the one in which Goethe and Schiller produced some of their leading works; the Baroque building became too small to admit the increasing numbers of visitors to Weimar, and it was demolished in 1907 and replaced by a larger one with better technical facilities. That theater was bombed in World War II and rebuilt in its present form in 1948. It reopened with a performance of Goethe's *Faust,* which was written in Weimar.

Adjacent to the National Theater is the surprisingly modest home of Countess Anna Amalia, the **Wittumspalais.** Within this exquisite Baroque house you can see the drawing room where her soirées were held, complete with the original cherrywood table at which the company sat. The east wing of the house contains a small museum that is a fascinating memorial to those cultural gatherings. *For information, call Weimar Classics Foundation, tel. 03643/7670. Admission: DM 3 adults, DM 2 children. Open Tues.–Sun. 9–noon and 1–5.*

Goethe spent 57 years in Weimar, 47 years in the house that has since become a shrine for millions of visitors. The **Goethehaus** is at the entrance of the street called Frauenplan, two blocks south of Theaterplatz. It's now a museum containing a collection of writings that illustrate not only the great man's literary might but his interest in the sciences, particularly medicine, and his administrative skills (and frustrations) as Weimar's exchequer. You'll see the desk at which Goethe stood to write (he liked to work standing up), his classical sculpture collection that fills the rooms, his own paintings (he was an accomplished watercolorist), and the modest bed in which he died. The rooms are dark and often cramped, but an almost palpable intellectual intensity seems to illuminate them. *Frauenplan 1, tel. 03643/5450. Admission: DM 5 adults, DM 3 children. Open Tues.–Sun. 9–5.*

Around the corner from Goethe's house, on a tree-shaded square, is Schiller's sturdy, green-shuttered home, in which he and his family spent a happy, all-too-brief three years (Schiller died there in 1805). Schiller's study was tucked up underneath the mansard roof, a cozy room dominated by his desk, where he probably completed *William Tell*. Much of the remaining furniture and the collection of books were added later, although they all date from around Schiller's time. *Neugasse, tel. 03643/5450. Admission: DM 5 adults, DM 3 children. Mon. and Wed.–Sun. 9–5.*

On the nearby central town square, **Marktplatz,** you'll find another historic Weimar house, the home of the painter Lucas Cranach the Elder, who lived there during his last years, 1552–53. Its wide, imposing facade is richly decorated and bears the coat of arms of the Cranach family. It now houses a modern art gallery.

Around the corner to the left is Weimar's 16th-century **Residenzschloss** (Grand Ducal Palace), with its restored classical staircase, festival hall, and falcon gallery. The tower on the southwest projection dates from the Middle Ages but got its Baroque overlay circa 1730. The castle houses eastern Germany's third-largest art collection, including several fine works by Cranach and many early 20th-century pieces by such artists as Böcklin, Liebermann, and Beckmann. *Tel. 03643/ 61831. Admission: DM 3 adults, DM 2 children. Open Tues.– Sun. 9–noon and 2–5. Closed Tues. Nov.–Mar.*

As in so many East German towns, Weimar's old town center has been reconstructed. Stop by the late-Gothic **Herderkirche,** named after 18th-century theologian and philosopher Johann Gottfried Herder, who was the church's chief pastor. Its large winged altar was started by Lucas Cranach the Elder and finished by his son in 1555. Herder died in 1803 and is buried in the church.

A short walk south, past Goethehaus and across Wieland Platz, takes you to the cemetery where Goethe and Schiller are buried, the **Historischer Friedhof** (Historic Cemetery). Their tombs are in the vault of a classical-style chapel in the leafy cemetery, where virtually every gravestone commemorates a famous citizen of Weimar. The Goethe-Schiller vault can be visited daily (except Tues.) 9–1 and 2–5.

On the other side of the Ilm, amid meadowlike parkland, you'll find Goethe's beloved **Gartenhaus** (Garden House), where he met with his mistresses and wrote much poetry and began his masterpiece *Iphigenie auf Tauris* (admission: DM 3 adults, DM 2 children; open daily 9–noon and 1–5). Goethe is said to have felt very close to nature here, and you can soak up the same rural atmosphere today on footpaths along the peaceful little river, where time seems to have stood still. Just across the river from the Gartenhaus is a generous German tribute to another literary giant, William Shakespeare, a 1904 statue showing him jauntily at ease on a marble plinth and looking remarkably at home in his foreign surroundings.

Just south of the city, the lovely 18th-century yellow **Belvedere Palace** once served as a hunting and pleasure castle; today you'll find a Baroque museum inside. The formal gardens were in part laid out according to Goethe's concepts. *Tel. 03643/ 64039. Admission: DM 4 adults, DM 2 children. Open Apr.– Oct., Wed.–Sun. 10–6.*

In the Ettersberg hills just north of Weimar is a blighted patch of land that contrasts cruelly with the verdant countryside that so inspired Goethe: **Buchenwald.** This was one of the most infamous Nazi concentration camps, where 65,000 men, women and children from 35 countries met their deaths through forced labor, starvation, disease, and gruesome medical experiments. Each is commemorated today by a small stone placed on the outlines of the barracks, which have long since disappeared from the site, and by a massive memorial tower built in a style that some critics find reminiscent of the Nazi megalomania it seeks to condemn. The tower stands on the highest point of Buchenwald, approached by a broad, long flight of steps and sheltering at its base a sculpted group representing the victims of Buchenwald. *Campsite admission: free. Open Tues.–Sun. 9:45–4:30. Bus tours to the site are organized by Weimar's tourist office, Weimar-Information, Markstr. 4 (tel. 03643/762–342).*

Twenty-five kilometers (15 miles) west of Weimar (take the B-7 route, running parallel to the autobahn) lies one of the most picturesque and best-preserved cities of Thuringia: the "flowers and towers" city of **Erfurt.** Erfurt emerged relatively unscathed from World War II, most of its innumerable towers intact (although restored in the early 1970s). Flowers? Erfurt is the center of the eastern German horticultural trade and Europe's largest producer of flower and vegetable seeds, a tradition begun by a local botanist, Christian Reichart, who pioneered seed research. The city outskirts are smothered in greenhouses and plantations, and one of Germany's biggest horticultural shows, the Internationale Gartenbauaustellung, takes place here every year from the end of March through September.

With its highly decorative and colorful facades, this is a fascinating city to discover on foot, and a photographer's delight. Erfurt is dominated by its magnificent cathedral, the 14th-century Gothic **Dom,** reached by a broad staircase from the expansive cathedral square. The Romanesque origins of the cathedral (Romanesque foundations can still be seen in the crypt) are best preserved in the choir, where you'll find glorious stained-glass windows and some of the most beautifully carved choir stalls in all Germany. They have a worldly theme, tracing the vintner's trade back through the centuries. Nearby, look for a remarkable group of freestanding figures: a man flanked by two women. The man is the 13th-century Count von Gleichen. But the two women? There are two stories: One, the respectable version, has it that the women are the count's wives, one of whom he married after the death of the other. The other, possibly older story claims that one of the women is the count's wife, the other his mistress, a Saracen beauty who saved his life under mysterious circumstances during a crusade. The cathedral's biggest bell, the Gloriosa, is the largest free-swinging bell in the world. Cast in 1497, it took three years to install, in the tallest of the three sharply pointed towers, painstakingly lifted inch by inch with wooden wedges. No chances are taken with such a heavy treasure; the bell is rung only on special occasions. *Admission to Dom: DM 2. Open May–Oct., Mon.–Sat. 10–5; Nov.–Apr. Mon.–Sat. 10–4. Tour available after mass at 10:30 AM.*

Next to the cathedral and linked to it by a 70-step open staircase is the Gothic church of **St. Severus.** Step inside, if only to admire the extraordinary font, a masterpiece of intricately carved sandstone that reaches practically to the roof of the church.

The cathedral square is bordered by attractive old houses dating from the 16th century. Behind the predominantly neo-Gothic city hall, the **Rathaus,** you'll find Erfurt's outstanding attraction, the **Krämerbrücke** (Shopkeepers' Bridge), spanning the Gera River. You'd have to travel to Florence in Italy to find anything else like this, a Renaissance bridge incorporating shops and homes. Built in 1325 and restored in 1967–73, the bridge served for centuries as an important trading center where goldsmiths, artisans, and merchants plied their wares. Today antiques shops are in the majority among the timber-framed houses that are incorporated into the bridge, some dating from the 16th century. The area around the bridge is crisscrossed with ancient streets lined with picturesque and often crumbling homes. The area is known as **Klein Venedig** (Little Venice), not because of any real resemblance to the lagoon city but for the recurrent flooding caused by the nearby river.

On the way back to the center of town from the Krämerbrücke, follow Gotthardstrasse and you'll pass the **St. Augustine cloisters,** where the young Martin Luther spent formative years. Today it's a seminary. In nearby Johannisstrasse you'll find Erfurt's interesting local-history museum, housed in a late-Renaissance house, **Zum Stockfisch.** *Johannisstr. 169, tel. 0361–23311. Admission DM 1 adults, 50 pf children. Open Sun.–Thurs. 10–6.*

Johannisstrasse brings you to the pedestrian-zoned **Anger,** an old street lined with restored Renaissance houses. The **Bartholomäusturm,** base of a 12th-century tower, holds a 60-bell carillon.

Just outside of the center is the **Erfurter Gartenbau-und ausstellung** (Erfurts Garten and Exhibition Center) (admission: DM 4; open daily 10–6). Slightly farther afield is **Schloss Molsdorf,** one of the most stunning Rococo castles in Thuringia, set in a lovely park in the village of Molsdorf. The complex dates from 1736–45 but has been considerably renovated since. *Tel. 036202/505. Grounds open daily, castle open Tues.–Sun. 10–5. Tours are given hourly.*

❸❽ **Eisenach,** 58 kilometers (36 miles) west on either the main B–7 highway or the autobahn E–63 (or an hour's journey by rail), is a historic old city that has managed to retain its medieval atmosphere better than most cities in eastern Germany. Standing in its ancient market square, ringed by half-timbered houses, it's difficult to imagine that this town was an important center of the eastern German automobile industry, home of the now-shunned Wartburg. The solid, noisy staple of the East German auto trade was named after the famous castle that broods over Eisenach, high atop one of the foothills of the Thuringian Forest.

Begun in 1067 (and added to throughout the centuries), **Wartburg Castle** hosted the German minstrels Walter von der Vogelweide and Wolfram von Eschenbach, Martin Luther, Richard Wagner, and Goethe. Johann Sebastian Bach was born in Eisenach in 1685 and must have climbed the hill to the castle often. Legend has it that von der Vogelweide, Germany's most famous minstrel, won a celebrated song contest here, the "contest of the Minnesingers" immortalized by the Romantic writer

Novalis and Wagner's *Tannhäuser*. Luther sought shelter within its stout walls from papal proscription, and from May 1521 until March 1522 translated the New Testament from Greek to German, an act that paved the way for the Protestant Reformation. The study in which Luther worked can be visited; it's basically the same room that he used, although the walls have been scarred by souvenir hunters who, over the centuries, scratched away the plaster and much of the wood paneling. Luther's original desk was vandalized, and the massive table before you is a later addition, although a former possession of the Luther family.

There's much else of interest in this fascinating castle, including a portrait of Luther and his wife by Cranach the Elder, and a very moving sculpture, the *Kneeling Angel*, by the great 15th-century artist Tilman Riemenschneider. The 13th-century great hall is breathtaking; it's here that the minstrels are said to have sung for courtly favors. Don't leave without climbing the belvedere for a panoramic view of the distant hills of the Harzgebirge (Harz Mountains) and Thüringer Wald (Thuringian Forest) and soak in the medieval atmosphere of the half-timbered, cottage-style interior courtyards of the castle. *Tel. 03643/5450. Admission: DM 3 adults, DM 1.50 children. Open Nov.–Feb., daily 9–5, Mar.–Oct., daily 8:30–5:30.*

The castle, accessible only from the north bridge, is an easy stroll from the center of town, along Friedrich-Engels-Strasse and Reuterweg. On the way you'll pass the **Reuter-Wagner Museum,** at Reuterweg 2, which has a comprehensive exhibition on Wagner's life and work (DM 1.05 adults, 55 pf children; open weekdays 9–12:30 and 2–5, Sun. 9–4). The town also has two museums devoted to Luther and Bach: the **Lutherhaus,** Lutherplatz 8 (open Mon.–Sat. 9–1 and 2–5, Sun. 2–5) and the **Bachhaus,** Frauenplan 21, which is devoted to the entire Bach family and includes a collection of historical musical instruments (open Mon., Tues., Thurs., and Fri. 9–5; weekends 9–12:30 and 1–5). At Johannesplatz 9, look for what is allegedly the narrowest house in East Germany, built in 1890; the width is just over 2 meters (6 feet, 8 inches), the height 7½ meters (24½ feet), and the depth 10½ meters (34 feet).

Our tour of the southern part of eastern Germany ends here. You can continue west on E40 into western Germany, which leads into Route 5 to Frankfurt-am-Main. To return to Berlin, the fastest route is east on E40 and north on E51. For a change of scenery, turn off E40 onto Route 4 north to Nordhausen, where you'll pick up Route 81 to Magdeburg (*see* Excursions from Berlin, Chapter 4, *above*), and from there the E30 autobahn back into Berlin.

What to See and Do with Children

In **Dresden,** the penguin house at the zoo is particularly appealing; the zoo houses about 2,000 animals of some 500 species. *Open summer 8–5:30, winter 8–4:30.*

Automobiles have been manufactured since 1896 at **Eisenach,** the third-oldest production center in Germany. The automobile works operates an exhibition hall, showing cars from earlier years. Even the most recent car manufactured here, the Wartburg, looks none too modern by Western standards. *Open daily 9–7.*

Also in Eisenach, at the Wartburg Castle, kids can ride donkeys from the *Eselstation* at the start of the pathway to the castle.

Off the Beaten Track

Hellerau, 10 kilometers (6 miles) west of Dresden, on the Elbe River is the site of one of Europe's first experiments in William Morris-style "garden towns." It was founded in 1910 by Walt Dohrn, but the experiment (a furniture factory employing "happy, fullfilled workers" housed in idyllic rural cottages) foundered with his death in a Swiss skiing accident in 1914. Hellerau took off again between the two world wars, but since the end of World War II, the premises that made it famous—an avant-garde theater and an international boarding school—have been a Red Army barracks. The Soviets have been moving out and there are plans to turn Hellerau into a European cultural center.

The **Feengrotte** (Fairy Grotto) at **Saalfeld,** near Gera, is a unique underground lake, transformed into a spectacular fairyland of colored stalactites as you travel through by boat.

Shopping

Souvenirs to buy in Saxony and Thuringia include wooden carvings, old books and prints, and glass Christmas ornaments. You can look for porcelain, but much of the good Meissen is exported. The gift shop at the Meissen factory occasionally has very good seconds that are (relative) bargains. There's also a large Meissen shop in the Bellevue Hotel in Dresden. Neither shop is equipped to ship, so be prepared to carry your purchases home very gingerly. What the shops offer is mainly Dresden, which at its finest rivals Meissen, or Thuringian china, only for lovers of Rococo design. None of it—if it's good—is inexpensive.

In **Leipzig,** shop on Grimmaischestrasse and the arcades along Sachsenplatz and the Markt. You'll find an excellent bookstore run by the Evangelical church opposite the entrance to Leipzig's St. Thomas church. **Dresden's** shopping districts include Ernst-Thälmann-Strasse, the nearby Neumarkt, and Strasse der Befreiung.

Dining and Lodging

Dining

Many of the best restaurants are in the larger hotels. Regional specialties include *Thüringer Sauerbraten mit Klössen* (roast corned beef with dumplings), *Bärenschinken* (cured ham), and *Harzer Köhlerteller mit Rostkartoffeln* (charcoal-grilled meat with roast potatoes). Seafood is plentiful in the lake areas.

Highly recommended restaurants in each price category are indicated with a star ★.

Category	Cost*
Very Expensive	over DM 40
Expensive	DM 25–DM 40
Moderate	DM 15–DM 25
Inexpensive	under DM 15

*per person for a three-course meal and a beer or glass of wine

Lodging

The choice of hotels in Saxony and Thuringia remains limited, and although private householders may now rent rooms, these are also hard to come by, as the demand is far greater than the supply. Contact the local tourist information offices for names of bed and breakfasts.

Note that during the Leipzig fair—early March and early September—all Leipzig hotels increase their prices.

Highly recommended hotels are indicated by a star ★.

Category	Cost*
Very Expensive	over DM 230
Expensive	DM 190–DM 230
Moderate	DM 130–DM 190
Inexpensive	under DM 130

*Prices are for two people in a double room.

Chemnitz
Lodging

Chemnitzer Hof. Look carefully at this older hotel (built in 1930, now on the national register) and you'll spot its origins in the early Bauhaus style, in which ornamentation was discarded in favor of abstract design. Inside, rooms are attractive and the service friendly. You'll be in the heart of the city; you might enjoy the sense of living in another era. *Theaterplatz 4, tel. 0371/6840. 106 rooms with bath. Facilities: 2 restaurants, Bierstube, bar, nightclub, sauna, garage. AE, DC, MC, V. Very Expensive.*

Kongress. This modern 26-story skyscraper close to the town center stands in dramatic contrast to the rest of the city, but you'll find comfortable rooms in friendly surroundings here. Preferred rooms are on the upper floors, overlooking the city. The restaurants, at least under the old regime, leaned heavily toward Russian cuisine. *Karl-Marx-Allee, tel. 0371/6830. 369 rooms with bath. Facilities: 4 restaurants, café, bar, nightclub, sauna, solarium, fitness room, garage. AE, DC, MC, V. Very Expensive.*

Moskau. Accommodations in this modern but plain blocklike structure near the town center are not particularly fancy, but you'll find everything you need. The outdoor cafés in summer are particularly relaxing. *Strasse der Nationen, tel. 0371/6810. 111 rooms with bath. Facilities: restaurant, cafés, nightclub, sauna, garage. AE, DC, MC, V. Moderate.*

Dresden
Dining

Kügelnhaus. The complex here includes a grill, coffee bar, restaurant, and historic beer cellar, all justifiably popular, so go early or book ahead. *Hauptstr., tel. 0351/52791. Reservations advised. Dress: informal. No credit cards. Moderate.*

Sekundogenitur. This famous complex consisting of a restaurant, now connected to the Dresdner Hof hotel complex (*see* Lodging, *below*), is on the banks of the Elbe. There is outside dining when the weather permits. The Wiener schnitzel is excellent. *Brühlsche Terrasse, tel. 0351/495–1772 or 0351/48410. Reservations advised. Dress: informal. No credit cards. Closed Mon. Moderate.*

Lodging **Bellevue.** Across the river from the Zwinger Palace, opera, and main museums, this fairly new hotel cleverly incorporates an old restored town house. The hotel views of the historic center are terrific, the rooms luxurious, and the service good. The Café Pöppelmann is especially recommended for its atmosphere and hearty dishes. *Meissnerstr., Grosse Meissner Str., 8060 Dresden, tel. 0351/56620. 328 rooms with bath. Facilities: 4 restaurants, bar, café, indoor pool, sauna, solarium, fitness room, bowling, jogging course, boutiques. AE, DC, MC, V. Very Expensive.*

Dresdner Hof. The city's newest hotel fits snugly into a corner of the old town and is only a short distance from the Zwinger palace, Albertinum, and other major sights. Housing a wine cellar, several bars, a bistro, and smart restaurants, it offers every possible comfort. The lobby is a stunning black-and-white evocation of Jugendstil. *An der Frauenkirche 5, tel. 0351/48410. 340 rooms with bath. Facilities: 7 restaurants, 2 bars, café, Bierclub, nightclub, indoor pool, sauna, solarium, fitness room, spa, garage. AE, DC, MC, V. Very Expensive.*

Newa. This modern monolith offers less charm than the Dresdner Hof or the Bellevue but is a good choice for comfort and is close to the main train station. The Newa is on the package-tour route and is often booked well in advance. In keeping with the name, the restaurants emphasize Russian cuisine; the main specialty restaurant enjoys a fairly good reputation. *St.-Petersburger-Str. 34, tel. 0351/496–7112. 314 rooms with bath. Facilities: 2 restaurants, bar, café, sauna, garage. AE, DC, MC, V. Expensive.*

Astoria. A half mile from the city center but close to the Dresden Zoo (take bus No. 72 from the main train station), the Astoria is a modern five-story hotel with a garden terrace. The staff is pleasant, but the decor hardly fancy—"minimalist" describes it best. *Strehlener Platz 2, tel. 0351/471–5171. 82 rooms, most without bath. Facilities: restaurant, bar, shop. AE, DC, MC, V. Moderate.*

Interhotel Prager Strasse. This modern complex of two hotels in tandem, the **Königstein** and **Lilienstein,** is named for the two promontories overlooking the Elbe River south of the city. The hotels are side by side on a pedestrian street between the train station and the city center. Rooms are modern if unexciting; the favored rooms (for the view) overlook the Prager Strasse, although the back rooms are slightly quieter. *Prager Str., tel. 0351/48560. 300 rooms each. Facilities: 3 restaurants, sauna, garage. AE, DC, MC, V. Moderate.*

Parkhotel Weisser Hirsch. You'll be a considerable distance from the city center here (if driving, take Bautzenerstrasse from Platz der Einheit) in pleasant country surroundings. Facilities are simple, but the parklike setting makes up for the lack of luxury. *Bautzner Landstr. 7, tel. 0351/36–852. 54* *rooms, none with full bath. Facilities: restaurant, café (dancing in evenings). No credit cards. Inexpensive.*

Eisenach **Gastmahl des Meeres.** You're always well served at this popular
Dining fish restaurant chain in eastern Germany, and Eisenach's version is among the best. It's a large, friendly place, smothered in flowers as fresh as the fish that's caught from the restaurant's tanks. *Auf der Esplanade, tel. 030/3885. No reservations. Dress: informal. MC. Closed weekends. Moderate.*

Waldschanke. This charming old restaurant is difficult to find, hidden away in a wood on the outskirts of town, but the hunt is well worth it (follow the Wartburgallee for about a mile and then watch for the signs to Prinzenteich). You'll eat lakeside in a former hunting lodge, and if you're lucky, fresh-caught fish or in-season venison will be on the menu. *Johannistal 57, tel. 030/ 4465. Reservations advised. Dress: informal. No credit cards. Closed Thurs. and Fri. Moderate.*

Lodging **Auf der Wartburg.** In this historic castle, where Martin Luther, Johann Sebastian Bach, and Richard Wagner were also guests, you'll get a splendid view over the town and the surrounding countryside. The standard of comfort is above average, and antiques and Oriental rugs mix with modern, moderately stylish furnishings. The hotel runs a shuttle-bus service to the rail station. *Wartburg, tel. 03691/5111. 30 rooms, most with bath. Facilities: restaurant. No credit cards. Moderate.*

Hospiz "Glockenhof-Sophienhof." At the base of the Wartburg Castle, this hostel, run by the Evangelical church, occupies a half-timbered brick-roofed house that radiates personality fitting to the town. Facilities are modest, but rooms are pleasant. *Grimmelgasse 4, tel. 03691/3562. 23 rooms, most with bath. Facilities: restaurant. No credit cards. Inexpensive.*

Erfurt **Hohe Lilie.** Sweden's King Gustav Adolph established his court
Dining in the Renaissance building housing this first-class restaurant. The atmosphere is aptly regal—and so are the prices. But the menu offers good value for money, and some of the dishes—the steak "Erfurtas" for instance—are, by eastern German standards, quite exceptional. *Domplatz 31, tel. 0361/22578. Reservations necessary. Jacket and tie required. AE, DC, MC, V. Expensive.*

Vital. If the Hohe Lilie is too expensive, or booked up, try the nearby Vital. Good portions of typical Thuringian fare (lots of local sausage) are served in simple but pleasant surroundings. Even after German unification it was possible to eat well here for less than DM 20, but prices are bound to rise. *Domplatz 3, tel. 0361/24317. Reservations advised. Dress: informal. No credit cards. Inexpensive.*

Dining and Lodging **Erfurter Hof.** This inviting house in a traditional elegant style is under historic preservation, but the interior has been fully renovated to bring it up to modern standards. You're right at the train station and an easy stroll from the town center. The restaurant features cuisine of the Thuringen region, with an emphasis on fish and grilled meats. *Am Bahnhofsvorplatz 1–2, tel. 0361/5310. 197 rooms, all with bath. Facilities: 2 restaurants, café, wine cellar, bar, nightclub, sauna, garage. AE, DC, MC, V. Very Expensive.*

Kosmos. This recent multistory intruder from outer space is out of place in this town, but you'll be halfway between the train station and the town center. At least the views are splendid; ask for a room on an upper floor overlooking the old city.

The prices at Orbis restaurant and Galaxie café are not as far out as the names would imply. *Juri-Gagarin-Ring 126–127, tel. 0361/551–294. 320 rooms, all with bath. Facilities: restaurant, café, bar, sauna, garage. AE, DC, MC, V. Moderate–Expensive.*

Gera
Lodging

Gera. The rooms inside this centrally located modern monolith are fortunately far more inviting than the nondescript facade suggests. The specialty restaurants—Ganymed (French), Lotos (East Asian), Elsertal (German), and Bierhöler (local Thüringen cuisine)—have good reputations. Guest rooms are standard but comfortable. Book ahead around Leipzig fair time. *Strasse der Republik, tel. 0365/6930. 330 rooms with bath. Facilities: 3 restaurants, Bierstube, café, sauna, solarium, garage. AE, DC, MC, V. Very Expensive.*

Halle
Lodging

Stadt Halle. Inside, this central hotel is considerably more appealing than the rather cold facade would lead you to believe. Rooms offer the standard comforts, but several of the public rooms, such as the Ufa restaurant (Russian specialties, and from the central Russian republic of Bashkir at that) and the Messe Club bar, are quite attractive. Halle also takes overflow from Leipzig at fair time, so plan and book accordingly. *Ernst-Thälmann-Pl., tel. 0345/25050. 345 rooms with bath. Facilities: 2 restaurants, café, bar, nightclub, garage. AE, DC, MC, V. Very Expensive.*

Leipzig
Dining

Paulaner. Intimate, attractive, and quiet, this small place offers a limited selection of good local food. *Klostergasse 3, tel. 0341/211–3115. Reservations advised. Dress: informal. No credit cards. Expensive.*

Sakura. Located in the Hotel Merkur (*see* Lodging, *below*), the Sakura offers good Japanese cuisine, perhaps out of respect for the Japanese firm that designed and built the hotel. *Gerberstr. 15 (in Hotel Merkur), tel. 0341/799. Reservations required. Jacket advised. AE, DC, MC, V. Expensive.*

Altes Kloster. Game is featured in this fascinating restaurant, once part of a cloister. The Old World ambience enhances the excellent food. *Klostergasse 5, tel. 0341/282–252. Reservations advised. Jacket and tie required. No credit cards. Moderate.*

★ **Auerbachs Keller.** This historic restaurant (built 1530) in the city center is immortalized in Goethe's *Faust.* The menu features regional dishes from Saxony, often with Faustian names. There is a good wine list. Both a visit and a reservation are musts. *Grimmaische Str. 2–4, tel. 0341/211–6034. Jacket and tie required. AE, DC, MC, V. Moderate.*

Burgkeller. Romanian specialties are served here in the Doina Restaurant; the keller, at least, is authentic German. *Naschmarkt 1–3, tel. 0341/295639. Reservations not necessary. No credit cards. Moderate.*

Kaffeebaum. Reputedly the country's oldest café (established 1694), Kaffeebaum has a limited menu, but the atmosphere of this Burgerhaus plus its regulars make a visit worthwhile. *Fleischergasse 4, tel. 0341/200452. Reservations advised. No credit cards. Moderate.*

Ratskeller. This large restaurant, which also has a *Jagdzimmer* (Hunting Room), prides itself on its good *bürgerliche* (plain-and-hearty) cooking. Specialties include the popular *Ratskeller Topf,* a savory stew with vegetables; homemade pasta; and *Schweineschnitzel* (pork cutlet). *Lotterstr. 1, tel. 0341/791–*

6201. Reservations advised. No credit cards. Closed Sun. dinner. Moderate.

Lodging   **Astoria.** Many prefer this older hotel for its solid comfort and atmosphere in the grand style, as well as for its central location by the main train station. There's considerable traffic in the area, so you'll do best with a quieter room on the side rather than the front. The Galerie restaurant literally puts you into an art museum of Social Realist murals for lunch or dinner. *Platz der Republik 2, tel. 0341/72220, fax 0341/722-4747. 309 rooms with bath. Facilities: 2 restaurants, bar, dance café, nightclub, sauna, garage. AE, DC, MC, V. Very Expensive.*

Inter-Continental. The city's newest and by far most luxurious hotel is imposing for its high-rise profile as well as its Japanese restaurant and garden. Rooms in this Japanese-built hotel offer every luxury, including full air-conditioning, and you're close to the main train station. *Gerberstr. 15, tel. 0341/7990, fax 0341/799-1229. 440 rooms with bath. Facilities: 4 restaurants, 2 bars, coffee bar, nightclub, indoor pool, sauna, solarium, spa, bowling, shops, parking. AE, DC, MC, V. Very Expensive.*

Hotel am Ring. This hotel is the logical choice for those who want to be close to the opera house and concert hall. The hotel is modern and efficiently run. Rooms at the rear are quieter. *Palais Platz 5-6, tel. 0341/79520. 275 rooms with bath. Facilities: 2 restaurants, bar, nightclub, sauna, shops, parking. AE, DC, MC, V. Expensive.*

Stadt Leipzig. Considering its central location close to the main train station, this postwar modern monolith from the '60s is surprisingly quiet. Public rooms are attractive: dark wood paneling in the Vignette restaurant sets the tone for a quiet meal. *Richard-Wagner-Str. 1-6, tel. 0341/21450, fax 0341/284-037. 340 rooms with bath. Facilities: 3 restaurants, café, bar, nightclub, sauna, garage. AE, DC, MC, V. Expensive.*

International. This traditional hotel offers appropriate charm and friendly personnel. You're within steps of the heart of the city, and not far from the train station either. The spacious rooms offer old-fashioned comfort but with modern facilities. The sidewalk café is popular. *Tröndlinring 8, tel. 0341/71880. 108 rooms with bath. Facilities: restaurant, Bierstube, bar, café, garage. AE, DC, MC, V. Moderate.*

Zum Löwen. This is another of the postwar modern hotels built to handle Leipzig fair traffic, but in this case, the house is personable and cheerful, if not opulent. Around the corner from the Astoria, you'll be near the train station and within an easy stroll of the city center. *Rudolf-Breitscheid-Str., tel. 0341/72230. 108 rooms with bath. Facilities: restaurant. AE, DC, MC, V. Moderate.*

Parkhotel. The location directly across from the train station could hardly be better, but the accommodations are simple if not downright spartan—virtually none of the rooms have baths. *Richard-Wagner-Str. 7, tel. 0341/7821. 174 rooms, none with bath. Facilities: restaurant, parking. No credit cards. Inexpensive.*

Meissen   **Bahnhofshotel.** This small hotel is at the train station and con-
Dining and Lodging   venient to the center of town. Rooms have a dated modern decor but are attractive, with satisfactory baths. The restaurants remind one a bit of the train station, which is only appropriate. *Grossenhainer Str. 2, tel. 03521/558. 18 rooms with bath. Facilities: restaurant, parking. AE, DC, MC, V. Moderate.*

Weimar **Weisser Schwan.** This historic restaurant in the center of town,
Dining right by Goethehaus (*see* Exploring, *above*), dates from 1500.
Its various rooms, including the library, offer international and
Thuringian specialties, particularly fish and grilled meats.
*Frauenstorstr. 23, tel. 03643/61715. Reservations essential.
Jacket and tie advised. AE, DC, MC, V. Closed last Mon. of
month. Expensive.*

Elephantenkeller. In the ancient vaulted cellar restaurant of
the Elephant Hotel (*see* Lodging, *below*), you'll eat well on traditional Thuringian cuisine in surroundings that haven't
changed much since Goethe's day. Only the functional 1950s
style of some of the furnishings disturb the overall atmosphere
reinforced by the well-worn flagstones of the floor and the
squat sandstone pillars behind which many lunchtime deals are
being sealed in post-reunification Germany. Try the *Weimarer
Zwiebelmarkt* soup, an onion soup made with pork-knuckle
stock. *Markt 19, tel. 03643/61471. Reservations advised.
Dress: informal. No credit cards. Moderate.*

Ratskeller. This historic restaurant is located in the cellar of
the Stadthaus (City Hall), a Renaissance building dating from
the 17th century. The wholesome regional fare includes grilled
sausages with sauerkraut and onions, and Thuringian onion
soup. *Markt 10, tel. 03643/64142. Reservations not necessary.
AE, DC, MC, V. Moderate.*

Felsenkeller. In this warm, rustic, country-style restaurant
and drinking establishment in the Gasthaus Brauere, a variety
of warm dishes are offered at prices between DM 5 and DM 30.
The beer is brewed on the premises. *Humboldtstr. 37, tel.
03643/61941. Reservations not necessary. No credit cards. Inexpensive.*

Gastmahl des Meeres. Centrally located, this restaurant offers
a wide range of fish dishes, as well as meat. It has fast service
and friendly waiters but tends to get crowded between 1 PM and
2 PM, so its best to arrive early for lunch. *Herder Platz 16, tel.
03643/4521. No reservations. No credit cards. Inexpensive.*

Lodging **Belvedere.** Opened in 1990, this luxurious hotel is about 1½ kilometers (1 mile) outside of the town center, across from a gor-
geous wooded park—Goethe helped plan the layout—which is
worth a stroll even if you're not staying at the Belevedere.
Rooms are, if anything, are overly complete; you'll lack nothing, except proximity to Weimar's center. *Belvedere Allee, tel.
03643/2429. 300 rooms with bath. Facilities: 2 restaurants,
café, beer pub, three bars, indoor pool, sauna, solarium, fitness room, spa, bowling, garage. AE, DC, MC, V. Very Expensive.*

Elephant. This hotel, dating from 1696, is one of the Germany's
most famous; you'll follow the choice of Goethe, Schiller, Herder, Liszt—and Hitler—all of whom have been guests here. Behind the sparkling white facade are comfortable modern rooms,
thanks to recent renovations, but a feeling for the historic past
is ever present. Book well ahead. *Am Markt 19, tel. 03643/
61471. 116 rooms with bath. Facilities: 4 restaurants, bar,
nightclub, sauna, garage. AE, DC, MC, V. Expensive.*

Hospiz. This hostel run by the Evangelical church is only steps
away from Goethe's house. Rooms are modest, but so is the
price; the public rooms are attractively furnished with antiques. In 1991, bathrooms were added to the rooms and old
furniture was replaced. *Amalienstr. 2, tel. 03643/2711. 21*

rooms, *12 with bath. Facilities: restaurant, parking. No credit cards. Moderate.*

Russischer Hof. This charming hotel built in 1805 was modernized and expanded in 1989. The rooms are attractively furnished, each equipped with bath, shower, TV, and radio. *Goethe Platz 2, tel. 03643/62331. 85 rooms with bath. Facilities: 2 restaurants, bar, beer cellar, garage. AE, DC, MC, V. Moderate.*

The Arts and Nightlife

The Arts

Opera The opera in **Dresden** has regained its international reputation since the **Dresden Opera House** (Sächsische Statsoper Dresden, Theaterplatz, Postfach 8, 0–8012, Dresden), which was almost totally destroyed in World War II, was reopened in 1985 following an eight-year reconstruction. Just to see the magnificent house alone is worth the trip; a performance is that much better. Tickets are reasonably priced but also hard to get; they're often included in package tours. Try your luck at the evening box office (the *Abendkasse,* left of the main entrance, tel. 0351/4842323, 0351/4842328, or 0351/4842333) about a half hour before the performance; there are usually a few dozen tickets available.

Several smaller cities, notably **Chemnitz,** also have opera houses that turn out interesting performances, occasionally of relatively little known or contemporary works.

Music The Neues Gewandhaus in **Leipzig,** a controversial piece of architecture, is home to a splendid orchestra. Tickets to concerts are very difficult to obtain unless you reserve well in advance and in writing only (Gewandhaus zu Leipzig, Augustus-Platz, Leipzig 7010). Sometimes spare tickets are available at the box office a half hour before the evening performance. Of the music festivals in the area, the best-known are the Handel festival in **Halle** (June) and the Music Days in **Leipzig** (June), as well as the International Bach Festival held every four years during September and October. **Dresden** organizes an international Dixieland festival each May.

Nightlife

Leipzig comes to life particularly during fair time, although in the past this was as much to extract hard currency from the visitors as it was to entertain them. In most cities the leading hotels run nightclubs year-round (*see* Lodging, *above*), and many of these are not bad at all. In **Leipzig,** try the Merkur, Kongress, Chemnitzer Hof, and Moskau; in **Dresden,** the Dresdner Hof; in **Gera,** the Gera; in **Erfurt,** the Erfurter Hof; and in **Weimar,** the Belvedere and Elephant hotels.

Index

Fodor's Travel Guides

Available at bookstores everywhere, or call 1–800–533–6478, 24 hours a day.

U.S. Guides

Alaska

Arizona

Boston

California

Cape Cod, Martha's Vineyard, Nantucket

The Carolinas & the Georgia Coast

Chicago

Colorado

Florida

Hawaii

Las Vegas, Reno, Tahoe

Los Angeles

Maine, Vermont, New Hampshire

Maui

Miami & the Keys

New England

New Orleans

New York City

Pacific North Coast

Philadelphia & the Pennsylvania Dutch Country

The Rockies

San Diego

San Francisco

Santa Fe, Taos, Albuquerque

Seattle & Vancouver

The South

The U.S. & British Virgin Islands

The Upper Great Lakes Region

USA

Vacations in New York State

Vacations on the Jersey Shore

Virginia & Maryland

Waikiki

Walt Disney World and the Orlando Area

Washington, D.C.

Foreign Guides

Acapulco, Ixtapa, Zihuatanejo

Australia & New Zealand

Austria

The Bahamas

Baja & Mexico's Pacific Coast Resorts

Barbados

Berlin

Bermuda

Brazil

Brittany & Normandy

Budapest

Canada

Cancun, Cozumel, Yucatan Peninsula

Caribbean

China

Costa Rica, Belize, Guatemala

The Czech Republic & Slovakia

Eastern Europe

Egypt

Euro Disney

Europe

Europe's Great Cities

Florence & Tuscany

France

Germany

Great Britain

Greece

The Himalayan Countries

Hong Kong

India

Ireland

Israel

Italy

Japan

Kenya & Tanzania

Korea

London

Madrid & Barcelona

Mexico

Montreal & Quebec City

Morocco

Moscow & St. Petersburg

The Netherlands, Belgium & Luxembourg

New Zealand

Norway

Nova Scotia, Prince Edward Island & New Brunswick

Paris

Portugal

Provence & the Riviera

Rome

Russia & the Baltic Countries

Scandinavia

Scotland

Singapore

South America

Southeast Asia

Spain

Sweden

Switzerland

Thailand

Tokyo

Toronto

Turkey

Vienna & the Danube Valley

Yugoslavia

Special Series

Fodor's Affordables

Caribbean

Europe

Florida

France

Germany

Great Britain

London

Italy

Paris

**Fodor's Bed &
Breakfast and
Country Inns Guides**

Canada's Great
Country Inns

California

Cottages, B&Bs and
Country Inns of
England and Wales

Mid-Atlantic Region

New England

The Pacific
Northwest

The South

The Southwest

The Upper Great
Lakes Region

The West Coast

The Berkeley Guides

California

Central America

Eastern Europe

France

Germany

Great Britain &
Ireland

Mexico

Pacific Northwest &
Alaska

San Francisco

**Fodor's Exploring
Guides**

Australia

Britain

California

The Caribbean

Florida

France

Germany

Ireland

Italy

London

New York City

Paris

Rome

Singapore & Malaysia

Spain

Thailand

Fodor's Flashmaps

New York

Washington, D.C.

Fodor's Pocket Guides

Bahamas

Barbados

Jamaica

London

New York City

Paris

Puerto Rico

San Francisco

Washington, D.C.

Fodor's Sports

Cycling

Hiking

Running

Sailing

The Insider's Guide
to the Best Canadian
Skiing

Skiing in the USA
& Canada

**Fodor's Three-In-Ones
(guidebook, language
cassette, and phrase
book)**

France

Germany

Italy

Mexico

Spain

**Fodor's
Special-Interest
Guides**

Accessible USA

Cruises and Ports
of Call

Euro Disney

Halliday's New
England Food
Explorer

Healthy Escapes

London Companion

Shadow Traffic's New
York Shortcuts and
Traffic Tips

Sunday in New York

Walt Disney World
and the Orlando Area

Walt Disney World
for Adults

**Fodor's Touring
Guides**

Touring Europe

Touring USA:
Eastern Edition

**Fodor's Vacation
Planners**

Great American
Vacations

National Parks
of the East

National Parks
of the West

**The Wall Street
Journal Guides to
Business Travel**

Europe

International Cities

Pacific Rim

USA & Canada

WHEREVER YOU TRAVEL, *H*ELP IS NEVER FAR AWAY.

From planning your trip to replacing
lost Cards, American Express® Travel Service
Offices* are always there to help.

BERLIN
Kurfuerstendamm 11
30-882-7575

Friedrichstrasse 172
30-238-4102, 4103, 4104, 4105

DRESDEN
Grosse Meissner Strasse 15
(At Hotel Bellevue)
51-566-2865, 2868

INTRODUCING

Fodor's
WORLDVIEW
TRAVEL UPDATE

AT LAST, YOUR OWN PERSONALIZED LIST OF WHAT'S GOING ON IN THE CITIES YOU'RE VISITING.

KEYED TO THE DAYS WHEN YOU'RE THERE, CUSTOMIZED FOR YOUR INTERESTS, AND SENT TO YOU BEFORE YOU LEAVE HOME.

EXCLUSIVE FOR PURCHASERS OF FODOR'S GUIDES...

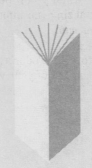

Fodor's WORLDVIEW
TRAVEL UPDATE

Introducing a revolutionary way to get customized, time-sensitive travel information just before your trip.

Now you can obtain detailed information about what's going on in each city you'll be visiting <u>before</u> you leave home—up-to-the-minute, objective information about the events and activities that interest you most.

Your Itinerary:
Customized repor
available for 160
destinations

This is a special offer for purchasers of Fodor's guides – a customized Travel Update to fit your specific interests and your itinerary.

Travel Updates contain the kind of time-sensitive insider information you can get only from local contacts – or from city magazines and newspapers once you arrive. But now you can have the same information before you leave for your trip.

The choice is yours: current art exhibits, theater, music festivals and special concerts, sporting events, antiques and flower shows, shopping, fitness, and more.

The information comes from hundreds of correspondents and thousands of sources worldwide. Updated continuously, it's like having your own personal concierge or friend in the city.

You specify the cities and when you'll be there. We'll do the rest — personalizing the information for you the way no guidebook can.

It's the perfect extension to your Fodor's guide and the best way to make the most of your valuable travel time.

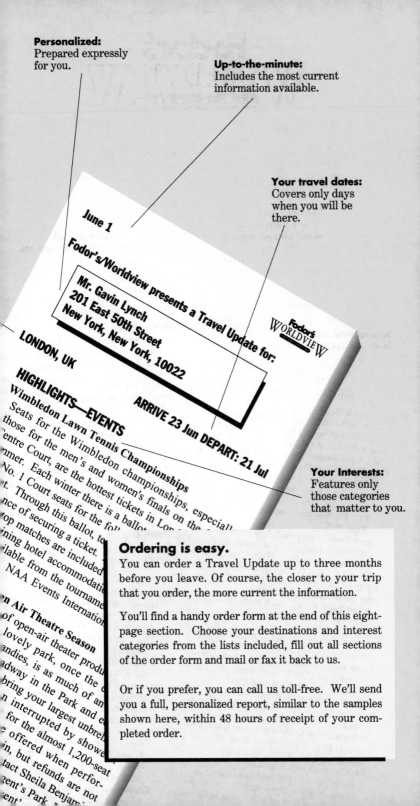

Personalized:
Prepared expressly
for you.

Up-to-the-minute:
Includes the most current
information available.

Your travel dates:
Covers only days
when you will be
there.

June 1

Fodor's/Worldview presents a Travel Update for:

Mr. Gavin Lynch
201 East 50th Street
New York, New York, 10022

Fodor's
WORLDVIEW

LONDON, UK

ARRIVE 23 Jun DEPART: 21 Jul

Your Interests:
Features only
those categories
that matter to you.

HIGHLIGHTS—EVENTS

Wimbledon Lawn Tennis Championships

Seats for the Wimbledon championships, especiall
those for the men's and women's finals on the
entre Court, are the hottest tickets in Lon
mmer. Each winter there is a ballo
No. 1 Court seats for the fol'
t. Through this ballot, t
nce of securing a ticket,
op matches are included
ining hotel accommodati
ilable from the tourname
NAA Events Internation

n Air Theatre Season
of open-air theater produ
lovely park, once the
andies, is as much of an
adway in the Park and e
bring your largest unbr
n interrupted by showe
for the almost 1,200-seat
e offered when perfor-
n, but refunds are not
tact Sheila Benjam
ent's Park
ent'

Ordering is easy.

You can order a Travel Update up to three months
before you leave. Of course, the closer to your trip
that you order, the more current the information.

You'll find a handy order form at the end of this eight-
page section. Choose your destinations and interest
categories from the lists included, fill out all sections
of the order form and mail or fax it back to us.

Or if you prefer, you can call us toll-free. We'll send
you a full, personalized report, similar to the samples
shown here, within 48 hours of receipt of your completed order.

**Special concerts—
who's performing
what and where**

**One-of-a-kind,
one-time-only events**

**Special interest,
in-depth listings**

Children — Events
Angel Canal Festival
The festivities include a children's funfa
entertainers, a boat rally and displays on t
water. Regent's Canal. Islington. N1. Tub
Angel. Tel: 267 9100. 11:30am-5:30pm. 7/0

Blackheath Summer Kite Festival
Stunt kite displays with parachuting ted
bears and trade stands. Free admission. SE
BR: Blackheath. 10am. 6/27.

Megabugs
Children will delight in this infestation
giant robotic insects, including a prayin
mantic 60 times life size. Mon-Sat 10am
6pm; Sun 11am-6pm. Admission 4.5
pounds. Natural History Museum, Cromwe
Road. SW7. Tube: South Kensington. Tel
938 9123. Ends 10/01.

Childminders
This establishment employs only women
providing nurses and qualified nannies to

Music — Jazz & Blues
Tito Puente's Golden Men of Latin Jazz
The father of mambo and Cuban rumba king
comes to town. Royal Festival Hall. South Bank.
SE1. Tube: Waterloo. Tel: 928 8800. 8pm. 7/15.

Georgie Fame and The New York Band
Riding a popular tide with his latest album, the
smoky-voiced Fame and his keyboard are on a
tour yet again. The Grand. Clapham Junction.
SW11. BR: Clapham Junction. Tel: 738 9000.
7:30pm. 7/07.

Jacques Loussier Play Bach Trio
The French jazz classicist and colleagues.
Kenwood Lakeside. Hampstead Lane.
Kenwood. NW3. Tube: Golders Green, then bus
210. Tel: 413 1443. 7pm. 7/10.

Tony Bennett and Ronnie Scott
Royal Festival Hall. South Bank. SE1. Tube:
Waterloo. Tel: 928 8800. 8pm. 7/11.

Santana
Royal Festival Hall. South Bank. SE1. Tube:
Waterloo. Tel: 928 8800. 8pm. 7/12.

Count Basie Orchestra and Nancy Wilson Trio
Royal Festival Hall. South Bank. SE1. Tube
Waterloo. Tel: 928 8800. 8pm. 7/14.

King Pleasure and the Biscuit Boys
Royal Festival Hall. South Bank. SE1. Tube
Waterloo. Tel: 928 8800. 6:30 and 9pm. 7/16.

Al Green and the London Community Gospel Choir
Royal Festival Hall. South Bank. SE1. Tube
Waterloo. Tel: 928 8800. 8pm. 7/13.

BB King and Linda Hopkins
Mother of the blues and successor to Bessi
Smith, Hopkins meets up with "Blues Boy
Royal Festival Hall. South Bank. SE

Music — Classical
Marylebone Sinfonia
Kenneth Gowen conducts music by P
and Rossini. Queen Elizabeth Hall.
Bank. SE1. Tube: Waterloo. Tel: 928
7:45pm. 7/16.

London Philharmonic
Franz Welser-Moest and George Ber
conduct selections by Alexander C
Messiaen, and some of Benjamin's ow
positions. Queen Elizabeth Hall. South
SE1. Tube: Waterloo. Tel: 928 8800. 8

London Pro Arte Orchestra and Forest
Murray Stewart conducts selecti
Rossini, Haydn and Jonathan Willcock
Queen Elizabeth Hall. South Ban
Tube: Waterloo. Tel: 928 8800. 7:45pr

Kensington Symphony Orchestra
Russell Keable conducts Dvorak's

Here's what you get . . .

Detailed information about what's going on — precisely when you'll be there.

Show openings during your visit

Reviews by local critics

Exhibitions & Shows—Antique & Flower
Westminster Antiques Fair
Over 50 stands with pre-1830 furniture and other Victorian and earlier items. Thu-Fri 11am-8pm; Sat-Sun 11am-6pm. Admission 4 pounds, children free. Old Royal Horticultural Hall. Vincent Square. SW1. Tel: 0444/48 25 14. 6-24 thru 6/27.

Royal Horticultural Society Flower Show
The show includes displays of carnations, summer fruit and vegetables. Tue 11am-7pm; Wed 10am-5pm. Admission Tue 4 pounds, Wed 2 pounds. Royal Horticultural Halls. Greycoat Street and Vincent Square. SW1. Tube: Victoria. 7/20 thru 7/21.

[Ha]mpton Court Palace International Flower Show
Major international garden and flower show [ta]king place in conjunction with the British

[The]ater — Musical
Sunset Boulevard
In June, the four Andrew Lloyd Webber musicals which dominated London's stages in the 1980s (Cats, Starlight Express, Phantom of the Opera and Aspects of Love) are joined by the composer's latest work, a show rumored to have his best music to date. The 1950 Billy Wilder film about a helpless young writer who is drawn into the world of a possessive, aging silent screen star offers rich opportunities for Webber's evolving style. Soaring, aching melodies, lush technical effects and psychological thrills are all expected. Patti Lupone stars. Mon-Sat at 8pm; matinee Thu-Sat at 3pm. In-person sales only at the box office; credit card bookings, Tel: 344 0055. Admission 15-32.50 pounds. Adelphi Theatre. The Strand. WC2. Tube: Charing Cross. Tel: 836 7611. Starts: 6/21

Leonardo A Portrait of Love
A new musical about the great Renaissance arti[st] and inventor comes in for a London premier[e] tested by a brief run at Oxford's Old Fire Stati[on] [au]tumn. The work explores the relations [...] [da Vi]nci and the woman [...]

[S]pectator Sports — Other Sports
Greyhound Racing: Wembley Stadium
This dog track offers good views of greyhound racing held on Mon, Wed and Fri. No credit cards. Stadium Way. Wembley. HA9. Tube: Wembley Park. Tel: 902 8833.

Benson & Hedges Cricket Cup Final
Lord's Cricket Ground. St. John's Wood Road. NW8. Tube: St. John's Wood. Tel: 289 1611. 11am. 7/10.

[Busi]ness-Fax & Overnight Mail
Post Office, Trafalgar Square Branch
Offers a network of fax services, the Intelpost system, throughout the country and abroad. Mon-Sat 8am-8pm, Sun 9am-5pm. William IV Street. WC2. Tube: Chari[ng] Cross. T[...]

Alberquerque • Atlanta • Atlantic City • N[...]
Baltimore • Boston • Chicago • Cincinnati
Cleveland • Dallas/Ft.Worth • Denver • De[...]
• Houston • Kansas City • Las Vegas • Los
Angeles • Memphis • Miami • Milwaukee •
New Orleans • New York City • Orlando • [...]
Springs • Philadelphia • Phoenix • Pittsburg[...]
Portland • Salt Lake • San Antonio • San Di[...]
• San Franc[...] • Se[...]le • [...]ouis • Tamp[...]
Oslo • Wash[...] • [...]lu • Island [...]
Hawaii • Kauai • Maui • Abacos • Bimini [...]
Ber[...] Countryside • [...]a[...]
Antigua & B[...] • Hamilton • [...]lar[...]
[...] • [...]vis • [...]ort[...]
[...] Gorda • Barbados • Dominica • Gren[...]
[...]cia • St. Vincent • Trinidad & Tobago [...]
[...]ymans • Puerto Plata • Santo Doming[...]
[...] Aruba • Bonaire • Curacao • St. Ma[...]
[...]ec City • Montreal • Ottawa • Toron[...]
[...]Vancouver • Guadeloupe • Martiniqu[...]
[...]helemy • St. Martin • Kingston • Ixta[...]
[...]o Bay • Negril • Ocho Rios • Ponce [...]
[...]n • Grand Turk • Providenciales • S[...]
[...] St. John • St. Thomas • Acapulco • [...]
[...] & Isla Mujeres • Cozumel • Guadal[...]
[...]a • Los Cabos • Manzanillo • Mazatl[...]
[...] City • Monterrey • Oaxaca • Puerto [...]
[...]do • Puerto Vallarta • Veracruz • [...]
[...]dam • Athens • [...]

Fodor's WORLDVIEW TRAVEL UPDATE

Interest Categories

For <u>your</u> personalized Travel Update, choose the categories you're most interested in from this list. Every Travel Update automatically provides you with *Event Highlights* – the best of what's happening during the dates of your trip.

1.	**Business Services**	Fax & Overnight Mail, Computer Rentals, Photocopying, Secretarial , Messenger, Translation Services

Dining

2.	**All Day Dining**	Breakfast & Brunch, Cafes & Tea Rooms, Late-Night Dining
3.	**Local Cuisine**	In Every Price Range—from Budget Restaurants to the Special Splurge
4.	**European Cuisine**	Continental, French, Italian
5.	**Asian Cuisine**	Chinese, Far Eastern, Japanese, Indian
6.	**Americas Cuisine**	American, Mexican & Latin
7.	**Nightlife**	Bars, Dance Clubs, Comedy Clubs, Pubs & Beer Halls
8.	**Entertainment**	Theater—Drama, Musicals, Dance, Ticket Agencies
9.	**Music**	Classical, Traditional & Ethnic, Jazz & Blues, Pop, Rock
10.	**Children's Activities**	Events, Attractions
11.	**Tours**	Local Tours, Day Trips, Overnight Excursions, Cruises
12.	**Exhibitions, Festivals & Shows**	Antiques & Flower, History & Cultural, Art Exhibitions, Fairs & Craft Shows, Music & Art Festivals
13.	**Shopping**	Districts & Malls, Markets, Regional Specialities
14.	**Fitness**	Bicycling, Health Clubs, Hiking, Jogging
15.	**Recreational Sports**	Boating/Sailing, Fishing, Ice Skating, Skiing, Snorkeling/Scuba, Swimming
16.	**Spectator Sports**	Auto Racing, Baseball, Basketball, Football, Horse Racing, Ice Hockey, Soccer

Please note that interest category content will vary by season, destination, and length of stay.

Destinations

The Fodor's/Worldview Travel Update covers more than 160 destinations worldwide. Choose the destinations that match your itinerary from this list. (Choose bulleted destinations only.)

United States (Mainland)
- Albuquerque
- Atlanta
- Atlantic City
- Baltimore
- Boston
- Chicago
- Cincinnati
- Cleveland
- Dallas/Ft. Worth
- Denver
- Detroit
- Houston
- Kansas City
- Las Vegas
- Los Angeles
- Memphis
- Miami
- Milwaukee
- Minneapolis/ St. Paul
- New Orleans
- New York City
- Orlando
- Palm Springs
- Philadelphia
- Phoenix
- Pittsburgh
- Portland
- St. Louis
- Salt Lake City
- San Antonio
- San Diego
- San Francisco
- Seattle
- Tampa
- Washington, DC

Alaska
- Anchorage/Fairbanks/Juneau

Hawaii
- Honolulu
- Island of Hawaii
- Kauai
- Maui

Canada
- Quebec City
- Montreal
- Ottawa
- Toronto
- Vancouver

Bahamas
- Abacos
- Eleuthera/ Harbour Island
- Exumas
- Freeport
- Nassau & Paradise Island

Bermuda
- Bermuda Countryside
- Hamilton

British Leeward Islands
- Anguilla
- Antigua & Barbuda
- Montserrat
- St. Kitts & Nevis

British Virgin Islands
- Tortola & Virgin Gorda

British Windward Islands
- Barbados
- Dominica
- Grenada
- St. Lucia
- St. Vincent
- Trinidad & Tobago

Cayman Islands
- The Caymans

Dominican Republic
- Puerto Plata
- Santo Domingo

Dutch Leeward Islands
- Aruba
- Bonaire
- Curacao

Dutch Windward Islands
- St. Maarten

French West Indies
- Guadeloupe
- Martinique
- St. Barthelemy
- St. Martin

Jamaica
- Kingston
- Montego Bay
- Negril
- Ocho Rios

Puerto Rico
- Ponce
- San Juan

Turks & Caicos
- Grand Turk
- Providenciales

U.S. Virgin Islands
- St. Croix
- St. John
- St. Thomas

Mexico
- Acapulco
- Cancun & Isla Mujeres
- Cozumel
- Guadalajara
- Ixtapa & Zihuatanejo
- Los Cabos
- Manzanillo
- Mazatlan
- Mexico City
- Monterrey
- Oaxaca
- Puerto Escondido
- Puerto Vallarta
- Veracruz

Europe
- Amsterdam
- Athens
- Barcelona
- Berlin
- Brussels
- Budapest
- Copenhagen
- Dublin
- Edinburgh
- Florence
- Frankfurt
- French Riviera
- Geneva
- Glasgow
- Interlaken
- Istanbul
- Lausanne
- Lisbon
- London
- Madrid
- Milan
- Moscow
- Munich
- Oslo
- Paris
- Prague
- Provence
- Rome
- Salzburg
- St. Petersburg
- Stockholm
- Venice
- Vienna
- Zurich

Pacific Rim Australia & New Zealand
- Auckland
- Melbourne
- Sydney

China
- Beijing
- Guangzhou
- Shanghai

Japan
- Kyoto
- Nagoya
- Osaka
- Tokyo
- Yokohama

Other
- Bangkok
- Hong Kong & Macau
- Manila
- Seoul
- Singapore
- Taipei

Fodor's WORLDVIEW **Order Form**

THIS TRAVEL UPDATE IS FOR (Please print):

Name			
Address			
City	State		ZIP
Country	Tel # ( ) -		

Title of this Fodor's guide:

Store and location where guide was purchased:

INDICATE YOUR DESTINATIONS/DATES: Write in below the destinations you want to order. Then fill in your arrival and departure dates for each destination.

		Month Day	Month Day
(Sample) LONDON	From:	6 / 21	To: 6 / 30
1	From:	/	To: /
2	From:	/	To: /
3	From:	/	To: /

You can order up to three destinations per Travel Update. Only destinations listed on the previous page are applicable. Maximum amount of time covered by a Travel Update cannot exceed 30 days.

CHOOSE YOUR INTERESTS: Select up to eight categories from the list of interest categories shown on the previous page and circle the numbers below:

1   2   3   4   5   6   7   8   9   10   11   12   13   14   15   16

CHOOSE HOW YOU WANT YOUR TRAVEL UPDATE DELIVERED (Check one):

❏ Please mail my Travel Update to the address above **OR**

❏ Fax it to me at **Fax #** ( ) -

DELIVERY CHARGE (Check one)

	Within U.S. & Canada	Outside U.S. & Canada
First Class Mail	❏ $2.50	❏ $5.00
Fax	❏ $5.00	❏ $10.00
Priority Delivery	❏ $15.00	❏ $27.00

All orders will be sent within 48 hours of receipt of a completed order form.

ADD UP YOUR ORDER HERE. *SPECIAL OFFER FOR FODOR'S PURCHASERS ONLY!*

	Suggested Retail Price	Your Price	This Order
First destination ordered	$13.95	$ 7.95	$ 7.95
Second destination (if applicable)	$ 9.95	$ 4.95	+
Third destination (if applicable)	$ 9.95	$ 4.95	+
Plus delivery charge from above			+
		TOTAL:	$

METHOD OF PAYMENT (Check one):   ❏ AmEx   ❏ MC   ❏ Visa   ❏ Discover
❏ Personal Check   ❏ Money Order

Make check or money order payable to: Fodor's Worldview Travel Update

Credit Card # _____   **Expiration Date:** _____

Authorized Signature _____

SEND THIS COMPLETED FORM TO:
Fodor's Worldview Travel Update, 114 Sansome Street, Suite 700, San Francisco, CA 94104

OR CALL OR FAX US 24-HOURS A DAY
Telephone **1-800-799-9609** • Fax **1-800-799-9619** (From within the U.S. & Canada)
(Outside the U.S. & Canada: Telephone 415-616-9988 • Fax 415-616-9989)

(Please have this guide in front of you when you call so we can verify purchase.)

Offer valid until 12/31/94.